W9-CMZ-797

SUPPLEMENT 2002-2012

FORENSIC PSYCHOPHYSIOLOGY USING THE POLYGRAPH
Scientific Truth Verification – Lie Detection

James Allan Matte

FORENSIC PSYCHOPHYSIOLOGY USING THE POLYGRAPH
Scientific Truth Verification – Lie Detection

SUPPLEMENT 2002-2012

James Allan Matte

Forensic Psychophysiology Expert

President
Matte Polygraph Service, Inc.
Williamsville, New York 14221-6915

Member, American Polygraph Association
Member, New York State Polygraph Examiners Association
Member, American Society for Testing and Materials
Member, Society for Psychophysiological Research
Member, Association for Psychological Science
Honorary President, British Polygraph Association
Honorary Life Member, Pennsylvania Polygraph Association
Former Special Agent, USAF Office of Special Investigations (OSI)
Retired Special Agent, U. S. Army Criminal Investigation Division Command (CID)
Member, The Authors Guild, Inc.

J. A. M. Publications
Williamsville, New York · U. S. A.

Published and Distributed throughout the World by
J. A. M. Publications
43 Brookside Drive
Williamsville, New York 14221-6915
Tel: (716) 634-6645 – Fax: (716) 634-7204
E-Mail: editor@jampublications.com
Website URL: http://www.jampublications.com

ISBN: 1469907933
ISBN 13: 9781469907932

Library of Congress Control Number: 2012900878

Library of Congress Cataloging in Publication Data

Matte, James Allan
SUPPLEMENT 2002-2012 to
FORENSIC PSYCHOPHYSIOLOGY USING THE POLYGRAPH
Scientific Truth Verification – Lie Detection (1996) ISBN: 0-9655794-0-9.

Includes Bibliographical References.
1. Lie Detectors and Detection
2. Polygraph operators
3. Polygraphist
4. Psychophysiological Veracity Examination
5. Forensic Psychophysiology

Printed in the United States of America
J.A.M. Publications
Williamsville, New York

This Supplement 2002-2012 to Forensic Psychophysiology Using The Polygraph is divided into two sections: Section I, Contents of Supplement 2002, and Section II, Contents of Supplement 2012. Those who already have the previously published Supplement 2002, will notice that Appendix P, Q, S and the Glossary of Terms have been revised. Otherwise they may go directly to the Supplement 2012 contained herein which starts at page 79.

SECTION I

Contents of Supplement 2002

CHAPTER 2

History: Lie Detection, The Polygraph, And Psychophysiological Veracity (PV) Examinations

Page 46. Change first sentence in last paragraph which commences with "In 1966…" as follows:

In 1966, Backster commenced his extensive research related to observed electrical responses in plant life (see Figure II-10A) and at a cellular level in other living organisms. In 2003, Backster authored a book on his research titled "Primary Perception: Biocommunication with Plants, Living Foods, and Human Cells" published by White Rose Millennium Press, Anza, CA. ISBN: 0-966435435.

Page 47. Add Figure II-10A after first paragraph ending with "Backster 1995).

Figure II-10A. Robert E. Henson (left) Chief Instructor and Administrator for the Backster School of Lie Detection (1963-1993) and Cleve Backster observing electrical responses of a plant (philodendron) with the use of the galvanic unit from a Stoelting deceptograph.

Page 66. Add the following new paragraphs and table 1 after line 21.

In 1998, this writer (Matte) authored a study entitled "An Analysis of the Psychodynamics of the Directed Lie Control Question in the Control Question Technique" published in *Polygraph*, Vol. 27, Nr. 1, which reviews and evaluates existing studies of the Directed Lie Control Question (DLCQ) and further analyzes the psychodynamics of the DLCQ versus the Probable-Lie Control Question (PLCQ) to determine its construct and criterion validity. Table 1 titled "Comparison of PLCQ and DLCQ, Potential Response Elements" reflected below, depicts a construct validity analysis of the Probable-Lie Control Questions versus the Directed-Lie Control Question in the control question technique. The Table shows that the DLCQ contains five elements (Nr. 3, 4, 5, 8, 9) which may cause a false negative result, whereas the PLCQ contains none. Both the DLCQ and the PLCQ each contain three elements (PLCQ 1, 6, 7; DLCQ 2, 5, 8) which may elicit a response from the Innocent subject which indicates an approximate equal capacity to identify the Innocent examinee. This study further reflects that the negative effect of the evidentiary element of the DLCQ is exacerbated by the methodology of the DLCQ which particularly emphasizes the review of the DLCQ between the collection of each polygraph chart data (Horowitz, et al. 1997), thus inordinately increasing the strength of the DLCQ resulting in undue influence and alteration of the guilty examinee's psychological set. This routine manipulation of the examinee's psychological set, without specific evidence of a control question malfunction, raises the potential for a false negative result to a higher probability. This study concludes that "The Probable-Lie Control Question has been shown to be a valid and reliable control question in control question tests both in laboratory and field studies. The Directed-Lie Control Question however appears to lack construct validity in that it fails to demonstrate adequate capacity to function as a control question of less intensity than the relevant question for the guilty examinee. It further lacks criterion validity in that there appears to be inadequate data demonstrating a relationship between test outcomes and a criterion of ground truth supporting the effectiveness of the DLCQ for all examinees in control question tests. There exists a wholly insufficient body of data to support its use as a valid and reliable control question in control question tests." (Matte 1998).

This writer (Matte) and Dr. Ronald M. Reuss, authored a subsequent study entitled "Validation of Potential Response Elements in the Directed-Lie Control Question" published in *Polygraph*, Vol. 28, Nr. 2 (1999) which was designed to determine the validity of the hypothesis set forth in the aforementioned 1998. This was accomplished by simulating a psychophysiological veracity (PV) examination in which 117 guilty participants were queried about the focus and strength of their psychological set in each one of the nine potential response elements to either the DLCQ or its neighboring relevant question. This study further evaluated the psychological effect of discussing the DLCQ with the guilty examinee between the conduct of the tests (charts) or repetitions.

The results of this study "support the construct validity of all nine Potential Response Elements for the directed-lie control question contained in Table 1. The data in Table 2, reflects that 90% of the participants in the role of guilty polygraph subjects in this study did not have any fear of detection to the directed-lie questions, validating Potential Response Elements (PRE) number 1. Only 6% of the Guilty participants in this study feared an error would be made regarding the directed-lie as opposed to 93% of the guilty participants who were hopeful an error would be made regarding the directed-lie questions, validating PREs number 2 and 3. Ninety-one percent of the guilty participants were afraid that a physiological comparison would be made between their known-lies to the directed-lie questions and the relevant (crime) questions, validating PRE number 4; and 91% of the Guilty participants perceived the directed-lie questions as a threat to the outcome of the PV test in that it would help identify their lies to the relevant (crime) questions, validating PRE number 5. Thirty-eight percent of the guilty participants considered the directed-lie questions an equal threat to that of the relevant questions and 48% considered the directed-lie questions a greater threat than the relevant questions, while only 6% of the guilty participants considered the directed-lie questions to be of a lesser threat than the relevant questions. Eighty-three percent of the guilty participants did not think

TABLE 1
COMPARISON OF PLCQ AND DLCQ POTENTIAL RESPONSE ELEMENTS

Response Elements Subjects:	Focus of Psychological Set and Potential Response			
	PLCQ		DLCQ	
	Innocent	Guilty	Innocent	Guilty
1. Fear of Detection	Yes	No	No	No
2. Fear of Error	No	No	Yes	No
3. Hope of Error	No	No	No	Yes
4. Fear of Physiological Comparison	No	No	No	Yes
5. Perceived as Threat to Outcome of Test	No	No	Yes	Yes
6. Perceived Threat of Past Offense Reflecting on Capacity to Commit Current Offense	Yes	No	No	No
7. Shame-Embarrassment	Yes	No	No	No
8. Perceived Relationship with Relevant Question	No	No	Yes	Yes
9. Invitation to Countermeasures	No	No	No	Yes
Total Affirmatives	3	0	3	5
Potential Errors		False Negative		False Negative

that the directed-lie questions would expose similar prior offense(s) that they may have committed which might suggest that they had committed the current offense, thus validating PRE number 6. Ninety-two percent of the guilty participants did not feel that they would experience shame-embar-

TABLE 2
GROUP DLCQ QUESTIONNAIRE RESULTS

Groups	Questions & Participant Answers												
	1		2a		2b		3		4a		4b		
	Y	N	Y	N	Y	N	Y	N	Y	N	1	2	3
1	1	15	3	12	12	4	13	3	15	1	0	6	9
2	0	17	1	16	14	3	15	2	14	3	0	4	10
3	4	13	2	15	14	3	16	1	15	2	1	6	8
4	0	11	0	11	11	0	11	0	11	0	0	3	8
5	2	12	0	14	13	1	13	1	13	1	1	4	8
6	1	9	0	10	10	0	10	0	10	0	0	4	6
7	1	11	0	12	12	0	11	1	11	1	1	4	6
8	3	17	1	19	19	1	18	2	18	2	4	13	1
TOTALS	12	105	7	109	105	12	107	10	107	10	7	44	56
%	10	90	6	93	90	10	91	9	91	9	6	38	48

Groups	Questions & Participant Answers										
	5		6		7		8		9		
	Y	N	Y	N	Y	N	Y	N	a	b	c
1	1	15	0	16	16	0	14	2	3	13	0
2	2	15	1	16	16	1	14	3	3	13	1
3	3	14	3	14	14	3	15	2	3	13	1
4	0	11	0	11	11	0	11	0	0	11	0
5	4	10	0	14	14	0	12	2	2	12	0
6	3	7	1	9	10	0	8	2	2	8	0
7	0	12	2	10	11	1	11	1	3	9	0
8	7	13	2	18	19	1	19	1	1	17	2
TOTALS	20	97	9	108	111	6	104	13	17	96	4
%	17	83	8	92	95	5	89	11	15	82	3

Note: Percentages were rounded to the nearest whole number.

Some total responses in 4b have a deficit corresponding to the negative responses in 4a. Only affirmative answers in 4a require response in 4b. See Questionnaire.

rassment at being directed to lie to the directed-lie questions, validating PRE number 7. Ninety-five percent of the guilty participants perceived a relationship and connection between the directed-lie questions and the relevant (crime) questions, validating PRE number 8. Eighty-nine percent of the guilty participants would use a physical or mental countermeasure when asked the directed-lie question(s) during the PV test, validating PRE number 9. In addition, 82% of the guilty participants indicated that the discussion of the directed-lie questions between the administration of the tests (charts) would increase their apprehension about the directed-lie questions, which supports Backster's Zone Comparison Technique Rules contained in his Tri-Zone Reaction Combinations Table appended to this study, of which certain relevant combinations are articulated in the body of this study. This study supports the assertions reflected in Table 1 that five of the nine elements, specifically numbers 3, 4, 5, 8 and 9 may elicit the guilty examinee's psychological set onto the directed-lie questions with a corresponding potential response and possible false negative test result. It should be noted that any one of the aforesaid five elements has the potential of causing a false negative. The results of this study confirm the conclusions of a previous study by this author (Matte, 1998) that the directed-lie control question lacks construct and criterion validity and contains a significant number of potential response elements capable of producing false negatives. This study further indicated that, except for those instances where remedial action is necessary as articulated in Backster's Tri-Zone Reaction Combinations Table, the discussion of the directed-lie control question between charts (tests) is a prescription for false negative results." (Matte, Reuss 1999)

Charles Honts, a proponent of the DLCQ, conducted a meta-analysis (Honts 1999) of eleven laboratory studies that included a discussion of questions and/or the stimulation of comparison questions between the repetitions of the question list for comparison with eight laboratory studies where comparison questions were not discussed between repetitions. According to Honts' analysis of the results of those studies, the error rate was significantly reduced where questions were reviewed between repetitions, especially with guilty subjects where the error rate was reduced by 54%. Honts asserts that these results clearly support the review of questions between charts, and the attacks against its practice by Dr. Stanley Abrams in several court cases have had a negative impact on the admissibility of polygraph examinations in United States Courts of Law. A critical analysis of Honts' study (Matte 2000) reveals selective scholarship and a seriously flawed research methodology, which call into question the conclusions of Honts' study.

In a "Critical Analysis of Honts Study: The Discussion (Stimulation of Comparison Questions" authored by this writer (Matte) published in Polygraph, Vol. 29, Nr. 2 (2000), this author (Matte) points out that the use by Honts of several laboratory studies involving diverse polygraph techniques and methodology completely ignores that there may be many other significant factors responsible for the difference in accuracy and percentage of false negatives and positives. These factors could include the type of test used (multiple – or single-issue), types of comparison questions (current exclusive, non-current exclusive, non-exclusive, disguised, relevant-connected, directed-lie), the polygraph testing methodology including the pretest interview format, the test data analysis and the competency of the Polygraphist , to name a few. Furthermore, Honts' selection of studies where comparison questions were not discussed between charts is very limited and selective, The Szucko and Kleinmuntz (1981) study selected by Honts reflects the poverty of his selection process. The Szucko et al study used four examiner-trainees, which of itself should have eliminated the study from consideration inasmuch as it does not replicate a real-life examination. Furthermore, the integrity of the Szucko study has been seriously questioned, in that one of the participating examiners (chodkowski,

1986) challenged the facts as they were published. It is interesting to note that nowhere in the Szucko study does it state that the comparison questions were not discussed with the examinees between charts. Yet Honts states in his Study Selection that "The studies shown in Table 1 were selected for inclusion in the analysis because they met at least one of the following criterion: The method section of the study explicitly described the discussion of, or the lack of discussion of, comparison and/or relevant questions between question list repetitions." Thus many other studies which reflected significantly higher accuracy rates could have qualified for inclusion in Honts instant article. In a footnote #3, in Honts' study, he states that "When I attended the Backster School of Lie Detection in San Diego, in 1976 the review of questions and the stimulation of comparison questions between charts was considered to be a standard practice." Honts previously made a similar statement under oath in U.S. v. Gilliard. However, in a letter dated 18 September 1998, Cleve Backster contradicts Honts' statements articulated above regarding the review and stimulation of comparison questions between charts, stating that:

"After formulation and discussion of control (comparison) questions during the pre-test interview, further routine discussion of these questions will be avoided except as dictated by principles outlined in our Zone Comparison Indication-Remedy Table." (See Chapter 11, Page 352 for Backster Letter of 18 Sep 98 and Zone Comparison Indication-Remedy Table.)

Honts acknowledges that "Correlational studies and analysis are not as good as experiments in determining causation." The recently completed study by Matte and Reuss (1999) indicates that "the direct review or discussion of comparison questions between charts may increase the guilty examinee" apprehension regarding the DLCQ, thus creating a formula for false negative results." (Matte 2000)

Honts (2000) criticizes the Matte-Reuss (1999) study of the Directed-Lie Control Question (DLCQ) commencing with the heading "The Hypothetical Construct, Psychological Set" stating that "the notion of psychological set is a contrivance of the polygraph profession and has received little scientific validation. Moreover, psychological set is not a term that is currently much used in mainstream psychological science. While the hypothetical construct, psychological set, may have some heuristic value as a descriptive tool, it has no reality in science or the real world." However, in a recently published article (Matte and Grove, 2001) entitled "Psychological Set: Its Origin, Theory and Application" the "paper sets forth the historical origins of its application to forensic psychophysiology and shows how psychological set continues to be widely used and regarded in contemporary psychological, industrial/organizational and legal/political science communities." Honts argues that the aforesaid Matte-Reuss (1999) study of the DLCQ fails to replicate an actual polygraph examination hence not worthy of consideration, when it is clearly stated in the aforementioned study that "the present study differs from traditional analog studies in that it is not recording and measuring the participants' physiology, nor is it attempting to determine the accuracy of a PV Examination technique. This study is designed to determine the thought processes and attitudes of each programmed guilty participant regarding each of the nine potential response elements identified in Table 1, and the effects of discussing the directed-lie questions between charts (tests), based on the same facts that would be presented to them in an actual PV examination. The questionnaire in this study deliberately invites intellectual decisions which may generate emotions. Real-life case participants also have to make intellectual decisions which may generate emotions which in actual cases are then recorded and evaluated. In this study we were only interested in the thought processes and attitudes present when making those intellectual decisions. We were not interested in the emotional response that may follow on the test, but only in the intellectual decision that preceded it, and there is no reason to believe that they would be any different in either circumstance. We doubt that Question 8, for instance, would elicit a different response from a guilty participant in a real-life case, to wit: 'As a Guilty examinee, if you knew how to use a physical or mental countermeasure, would you have employed one when asked the Directed-Lie Question 3 and 4 during the test? Yes? or No?'" Honts states that "Essentially no discussion of the relevant issue is mentioned, with only 82 words being devoted to the entire section on the issues of the examination and the relevant questions." However Honts disregards the statement in the Matte-Reuss (1999) study that "The pretest interview including the review of the control and relevant test questions was included in the preparation of each participant." It is a well-known fact among Polygraphist s that the pretest interview includes everything from a full discussion of the relevant issue, an explanation of the psychophysiological aspects, to the review of all test questions with the examinee. In summary, Honts' criticism of the Matte-Reuss (1999) study is non-persuasive.

Dr. Stanley Abrams (1999) in his published article "A Response to Honts on the Issue of the Discussion of Questions Between Charts" makes a very strong case for the rejection of the Utah Directed-Lie Test, stating "Abrams has provided evidence supporting his view that this technique neither should be admitted into court nor employed as a polygraph technique because there is insufficient and conflicting research findings, there is a discussion of questions between charts, and there is an excessive emphasis placed on the directed lie which has resulted in false negative findings." Abrams documents several court cases (Abrams 1999 and 2001) wherein Charles Honts and David Raskin employing the Directed-Lie Test found the defendants truthful but were subsequently shown to be guilty. Abrams cites one particular case that caused damage to the polygraph profession in United States v. Cordoba wherein U. S. District Judge Gary Taylor stated "The blanket and non-critical approval of Defendant's test by Dr. Raskin, who is probably the strongest and best informed advocate for polygraph admissibility, illustrates that the polygraph industry lacks sufficient controlling standards to satisfy Daubert. If pro polygraph's best expert declines to find fault with an obviously faulty examination, that is strong evidence that there are insufficient controlling standards." For a list of more details and additional cases Abrams invites the reader to consult the testimony in U.S. v. Clayton and Dalley or Steve Griffith v. Muscle Improvement Inc.

Page 76. Delete paragraph 2 which starts with "On 11 September 1996…" and ends with "(Capps, 1996), and add the following paragraphs after line 11.

On 7 February 1998, the American Polygraph Association issued a position statement on voice stress analysis which reads in part as follows: (APA 1998)

"Recently there have been claims made that voice stress analysis is an accurate means of detecting deception. There is no independent research supporting the assertion that voice stress analysis is an accurate means of detecting deception. Based on the status of the current body of research, the APA does not endorse the use of voice stress analysis to determine or detect deception."

On 11 September 1996, the Department of Defense Polygraph Institute issued a position statement regarding voice stress analysis which reads in part as follows:

"Starting about 25 years ago, serious efforts were made to use the voice to detect deception. Many devices were marketed for this purpose. The most widely advertised devices have been the Psychological Stress Evaluator (PSE), the Hagoth, the Mark II Voice Stress Analyzer (VSA), and the Computerized Voice Stress Analyzer (CVSA). If effective, voice analysis offers many advantages over current polygraph methodology. Voice samples can be recorded without discomfort to the subject. Examinations could be conducted remotely, both in distance, using a telephone or radio link, or in time, using a tape recording. In rare cases, it could even be conducted after a person's death, if a recording made under proper technical, psychological, and investigative conditions existed. The recordings could also be conducted surreptitiously and would be of great benefit in intelligence and counterintelligence investigations, international negotiations, etc. If effective, voice stress analysis could significantly improve the nation's security."

"The Department of Defense Polygraph Institute has investigated the scientific value of voice stress analysis. We reviewed the research literature on voice stress analysis. Only one voice stress device, the CVSA, is being widely marketed. We purchased the CVSA, and sent two researchers to the CVSA school for training by the manufacturer. We conducted several studies on voice stress analysis, using standard laboratory voice equipment and software and also using the CVSA device. We solicited the manufacturer's advice in designing the CVSA studies, and used both our own scientists and CVSA practitioners recommended by the CVSA manufacturer to father the research data."

"Conclusions:

1. To date, we have found no credible evidence in information furnished by the manufacturers, the scientific literature, or in our own research, that voice stress analysis is an effective investigative tool for determining deception.

2. A very few studies have found that voice stress analysis worked better than chance at detecting deception. Unfortunately, these results are not consistent, nor are the reported accuracies nearly as good as those normally reported for the polygraph. Hundreds of studies have shown that when properly trained examiners use the polygraph under controlled conditions, their decisions can be highly accurate in discriminating between truthful and deceptive people.

3. The preponderance of evidence indicates the polygraph is far more accurate at detecting deception than is voice stress analysis. No Department of Defense agency uses any form of voice stress analysis for investigative purposes." (Capps, 1996).

In July 1998, the American Association of Police Polygraphist s (AAPP) issued a position statement on Voice Stress Analysis which reads in part as follows:

"To date, the AAPP has found no scientific studies or independent research which support voice stress analysis as a method of discriminating between truth and deception." "Ultimately, every procedure and process employed by a law enforcement agency must be able to withstand the in-depth scrutiny of judicial proceedings. In making a determination of acceptability, the courts will weigh the available scientific data. 'Testimonials' without the support of reliable scientific information will not meet the standards for acceptable evidence. Polygraph is the only deception detection device which as the scientific support and has earned judicial acceptance for expert testimony. In addition to jeopardizing criminal proceedings, the use of methods and equipment which have not been proven to be impartial, valid and reliable may expose a law enforcement agency to potential civil liability. As law enforcement processionals and public servants, it is our duty and responsibility to protect and uphold the individual civil rights of the citizens which we serve. The AAPP joins with other professional national and state polygraph associations which require their members to utilize proven professional procedures and instrumentation. Until voice stress analysis is supported by scientific research that conclusively demonstrates its validity and reliability, the American Association of Police Polygraphist s will not endorse the use of such equipment in the law enforcement community." (APA 1998; AAPP 2002)

In an article authored by N. Joan Blackwell published in APA Newsletter, Vol. 31, Nr. 4 (1998), the author describes "Work done by the Walter Reed Army Institute of Research (WRAIR) has shown there to be various saliva and blood chemistry markers for psychological stress. Dr. Victor Cestaro, Department of Defense Polygraph Institute (DoDPI), recently conducted a joint research study with WRAIR, which compared known biomedical indices to those measures used for detecting deception by the Computerized Voice Stress Analyzer (CVSA), one of the two systems currently utilized by numerous law enforcement agencies. Speech samples, along with blood and saliva samples, were collected from soldiers during a stressful soldier of the month interview. Voice, blood, and saliva samples were also collected at three intervals preceding and three intervals after the interview. Analysis of the blood and saliva samples for all participants showed the cortisol (a powerful hormone produced by the adrenal gland during times of stress) level to be at its peak during the treatment, or stress, phase of the study. Heart rate data collected during this study also correlated with the biochemical measures. Three trained CVSA examiners were than asked to analyze the voice recordings of each subject. There was found to be no agreement among the examiners' decisions. One frequently scored the least stressful periods (according to the biomedical results) as the most stressful. A second examiner's scores were considered to be completely random. The remaining examiner's scores were inverse to expected values, i.e., he consistently scored the treatment condition lower than any other phase. Thus, biomedical measures and speech data were collected in a proven stress inducing situation and voice stress scores did not track stress level conditions." " It can be concluded that there is no scientific evidence to date, either from this study or others, which would indicate that the CVSA or any other voice stress analyzer can detect stress (or deception) at other than chance levels." (Blackwell 1998)

Donald J. Krapohl, Editor of the American Polygraph Association (APA) (1998-2001) authored and published an article on research studies that "investigated voice stress as a deception detection approach." This article is published in toto herein with permission of the author and the APA. (Krapohl, 2002)

"Various investigative techniques for detecting deception have appeared in the past 80 years. Some were developed by scientists and researchers, like reaction time tests, the polygraph, and brain wave methods. Others were proffered by manufacturers without the help of researchers, such as the B&W lie detector and the various voice stress devices. The most recent method being heralded as the new lie detector is the Computer Voice Stress Analyzer (CVSA). What separates the CVSA from previous voice stress methods is that the display is on a computer screen, versus on paper. There are no validated algorithms or scoring systems, or sophisticated analytical methods. These shortcomings have not prevented the manufacturer from making remarkable claims regarding the efficacy of its product. But, are they true? Those of us in the detection of deception profession would like to believe it, because switching to this new device would allow us to better serve our clients and agencies in a shorter time. Before we accept the self-endorsements of the manufacturer, it is best that we first look at what scientists have to say."

"Below is a list of the university-grade research studies that have investigated voice stress as a deception detection approach. Some studies looked at the CVSA device in particular, while others investigated whether voice stress analysis in general could be used to detect stress or deception. Copies of these studies can be obtained at many university libraries."

"Brenner, M., Branscomb, H., & Schwartz, G. E. (1979). Psychological stress evaluator: Two tests of a vocal measure. Psychophysiology, 16(4). 351-357.
Conclusion: Validity of the analysis for practical lie detection is questionable."

"Cestaro, V. L. (1995). A Comparison Between Decision Accuracy Rates Obtained Using the Polygraph Instrument and the Computer Voice Stress Analyzer (CVSA) in the Absence of Jeopardy. (DoDPI95-R-0002). Fort McClellan, AL: Department of Defense Polygraph Institute.
Conclusion: Accuracy was not significantly greater than chance for the CVSA."

"DoDPI Research Division Staff, Meyerhoff, J. L., Saviolakis, G. A., Koenig, M. L., & Yourick, D. L. (Ion press). Physiological and Biochemical Measures of Stress Compared to Voice Stress Analysis Using the Computer Voice Stress Analyzer (CVSA). (DoDPI-R-0001). Department of Defense Polygraph Institute.
Conclusion: Direct test of the CVSA against medical markers for stress (blood pressure, plasma ACTH, salivary cortisol) found that CVSA examiners could not detect known stress. This project was a collaborative effort with Walter Reed Army Institute of Research."

"Fuller, B. F. (1984). Reliability and validity of an interval measure of vocal stress. Psychological Medicine. 14(1), 159-166.
Conclusion: Validity of voice stress measures was poor."

"Janniro, M. J., & Cestaro, V. L. (1996). Effectiveness of Detection of Deception Examinations Using the Computer Voice Stress Analyzer. (DoDPI95-P-0016). Fort McClellan, AL: Department of Defense Polygraph Institute. DTIC AD Number A318986.
Conclusion: Chance-level detection of deception using the CVSA as a voice stress device."

"Hollien, H., Geison, L., & Hicks, J. W., Jr. (1987). Voice stress analysis and lie detection. Journal of Forensic Sciences, 32(2), 405-418.
Conclusion: Chance-level detection of stress. Chance-level detection of lies."

"Horvath, F. L. (1978). An experimental comparison of the psychological stress evaluator and the galvanic skin response in detection of deception. Journal of Applied Psychology, 63(3), 338-344.
Conclusion: Chance-level detection of deception."

"Horvath, F. S. (1979). Effect of different motivational instructions on detection of deception with the psychological stress evaluator and the galvanic skin response. Journal of Applied Psychology, 64(3, June), 323-330.
Conclusion: Voice stress did not detect deception greater than chance."

"Kubis, J. F. (1973). Comparison of Voice Analysis and Polygraph as Lie Detection Procedures. (Technical Report No. LWL-CR-03B70, Contract DAAD05-72-C-0217). Aberdeen Proving Ground, MD: U.S. Army Land Warfare Laboratory.
Conclusion: Chance-level detection of deception for voice analysis."

"Lynch, B. E., & Henry, D. R. (1979). A validity study of the psychological stress evaluator. Canadian Journal of Behavioural Science, 11(1), 89-94.
Conclusion: Chance level detection of stress using the voice."

"O'Hair, D., Cody, M. J., & Behnke, R. R. (1985). Communication apprehension and vocal stress as indices of deception. The Western Journal of Speech Communication, 49, 286-300.
Conclusions: Only one subgroup showed a detection rate significantly better than chance, and it did so by the thinnest or margins. Use of questionable statistical methods in this study suggests the modest positive findings would not be replicated in other research. See next citation."

"O'Hair, D., Cody, M. J., Wang, S., & Chao, E. Y. (1990). Vocal stress and deception detection among Chinese. Communication Quarterly, 38(2, Spring), 158ff.
Conclusion: Partial replication of above study. Vocal scores were not related to deception."

"Suzuki, A., Watanabe, S., Takeno, Y., Kosugi, T., & Kasuya, T. (1973). Possibility of detecting deception by voice analysis. Reports of the National Research Institute of Police Science, 26(1, February), 62-66.
Conclusion: Voice measures were not reliable or useful."

"Timm, H. W. (1983). The efficacy of the psychological stress evaluator in detecting deception. Journal of Police Science and Administration, 11(1), 62-68.
Conclusion: Chance-level detection of deception."

"Waln, R. R., & Downey, R. G. (1987). Voice stress analysis: Use of telephone recordings. Journal of Business and Psychology, 1(4), 379-389.
Conclusions: Voice stress methodology did not show sufficient reliability to warrant its use as a selection procedure for employment."

Page 76. Typographical error at paragraph 3, line 5 from bottom of paragraph.

Change buffalo to read "Buffalo."

Pages 88-101. Add the following References in alphabetical order at appropriate pages.

Abrams, S. (1991) The directed lie control question. Polygraph, 20: 26-31.

Abrams, S. (1999). A Response to Honts on the Issue of the Discussion of Questions Between Charts. Polygraph, 28(3): 223-229.

Abrams, S. (2001). Statistics and Other Lies. Polygraph, 30(1): 1-10.

American Polygraph Association (1998, July 19). Polygraph vs. Voice Stress. APA website: http://www.polygraph.org/voice.htm.

American Association of Police Polygraphist s (2002, February 6). Telephone and electronic mail communication between Gordon Moore, President of AAPP and J. A. Matte.

Blackwell, N. J. (1998, July-August). Truth=Polygraph+Research. American Polygraph Association Newsletter, 31(4): 20.

Capps, M. H. (1996, September 11). Voice Stress Analysis Position Statement.

Department of Defense Polygraph Institute. Fort McClellan, AL.

Chodkowski, R. E. (1986, February 22). Personal communication with Dr. Frank Horvath.

Griffith, et al., v. Muscle Improvement, Inc., et al. Superior Court for the State of California for the County of Los Angeles, No. BC215080, 1996.

Griffith v. Milgaar. Boise, Idaho MB&C, File No. 4502.00, 1996.

Hoffman, M, Naefeh, S. & White, G. W. (1989). The Mormon Murders. Onyx Books.

Honts, C. R. (1999). The discussion of questions between list repetitions (charts) is associated with increased test accuracy. Polygraph, 28(2): 117-123.

Honts, C. R. (2000). A brief note on the misleading and the inaccurate: A rejoinder to Matte (2000) with critical comments on Matte and Reuss (1999). Polygraph, 29(4): 321-325.

Honts, C. R. & Raskin, D. C. (1988). A field study of the validity of the directed lie control question. Journal of Police Science and Administration, 16: 56-61.

Horowitz, S. W., Kircher, J. C., Honts, C. T., Raskin, C. D. (1997). The role of comparison questions in physiological detection of deception. Psychophysiology, 34(1): 108-115.

Krapohl, D. J. (2002). Voice stress analysis research. Tech Talk. APA website: http://www.polygraph.org/Tech%20Talk.htm. Reprinted from APA Newsletter with permission.

Matte, J. A. (1998). An analysis of the psychodynamics of the directed lie control question in the control question technique. Polygraph, 27(1): 56-67.

Matte, J. A., Reuss, R. M. (1999). Validation of potential response elements in the directed-lie control question. Polygraph, 28(2): 124-142.

Matte, J. A. (2000). A critical analysis of Honts' study: The discussion (stimulation) of comparison questions. Polygraph, 29(2): 146-150.

Matte, J. A., Grove, R. N. (2001). Psychological Set: Its origin, theory and application. Polygraph, 30(3): 196-203).

Szucko, J. J., Kleinmuntz, B. (1981). Statistical versus clinical lie detection. American Psychologist, 36(5): 488-496.

U. S. v. Clayton and Dalley. U.S. District Court, District of Arizona. No. 92-374-PCT- RCB, 1994.

U.S. v. Gilliard. U.S. District Court, District of Georgia. No. 196-19, 1996..

CHAPTER 3

RESEARCH AND THE SCIENTIFIC STATUS OF PV EXAMINATIONS

Page 112. Add the following paragraph after the first paragraph which ends with "clearly without merit." (Matte, Reuss 1990)

The number of confirmed deceptive cases in aforesaid study by Matte and Reuss (1990) for defense attorneys was 34 versus 13 for the police cases. In view of the small number of police cases in that 1990 study, a search of the files of the Buffalo Police Department for verified deceptive cases since 1990 was conducted for the purpose of acquiring a larger sample for comparison with the aforesaid data from defense attorney cases. Thirty-two confirmed deceptive cases were found, and they proved to have a mean chart score of –8.6. The difference in the mean scores of the defense cases and the police cases were not statistically significant, adding to the growing body of evidence against the Friendly Polygrapher hypothesis. (Matte, Armitage 2000).

Page 139. Add the following paragraph after paragraph four ending with "these studies."

The field studies cited above by Norman Ansley regarding "The Validity and Reliability of Polygraph Decisions in Real Cases" for the period 1980 to 1990 reflect that this group of eleven Control Question Tests contained several different CQT formats, with one appearing in four studies; namely the Backster Zone Comparison Technique, which averaged 97 percent accuracy. Yet in a recent publication (Kleiner 2002), David Raskin and Charles Honts, both advocates of the Directed-Lie Control Question Test, severely criticized the validity of the Backster ZCT, in their chapter of Kleiner's book on "The Comparison Question Test."

In their description and evaluation of the Backster ZCT, Raskin and Honts make several significant errors, such as "The set of questions is asked only twice, usually in the same order," which is not true. The *minimum* number of charts that must be conducted before a determination of truth or deception can be rendered is "two" but the number of charts can be as many as four, depending on the quality of the charts collected from the examinee. Furthermore, the relevant questions are rotated in their position with each chart run so that each relevant question is eventually compared with each control (comparison) question.

Raskin and Honts erroneously describe the two probable-lie control (comparison) questions using the same two words "Before" 1997 or "Before" age 27, when in fact the standard wording for the past 40 years has been "Between the ages of ( ) and ( ), do you remember ever ……." and the second control question worded "During the first ( ) years of your life, do you remember ever………". The difference in the wording of the two control questions, starting with the first word is important in that it immediately identifies and separates the two control questions as being entirely different, hence avoiding or delaying potential habituation to the control questions. Secondly, use of the word "remember" elicits mental exercise (see page 252) and provides the examinee with a rationale for giving a negative answer. They also fault the Backster control (comparison) questions as being too narrow in scope thus "increasing the risk of a false positive error" when in fact the Polygraphist has 20 pages of control questions (See chapter 16) to choose from, depending on the background of the examinee and the case information, thus providing the Polygraphist with a wide array of choices in the selection of control questions. The Polygraphist is undoubtedly in the best position to determine which control question(s) under the existing circumstance will be most effective.

Raskin and Honts further state that "the Backster approach is mildly confrontational owing to its law enforcement orientation" which is not true inasmuch as the polygraphist in the standardized pretest interview (see Chapter 8) must inform the examinee that it is assumed by the polygraphist that the examinee is innocent of the offense for which he/she is being polygraphed and the polygraphist will maintain that assumption of his/her innocence until the examination is concluded. Furthermore, the polygraphist is prohibited from using any type of accusatory or interrogative approach during any portion of the PV examination.

Raskin and Honts further state "Backster severely reduced the amount of pretest discussion of the comparison questions to simply telling the subject that certain other questions needed to be asked. He also minimized the pretest explanation of the psychophysiological reasons why stronger reactions occur during deception. The latter changes reduce the face validity and accuracy of the test." Both of those assumptions by Raskin and Honts are in error as evidenced by the Standardized Pretest Interview reflected in Chapter 8 and this supplement.

Raskin and Honts criticize the effectiveness and usefulness of Backster's use of Symptomatic questions in his test format, citing Honts' unpublished (2000) study, but fail to mention a published study by Capps, Knill & Evans (1993), which revealed that the use of Symptomatic questions reduced the inconclusive rate by 66 percent. (See also Krapohl & Ryan 200la; Backster 2001; Matte 200la; Krapohl & Ryan 200lb; Matte 2001b).

Raskin and Honts recognize Backster's introduction of a numerical scoring system for the evaluation of the physiological data recorded on polygraph charts as a major advance in test evaluation. However they criticize the scoring rules, stating "There is a complex set of rules for this procedure, but they are extremely difficult to follow and are biased against the innocent subject." On the contrary, the chart interpretation rules are standardized, and the threshold or cut-off scores for arriving at a determination of truth or deception require only a plus 6 for two charts or plus 9 for three charts for a finding of truthfulness, while a minus 9 for two charts and a minus 13 for three charts are required for a finding of deception. The Utah ZCT does not require a lower score for the truthful (+ or – 6) as in the Backster ZCT, hence the Backster Technique recognizes that the control questions are structurally weaker than the relevant questions and incorporates that element into the scores (threshold) required to arrive at a determination, hence protecting the innocent from false positives.

Raskin and Honts erroneously state that "Backster assumed that if the test results are inconclusive, the 'probable-lie questions are perfectly formulated' and the problem is the wording of the relevant questions, which need to be strengthened (Backster, 1973). This automatic strengthening of the relevant questions rather than the probable-lie questions increases the risk of false positive errors." Nothing could be further from the truth. Backster's "Tri-Zone" Reaction Combinations which have been in effect since 1962, clearly indicate in Combination 'H' when there is no reactions to either the relevant or control (comparison) question (Inconclusive), that "No remedy necessary; red zone questions have been formulated as ideally as possible; red zone questions functioning as designed. Increase intensity of green zone questions by altering age categories or changing scope of green zone questions." It should be noted that Red Zone questions refer to Relevant questions and Green Zone questions refer to Control (comparison) questions.

Raskin and Honts further stated that "he weakened the power of the probable-lie questions to establish the truthfulness of the innocent suspect by including behaviors and terminology that would allow more subjects to truthfully answer with a denial." However, Raskin and Honts fail to describe those alleged "behaviors and terminology" which this author who is a 1972 graduate of the Backster School of Lie Detection and an Instructor since 1997 finds implausible and unsupported by the numerous published studies cited in Chapter 3 and a recent field study by this author using the files of the Virginia State Police that uses the Backster ZCT religiously, which attained a 100 percent accuracy, further validating the Backster Zone Comparison Technique.

Footnote: Cleve Backster has successfully testified in court against David Raskin in his use of the Directed-Lie Control Question Test, and has been an outspoken critic of its use in general.

Pages 147 thru 152. Add the following references in alphabetical order.

Backster, C. (2001). A response to Krapohl & Ryan's "Belated look at symptomatic questions." *Polygraph*, 30(3): 313-216

Krapohl, D. J., Ryan, A. H. (2001a). A belated look at symptomatic questions. *Polygraph*, 30(3): 206-212.

Krapohl, D. J., Ryan, A. H. (2001b). Final comment on the belated look at symptomatic questions. *Polygraph*, 30(3): 218-220.

Matte, J. A., Reuss, R. M. (1990). A field study of the "Friendly Polygraphist " concept. Polygraph, 19(1): 1-8.

Matte, J. A., Armitage, T. E. (2000). Addendum to 1990 field study of the friendly polygrapher hypothesis. *Polygraph*, 29(3): 267-270.

Matte, J. A. (In Press). A field study of three methods of comparison of control questions when relevant question elicits strong response. Submitted to Polygraph.

Matte, J. A. (2001a). Comments on Krapohl & Ryan criticism of Capps, Knill & Evans research. *Polygraph*, 30(3): 216-218.

Matte, J. A. (2001b). Reply to rejoinder by Donald J. Krapohl and Andrew H. Ryan. *Polygraph*, 30(3): 220-223.

Page 153. Reference Putnam, R. L. (1953) should be changed to read as follows:

Putnam, R. L. (1983).

Page 153. Reference Rafky, D. M., Sussman, R. C. (1985). Polygraphic…

Separate above reference from Putnam, R. L., as it is a separate reference.

Page 154. Add the following reference in alphabetical order.

Kleiner, M. (2002). Handbook of Polygraph Testing. San Diego, CA: Academic Press.

CHAPTER 5

EVOLUTION OF THE PSYCHOPHYSIOLOGICAL VERACITY EXAMINATION

Page 191. Add the following reference after (Hunter 1974) at the end of third paragraph.

(Hunter, F. L. 1974; Bongard, S., Pfeiffer, J. S., Al'Absi, M. Hodapp, V., and Linnenkemper, G. (1997).

Page 211. Add the following paragraphs after the last paragraph which ends with DLCQ.

In 1998, this writer (Matte) authored a study entitled "An Analysis of the Psychodynamics of the Directed-Lie Control Question in the Control Question Technique" (Matte 1998) which reviews and evaluates existing studies of the Directed Lie Control Question (DLCQ) and further analyzes the psychodynamics of the DLCQ versus the Probable-Lie Control Question (PLCQ) to determine its construct and criterion validity. (See Page 66, Chapter 2 for a detailed discussion of aforesaid study).

In 1999, this writer (Matte) and Dr. Ronald M. Reuss, authored a subsequent study entitled "Validation of Potential Response Elements in the Directed-Lie Control Question" (Matte, Reuss 1999), which was designed to determine the validity of the hypothesis set forth in the aforementioned 1998 study. The results of this study confirmed and validated the conclusions of the previously mentioned study (Matte 1998) and affirmed that of the nine potential elements capable of eliciting a response, five of them may elicit the guilty examinee's psychological set onto the directed-lie questions with a corresponding potential response and possible false negative test result. This study (Matte, Reuss 1999) further indicated that, except for those instances where remedial action is necessary as articulated in Backster's Tri-Zone Reaction Combinations Table, the discussion of the directed-lie control question between charts (tests) is a prescription for false negative results." (See pages 8-11 of this supplement and corresponding pages 66-70, Chapter 2 for a detailed discussion and tables reflecting the results of aforesaid study by Matte and Reuss 1999).

Charles Honts, a proponent of the DLCQ, conducted a meta-analysis (Honts (1999) of eleven laboratory studies that included a discussion of questions and/or the stimulation of comparison questions between the repetitions of the question list for comparison with eight laboratory studies where comparison questions were not discussed between repetitions. According to Honts' analysis of the results of those studies, the error rate was significantly reduced where questions were reviewed between repetitions, especially with guilty subjects. (for further details see page 11 of this supplement and corresponding page 69-70, Chapter 2 of this textbook.)

In a "Critical Analysis of Honts Study: The Discussion (Stimulation of Comparison Questions" authored by this writer (Matte 2000), this author (Matte) points out that the use by Honts of several laboratory studies involving diverse polygraph techniques and methodology completely ignores that there may be many other significant factors responsible for the difference in accuracy and percentage of false negatives and positives. These factors could include the type of test used (multiple- or single-issue), types of comparison questions (current exclusive, non-current exclusive, non-exclusive, disguised, relevant-connected, directed-lie), the polygraph testing methodology including the pretest interview format, the test data analysis and the competency of the Polygraphist, to name a few. The test structure, format and protocol used in the several studies compiled for a meta-analysis (Hunter, Schmidt & Jackson, 1982) should be near-identical so that only the item being tested (Discussion or non-Discussion of Questions Between Charts) is at variance. Other criticisms of Honts' study were set forth in aforementioned "Critical Analysis" which are articulated on Pages 12-13 of this supplement and corresponding page 70, Chapter 2 of this textbook.) Honts acknowledges (Honts 1999) that "Correlational studies and analysis are not as good as experiments in determining causation." The Matte and Reuss 1999 study indicates that "the direct review or discussion of comparison questions between charts may increase the guilty examinee's apprehension regarding the DLCQ, thus creating a formula for false negative results." (Matte 2000).

Pages 213-217. Add the following References in alphabetical order at appropriate pages.

Bongard, S., Pfeiffer, J. S., Al'Absi, M., Hodapp, V., and Linnenkemper, G. (1997). Cardiovascular responses during effortful active coping and acute experience of anger in women. *Psychophysiology*, 34: 459-466.

Hunter, J. E., Schmidt, F. L., Jackson, G. B. (1982). *Meta-analysis: Cumulating research findings across studies.* Beverly Hills, CA: Sage.

Honts, C. R. (1999). The discussion of questions between list repetitions (charts is associated with increased test accuracy. *Polygraph*, 28(2): 117-123.

Matte, J. A. (1998). An analysis of the psychodynamics of the directed lie control question in the control question technique. *Polygraph*, 27(1): 56-67.

Matte, J. A., Reuss, R. M. (1999). Validation of potential response elements in the directed-lie control question. *Polygraph*, 28(2): 124-142.

Matte, J. A. (2000). A critical analysis of Honts' study: The discussion (stimulation) of comparison questions. *Polygraph*, 29(2): 146-150.

CHAPTER 8

_____

FORMULATION, REVIEW, PRESENTATION AND ASSURANCE OF INTENDED INTERPRETATION OF TEST QUESTIONS CRITICAL TO EXAMINATION RESULTS.

Page 241. Add the following paragraph after last paragraph ending with "the deception syndrome."

In a study by Stephen Bongard, Jutta S. Pfeiffer, Mustafa Al'Absi, Volker Hodapp, and Gabi Linnenkemper (1997) entitled "Cardiovascular Responses During Effortful Active Coping and Acute Experience of Anger in Woman" the study revealed that active coping (mental arithmetic) elevated cardiovascular activity including increase in heart rate, systolic and diastolic blood pressure. The study further revealed that anger provocation also elevated cardiovascular activity, particularly the heart rate and diastolic blood pressure responses.

Page 244. Add the following standardized pretest interview consisting of several pages after the first paragraph which ends with "which is discussed later in this chapter."

STANDARDIZED METHODOLOGY PRECEDING COLLECTION
OF
PHYSIOLOGICAL DATA
IN
PSYCHOPHYSIOLOGICAL VERACITY EXAMINATIONS

INTRODUCTION

The most important part of the psychophysiological veracity (PV) examination is the pretest interview which precedes the collection of the physiological data. While several of the numerous variables that can affect the examination process which have been identified in chapter 9, *Forensic Psychophysiology Using The Polygraph*, are addressed through the psychologically structured test questions used in the collection of the physiological data, the remaining variables must be addressed with a psychologically structured methodology that will insure the psychological readiness of the examinee for the administration of the test in which the physiological data is collected. Failure to address all of the identified variables can seriously jeopardize the validity of the examination results. Case preparation which precedes the pretest interview is also of importance in selecting those test issues which meet the *Examination Reliability Rating* requirements, plus the scientific formulation of the test questions to be used in a validated psychologically structured test, in a controlled testing environment, with a timely calibrated polygraph instrument. The following methodology developed by this author is the result of an evolutionary process that spans twenty-five years of observation, practice, research, development and validation (Matte, Reuss 1989). This author does not claim that this is the only valid pretest methodology, but one that has proved extremely successful in addressing all of the identified impeding variables in PV examinations.

PART I

Case Preparation and Evaluation

Selection of Issues to be Tested:

Prior to the scheduled PV examination, the Polygraphist reviews the case file and applies the Examination Reliability Rating Table using a five-point rating results, on the basis of its combined Adequacy of Information, Case Intensity, and Distinctness of Issue. (Backster 1969, Matte 1980). (See Chapter 9, Page 269, and Chapter 11, Page 326). From the case file and agency/client ordering the test, the polygraphist should acquire background information including medical/psychological/criminal history of examinee. (See Chapter 11, Pages 327-328).

Formulation of Test Questions:

The formulation of the relevant and control questions must be in conformance with the requirements of the validated technique selected. Chapter 8 commencing on page 241 of *Forensic Psychophysiology Using The Polygraph* provides detailed guidance.

Examination Environment:

Examination room should be near soundproof or devoid of external noise to avoid orienting response to external stimuli during examination. Proper examination chair, adequate lighting and comfortable room temperature are essential. (See Chapter 9 for details)

Avoidance of Non-Participants in Examination Environment:

No one should be permitted inside the examination room except the examinee and the Polygraphist, unless there is a need for an interpreter-translator. All others directly involved in the case with a *need to know* may view the examination with the permission of the examinee and the Polygraphist through closed-circuit television or two-way mirror and speaker. However, the presence of a relative or close friend of the examinee, immediately outside of the examination room should be avoided. (See Chapter 9, pages 270-271 for detailed guidance).

Recording of PV Examination:

The complete, entire PV examination must be video recorded or when not possible, audio recorded, to provide continuous documentation of the PV examination to reviewing authorities to ascertain that no procedural violations were committed during any portion of the pretest interview and/or during the collection of the physiological data. (See Chapter 23, Pages 588-590 for detailed guidance).

PART II

PSYCHOLOGICAL STRUCTURE OF PRETEST INTERVIEW INITIAL CONTACT WITH SUBJECT

A.   Establishing Control of Examination:

Establish initial control by leading subject into examination room, stating "Please follow me." Then when entering examination room the polygraphist directs the examinee to *interview* chair by standing in front of *examination* chair (blocking it) and asking the examinee to "please have a seat in this chair, thank you." Thus the Polygraphist has politely established his/her initial authority/control over the interview/examination. The polygraphist maintains authority/control during the examination by his/her superior knowledge of forensic psychophysiology and adherence to a scripted validated methodology.

B.   Establishing Attitude of Examinee Towards PV Examination:

Attempt to identify the presence of anger on the part of the examinee regarding his/her submission to the PV examination. If there is evidence of anger by the examinee, every effort should be made by the polygraphist to diffuse it, and if unsuccessful, a rescheduling or abortion of the examination should be considered depending upon the degree and intensity of aforesaid emotion. A deceptive result ensuing from a PV examination conducted under such circumstance where the emotion of anger is present, should be regarded with extreme caution. (Hunter 1974; Bongard, et al 1997) (See Chapter 9, Page 273 for detailed guidance).

PRETEST INTERVIEW STRUCTURE

C.   Background Information Acquisition:

Use a clipboard to hold the Worksheet and writing pad. The clipboard should always be held at an angle that prevents the examinee from seeing pen on paper while the polygraphist is writing. Experience has shown that as long as the examinee cannot see pen on paper, he/she will not be inhibited from talking with the polygraphist. The importance of this procedure is fully explained in Chapter 8, *Forensic Psychophysiology Using The Polygraph* (Matte, 1996) which discusses in minute detail the procedure for the review of the test questions with the examinee, especially the control questions, which are summarily discussed herein in Section F. Use of the Backster ZCT Notepack or the Matte Quadri-Track ZCT Worksheet (Chapter 11, *Forensic Psychophysiology Using The Polygraph*) includes all of the essential data that must be acquired from the examinee during the pretest interview. Included is information regarding proof of the examinee's identity, his/her residence, education, limited medical history including current ailments and treatment, current prescribed drugs/medication and use of drugs/medication during the previous 15 hours, pregnancy when applicable, amount of sleep the night before the examination, and previous PV Examinations.

NOTE: Symptoms of coughing, sneezing, or sniffing caused by respiratoryailments such as the common cold, influenza, pneumonia, bronchitis, tuberculosis can adversely affect the validity of the pneumograph recordings and indirectly the other physiological recordings. (See Chapter 9, Page 283 for detailed guidance)

D.   Examinee's Version of the Incident:

(1) Listen to examinee's version of the incident without interruption, except for point clarification and/or resumption in the direction of examinee's version. Interrogation and/or challenge to the examinee's version must be totally avoided.

(2) The *Innocent Theme* which must prevail throughout the entire examination is introduced at this time by stating to the examinee: "I want you to know that I *presume* (not believe) that *all* examinees who come here for a PV examination are innocent and thus truthful regarding the target issue which is the issue for which you are being polygraphed, and I maintain that presumption of your innocence throughout the entire examination until all of the polygraph charts have been collected, analyzed and scored for a determination of truth or deception."

The above can be strengthened by relating a particular case where the evidence against the examinee was overwhelming, but nevertheless the results of the examination based on the physiological data showed truthfulness regarding the target issue and the charges were dropped.

NOTE: A display of disbelief in an Innocent (as later verified) examinee's version of the incident can be interpreted as an accusation of guilt regarding the target issue, which can arouse the emotion of *anger* towards the polygraphist. Published data and neurological evidence suggests that *fear* and *anger* both cause a strong arousal of the sympathetic subdivision of the autonomic nervous system. The best safeguard against the arousal of anger is to adopt the presumption of innocence throughout the PV examination until all physiological data has been collected, analyzed, quantified and truth or deception has been determined. (See Chapter 9, *Forensic Psychophysiology Using the Polygraph* for more details)

E.   Explanation of Polygraph Instrument and Related Physiology:* (See Note below)

(1) The attention of the examinee is now directed to the polygraph instrument and the physiology that it records. If an analog instrument is used, then the polygraphist activates the kymograph and remarks that the chart is moving but the pens are not because none of the instrument components are connected to anyone. If a computerized instrument is used, then the polygraphist may show the graph displayed on the monitor screen. Furthermore, the chart moves exactly at six inches per minute and the vertical lines on the chart are spaced at half inch intervals, which means that it takes five seconds for the tip of the cardio pen to travel from one vertical line to the next vertical. This permits the polygraphist to calculate pulse rate, question spacing, etc. The polygraphist then explains to the examinee what each pen records on the polygraph chart, in the following suggested manner. The polygraphist

should not underestimate the ability of the examinee to understand the following example, which not only establishes the role of the sympathetic and parasympathetic systems as being divorced from general nervousness, but also its role in detecting deception. It further increases the examinee's perception of the importance of the physiological data as being the sole determinant of truth or deception. This sets the stage for Section F, wherein the accuracy of the numerical scoring of the physiological data is reviewed in validation studies.

Example: The polygraph instrument is activated and the chart is moving.
"As you can see, the chart is moving but the pens are not. This is because none of the components are connected to anyone. But when they are, the pens will be continuously moving as they record your heart beat, pulse rate, pulse strength, pulse amplitude, variations in your galvanic skin resistance (or conductance) to a minute electrical current, caused by changes in the electrical potential in your system and sweat gland activity, and any inhibitions of your intercostal muscular diaphragm complex, which are all governed by the autonomic nervous system of which you have no direct conscious control. Within the autonomic nervous system there are two subdivisions which we examiners are particularly interested in. One is the sympathetic system which is a self-preservation mechanism whose role is to prepare our body for fight or flight from any serious threat to our well-being."

---

*NOTE: The detailed explanation herein of the physiology recorded by the polygraph instrument is offered as the preferred version whenever possible. Understandably, this version may be tailored and reduced to the examinee's level of understanding, i.e. intelligence, education. However, it must be said from this author's experience that very few examinees have found the enclosed explanation too lengthily, boring, or beyond their understanding. The enclosed explanation of the physiology serves an important role in the psychological preparation of the examinee, including the examinee's perception of the examination process and the competency of the attending forensic psychophysiology expert. Furthermore, a detailed explanation of the physiology involved enhances the value and effectiveness of the Control-Stimulation Test and allays the *fear of error* in the innocent examinee and stimulates the *fear of detection* in the guilty examinee.

"If your were walking in the woods (North America. Use animal predator from your region) and saw a grizzly bear advancing towards you, or heard the roar of a grizzly bear behind you and recognized it as a bear, the moment you recognized the threat with your eyes or ears, a signal would be sent from either receptor to the 'old brain' (pointing to the back of the head) which is primitive in nature; through evolution we developed the 'new brain' (pointing to the top of the head), but the pathway from the eyes or ears is still direct to the 'old brain' which activates the sympathetic system to prepare your body for fight or flight from that threat. Whatever you do, it will be with the greatest strength that your body can marshal for those few seconds when your life may well depend on it. Adrenaline (epinephrine)will cause your heart to beat stronger and faster, increasing blood pressure, pulse rate, and strength, thus furnishing more oxygenated blood to those areas of the body where it is vitally needed to meet the emergency, such as the brain when increased mental activity is demanded, and there will be a major redistribution of the blood in your body. For instance, norepinephrine from sympathetic nerves, constrict arterioles that force blood away from the skin surfaces in the outer extremities of the body, which for example may cause a person's face to blanche or turn pale. The flow of blood to the stomach is significantly reduced, which may give you the familiar sensation of stomach butterflies. Simultaneously, another hormone called epinephrine causes a dilation of blood vessels in the larger muscle groups to enable you to cope with the emergency.

"Nature provided another system to put the brakes on the sympathetic system otherwise your heart would beat itself out of your chest; it would be like a run-away train. So the second system is called the parasympathetic system whose role is to maintain the homeostasis or chemical balance if you will in your body. Whenever the sympathetic system activates, the parasympathetic system activates right behind it to bring you back to normal. You may think of the sympathetic system as the accelerator on your car, and the parasympathetic system as the brakes on your car. If you are traveling at 100 miles per hour and suddenly slam on the brakes, you are not going to come to a smooth stop. You will swerve as the car's body weight shifts forward. Similarly, when the sympathetic system activates, the parasympathetic system may overcompensate for the other's activity."

"You are probably wondering what these two systems have to do with this test. Well, everything. You see, your 'old brain' doesn't know the difference between a physical or psychological threat. It reacts the same way. You may feel butterflies in your stomach just before giving an important speech to a large audience, which is caused by 'fear'. Another person's face may turn pale when confronted with the potential loss of their freedom. Thus when a person lies to a question in a polygraph test, their sympathetic system will activate because they are afraid of the consequences if their lie is discovered. And of course, the parasympathetic system will also activate to bring you back to normal. That is the reason each test question is separated by a twenty second interval; to allow the two systems to manifest themselves on the chart before the next test question is asked. Therefore the polygraphist is seeking *physiological evidence* that the *sympathetic* and *parasympathetic* systems have activated to a particular test question indicating that they were attempting deception. And this has nothing to do with nervousness. The state of being nervous as a result of your anxiety about taking this test is constant throughout the test, whether you are very nervous, nervous or just mildly nervous. Whereas the sympathetic and parasympathetic responses are action specific. I expect that all examinees who come here for a polygraph test are nervous, but that will not affect the accuracy of the test."

F.   Validity Studies - Numerical Scoring Accuracy:

Explain the validity and reliability of the PV examination:

"You're probably wondering about the accuracy of the test. So let me show you this three-year validity study which was conducted on the Matte Quadri-Track Zone Comparison Technique."

There is a momentary increase in sweat gland activity in the hands, which is thought to enable man to have a better grip on things such as tree branches in his attempt to escape the threat. All of these things are governed by the autonomic nervous system of which you have no direct conscious control. You can see a person's face blanche, and you can feel butterflies in your stomach, but you can't see those other actions which nevertheless can all be recorded on this chart by this very sensitive instrument."

NOTE: The Polygraphist should preferably produce the study(ies) which pertain to the technique he is using in instant examination.

At this point the examinee is shown the study, either the 220-page study entitled "Validation Study on the Polygraph Quadri-Zone Comparison Technique" by James Allan Matte and Ronald M. Reuss, June 1989, or the summarized version (16-pages) published in *Polygraph*, Vol. 18, Nr. 4, 1989, entitled "A Field Validation Study of the Quadri-Zone Comparison Technique." The available study is opened to the page containing the Abstract, and the examinee is asked to read it (17 lines), or the polygraphist points to its highlight which reflects that the Quadri-Zone now renamed Quadri-Track ZCT correctly identified 91% of the Innocent as truthful with a 9% inconclusive, and no errors, and that it correctly identified 97% of the Guilty as deceptive with a 3% inconclusive, and no errors, thus it was 100% accurate in diagnosing the truthful and deceptive subjects. Other published studies validating the particular polygraph technique may also be shown to the examinee, to wit: Mangan, et al 2008; Shurany, et al 2009. The high validity and reliability of this technique is due to the fact that it requires a high score be attained before a definite conclusion can be rendered, otherwise inconclusive results are reported. This inconclusive area is a safeguard against making errors.

At this point the polygraphist shows the examinee a blank score sheet which reflects the spots where the scores are to be entered and how they are all tallied for a total score. The examinee is then shown the Conclusion Table on the same score sheet which reflects the Inconclusive score area, so that the examinee understands that this scoring system is very objective and furthermore the sole determinant of truth or deception regarding the target issue. This explanation serves to reinforce the objectivity of the test, the importance of the collection of the physiological data, and the futility of objecting to deceptive results during the post-test interview.

G. Review of All Test Questions in Test A Only:

At this point, the examinee is told that all of the test questions in Test A are now going to be reviewed with him/her word for word, and that no other questions will be asked of him/her during the actual test. In fact, a surprise question would invalidate the test, therefore he/she can rest assured that only those questions reviewed with him/her will be asked on the test. If there are other targets to be covered, they are incorporated into test(s) B and C in accordance with their combined adequacy of case information, case intensity and distinctness of issue, using the Examination Reliability Rating Table found in Chapter 11, *Forensic Psychophysiology Using The Polygraph*. When there are more than one test to be administered within the PV examination, the examinee is advised of each issue to be tested and that they will be covered as separate tests. The test questions contained in test(s) B and C are not discussed or reviewed with the examinee until it is time to administer those tests. Failure to advise an examinee of *all issues* that will be covered in the examination may cause the absorption of all issues by the examinee into test A, thus confounding the examinee's psychological set, whereas prior notification of each test will allow the examinee's selective attention to be focused on the specific issue being tested, knowing that the other issues will be covered in separate tests.

The first test question to be reviewed with the examinee is the Preparatory/Sacrifice Relevant Question (#39 in Matte QZCT or Backster ZCT). The second test question is the first Relevant question (#33), followed by the review of the second Relevant question (#35). The review of the two non-current exclusive control questions (#46 & 47) are preceded by the customary preamble. The next test question to be reviewed with the examinee is the Fear of Error question (Matte #23; Backster #M48) followed by the Hope of Error question (Matte #24; Backster #M37). <u>Care must be exercised to assure that these two "Inside-Track" questions are interpreted by the examinee as intended by acquiring feedback from the examinee as to his/her understanding of those two questions.</u> Furthermore, these two inside-track questions (Fear and Hope of Error) each have the suffix "regarding the target issue." See Matte 1996, Chap. 8, This is followed by the review of the Neutral question (#14J) used as the first test question. Finally, the two symptomatic questions (#25 & 26) are reviewed with the examinee. (*For a full discussion of the procedure used in the introduction/review of aforesaid test questions, please read Chapter 8, Forensic Psychophysiology Using The Polygraph.*)

H.   Victim Trauma Considerations:

With victims, formulation of the relevant questions should avoid traumatic and personally embarrassing words which might elicit a physiological response by their very nature. (See Chapter 9, Page 275 for detailed guidance)

I.   Shame:

It is imperative that, when testing is appropriate and legally permitted, the polygraphist recognize the potential for autonomic arousal to relevant questions by legitimate victims of transgressions which invoke *shame* such as rape, though not limited to sex offenses, and formulate the relevant questions in a manner that does not debase the victim/examinee and arouse or cause shame. (See Chapter 9, Page 276 for detailed guidance)

J.   Importance of Examinee Cooperation Explained:

(1)   Instructions To Examinee:
(a) Examinee must sit perfectly still during the collection of the physiological data. Wherever he/she places his/her feet, that's where they must remain during each test (chart) collected. There must not be any movement of the hands, fingers, legs, feet, body, arms or head. In fact there must not be any movement of the facial muscles except when answering Yes or No to the reviewed test questions.
(b) The examinee is advised that he/she is expected to be nervous during the test, and this condition may cause his/her mouth to get dry which may tempt him/her to clear his/her throat so that their answer may come out better. But he/she is cautioned not to clear his/her throat during the test because that will affect the tube component over his/her stomach. Besides, it doesn't matter how his/her answer comes out as long as the polyraphist can distinguish a Yes from a No answer. Furthermore, the examinee should not emphasize his/her answer by adding extra words such as "No I did not." The emphasis will not be heard by the polygraph instrument, therefore a simple Yes or No will suffice. In addition, the examinee is cautioned not to sigh or take deep breaths

during the examination. The examinee is informed that the instrument is so sensitive that a mere swallow, which is permitted if necessary, is reflected on the polygraph chart and quite apparent to the polygraphist.

(c) Inasmuch as the test questions will become familiar to the examinee through repetition of the tests and the fact that they were reviewed with the examinee, the examinee may be tempted to answer a question before it has been completely asked. The examinee should be cautioned to wait until the question is asked in its entirety before answering the question, but once heard, he/she should answer it immediately.

(d) The examinee is explained that a blood pressure cuff will be wrapped tightly around the examinee's left (or right) biceps and the cuff bladder will be inflated with air at the beginning of the test. The bladder will not be inflated as much as a doctor would because the polygraphist is not interested in the examinee's peak blood pressure. The bladder will be inflated with just enough air to record his/her mean blood pressure, thus the air will be locked in for the duration of the chart which is about four minutes. The examinee is further advised that immediately after the cuff bladder has been inflated with air, the polygraphist will message the cuff bladder to distribute the air evenly in the cuff. Twenty-five seconds after the last test question, the polygraphist will push a button on the polygraph instrument which will release the air out of the cuff bladder giving his/her arm a rest. But the examinee must not move his/her arm when that happens because he/she is still being monitored by the other components, but simply to sit still for about one minute until his/her arm has returned to normal and wait for the polygraphist's instructions.

(e) The examinee is asked if he/she is wearing contact lenses. If positive then the Closed Eyes Technique is not used and the examinee is permitted to keep his/her eyes open during the collection of the physiological data. No mention of the Closed Eyes Technique is made. The examinee is asked if he/she suffers from claustrophobia. If positive then the Closed Eyes Technique is not used. In the absence of either of above conditions, the examinee is explained that during the test his/her eyes will be closed so that he/she is not distracted by the movement of the polygraph pens through his/her peripheral vision. The examinee is not asked to close his/her eyes until just before the announcement that the test is about to begin during the testing phase.

NOTE: After the conduct of several charts or tests, some examinees display fatigue which may be enhanced by having his/her eyes closed. In such instances, the examinee is instructed to maintain his/her eyes open for the remainder of the test(s). This instruction should not be given while a chart or test is in progress.

(f) The examinee is explained that full cooperation in following all of the aforesaid instructions is expected from the innocent examinee who wants the polygraph instrument to accurately record his/her physiology and demonstrate his/her innocence. Thus the truthful are cooperative and follow directions. But the Deceptive examinee is usually uncooperative; does not follow instructions, and may attempt through subtle maneuvers to sabotage the test, because he/she does not want the instrument to accurately record his/her physiology which would reveal their deceit. Thus the *innocent* examinee *does not want an error to be made on the test.* He/she wants the test to be accurate. Whereas the *guilty* examinee *does want and hopes that an error will be made on his/her test* so that his/her deceit will not be detected. Therefore, to violate instructions is tantamount to waiving a big flag with the words 'Lie" on it. Thus full cooperation from this examinee is expected.

NOTE: Sub-paragraph (f) above reinforces clarification of the Fear/Hope of Error test questions. It also establishes an anti-countermeasure.

K.   Acquisition of Normal Physiological Specimen:

(1) The examinee is seated in the examination chair and all of the polygraph instrument sensors are placed on his/her person, commencing with the abdominal pneumo tube, followed by the thoracic pneumo tube. The blood pressure cuff is wrapped tightly around the examinee's biceps and the GSR/GSG electrodes are placed on the fingers of the examinee's opposite hand which should be fully supported by the arm rest. The examinee is then explained that the test is not going to be administered yet, inasmuch as the instrument must be warmed up and the polygraphist wants the examinee to get used to having the instrument components hooked up to him/her. The examinee is instructed to sit still and look straight ahead. The kymograph is activated and the recording of the two pneumograph channels is adjusted to ideal tracings on the polygraph chart. The polygrahist should allow at least 60 seconds of chart time recording the pneumograph tracings. During that time, the GSR/GSG channel is also adjusted to an ideal tracing and allowed to run for 60 seconds simultaneously with the pneumograph. Then the cuff bladder is inflated to 90mmHg and locked. The polygraphist then walks over to the examinee and messages the cuff bladder then upon his/her return to the instrument, should observe a significant reduction in the cuff pressure, usually to about 60mmHg. The polygraphist then should inflate the messaged cuff to about 75-80mmHg, and record the examinee's cardiograph tracing along with the other tracings for 60 seconds, at which time the cuff pressure is released, but the examinee is instructed to remain still, looking straight ahead for one minute. The GSR/GSG component is then turned off but pneumo tracings continue to be recorded for several seconds to acquire an additional sample of the examinee's breathing pattern. This Acquaintance Test chart is not cut off or torn from the instrument. This portion of the chart is to precede the Control-Stimulation Test which is to be administered next.

(2) With all of the components still on the examinee, he/she is now advised that a sensitivity test will now be administered to determine the examinee's capability and manner of response to a known lie. That the polygraphist wants to acquire from the examinee physiological evidence of his/her sympathetic and parasympathetic systems to a *known lie.* The Control-Stimulation Test is then administered.

NOTE: The role of the Control-Stimulation Test goes beyond its original purpose of assuring the innocent and stimulating the guilty. The Stimulation test also serves as a *Control test* to establish the examinee's capability and manner of response to a known lie under controlled conditions. It is important that the examinee perceives the Control-Stimulation Test as the means by which the polygraphist acquires a *known deception exemplar* from the examinee, thus will not relate that role to the exclusive (earlier-in-life) control questions which are used for comparison with its neighboring relevant questions. Hence the Control-Stimulation Test should be administered before any of the relevant tests related to the target issue(s). For a full explanation of the reasons for avoiding the association of the exclusive control question with the acquisition of a known deception exemplar, read "*An Analysis of the Psychodynamics of the Directed Lie Control Question in the Control Question Technique*" by James Allan Matte, 1998, published in *Polygraph*, <u>27</u>(1), and Validation of Potential Response Elements in the Directed-Lie Control Question, published in *Polygraph*, <u>28</u>(2), 1999.

(3) Upon completion of the Control-Stimulation Test which is administered with eyes closed unless not permitted, the cuff pressure is released but the examinee is instructed to remain still with eyes closed for one minute. During that one minute period or longer, the pneumograph components for both thoracic and abdominal continue to be recorded. After the one minute expiration, the chart is manually advanced to the knife edge and cuff off where the Control-Stimulation Test ended, but the thoracic and abdominal tracings continue to be recorded. The examinee is then instructed to open his/her eyes while the polygraphist walks with the polygraph chart towards the examinee and facing the examinee studies the chart for a few more seconds then announces the number picked by the examinee who then is requested to return the numbered cards to the polygraphist. The polygraphist then returns behind the polygraph instrument desk and examines the continuously moving chart still recording the examinee's breathing patterns in full view of the examinee. The instrument is then turned off. The examinee should now realize that a third exemplar of his uncontrolled breathing patterns has been acquired. The examinee is then requested to *sign all of the aforementioned charts*, including the third exemplar, as is customary for all polygraph charts collected during the PV examination. No comments should be made to the examinee regarding the collected physiological data. The examinee should now be ready for the administration of the first test regarding the target issue.

NOTE: This procedure articulated in paragraph (3) above is an anti-countermeasure in that a guilty-as-later verified examinee will now realize that the polygraphist has a verified sample or exemplar of his normal breathing pattern, thus will be reluctant to manipulate his breathing during the actual testing phase. This also provides the polygraphist with a means of comparison between the three samples for evidence of attempts at countermeasures, especially in the pneumograph tracings. It further provides the polygraphist with a record of the examinee's normal physiological tracing patterns if and when that issue is raised in court.

Page 248. Insert the following paragraph after paragraph 3 of Relevant Question Review, which ends with "understanding and interpretation of the test question."

In regards to the mixture of Yes and No answers to relevant test questions on the same single-issue test, we must consider in the structuring of a PV examination, the most sensitive, the most fearful, and the most illiterate of Innocent examinees, which raises the number of variables that must be addressed in the construct of the PV examination's methodology and psychological test structure. Thus the inconsistent reply format of Yes and No answers to relevant questions in a single-issue format can conceivably require additional attention from the Innocent examinee fearful of uttering the wrong answer that would inadvertently inculpate him/her through the misunderstanding of the question. The selective attention process of the Innocent examinee could also be altered by the examinee's hesitancy in determining which is the appropriate (truthful) answer to that particular question. We must not underestimate the intellectual and emotional processes that take place in PV examinations. Hence the best test construct is that which addresses all of the possible variables that may interfere with the logical, unimpeded flow of the examinee's psychological set.

Page 249. Insert the following paragraph after first paragraph ending with "numerical classification."

Intent Question: In Psychophysiological Veracity (PV) Examinations, an intent question refers to a relevant test question which lacks the element of *certainty* regarding the commission of an offense, thus determines only an *intent* to commit an offense. Intent questions should be avoided whenever possible. However there are exceptions and the use of the word *intent* and its derivatives can be successfully used when the proper circumstances are present. At other times a more positive synonym can be used, or the intent question can be totally avoided by restructuring the test question. Much depends on the nature of the allegation and the defense claim made by the defendant-examinee. If a defendant claims that the shooting which caused the death of a companion was accidental in that he didn't know that the gun was loaded when he pulled the trigger, the issue for testing should be whether or not he knew that the gun was loaded when he pulled the trigger rather than whether or not he intended to shoot (or injure) his companion when he pulled the trigger. However if a defendant claims that he knew the gun was loaded and deliberately pointed it at the victim but claims he did not *intentionally* pull the trigger in that it fired accidentally inasmuch as he was only trying to scare the victim, then the intent question is difficult to avoid. However the word *intentionally* can be substituted with the word *deliberately* when repeating the relevant question with different wording as required in single-issue tests (Backster and Matte Zone Comparison Techniques). While the intent question may sometimes appear necessary, it oftentimes can be avoided with adroit question formulation. For example, a defendant-examinee was accused of shoplifting a pair of sunglasses which she was found wearing on top of her head after she was checked out at the cash register of a department store. She claimed that she had forgotten about the sunglasses because she had a habit of wearing them on top of her head when not in use and thus did the same after trying them out. Instead of asking the defendant-examinee if she intended to steal the sun glasses, a more direct and less ambiguous approach would be to ask the defendant if she knew (was aware) at the time she was checked out by the cashier that she had in her possession a pair of sun glasses. In sex offenses, especially in child molestation cases, the allegations often include the touching by the adult defendant of the child's genitalia. If the defendant denies ever touching the child's genitalia, than the relevant test question(s) can be direct. However, if the defendant states that when bathing the child, his daughter, he may have inadvertently touched her, but never in a sexual manner, the question arises as to whether or not the defendant ever intentionally (deliberately) touch his daughter's genitals for sexual gratification. The test question can be even more precise and unambiguous with the insertion of the time frame alleged by the victim, when such time frame is considered reliable, but a precautionary time buffer should be factored into the formulation of the test question to allow for sincere errors in memory by the victim. However, use of *intent and its derivative* word in the Preparatory-Sacrifice Relevant question has been in regular use both in the Backster and Matte Zone Comparison Techniques inasmuch as they are not used for determination of truth of deception, and in control questions where ambiguity and uncertainty is a desired element. In the final analysis, the polygraphist   should whenever possible formulate the relevant test questions to incorporate the precise commission of the act rather than the examinee's intentions regarding the commission of the act.

Page 251. Add the following paragraph after line 3 of first paragraph:

The following sentence can also be added to the above explanation and introduction of the control (comparison) questions. "These two questions are also important in that they will reveal your character and potentiality for this sort of offense." Of course, prior to the introduction of the aforementioned preamble, the polygraphist   must at some point manipulate the examinee to present himself/herself as near a 10 on a scale of 0 to 10, 10 being the most honest, or morally correct, etc., so that the examinee will subsequently be reluctant to make any admissions to the control (comparison) questions that would be inconsistent with his prior character stance.

Pages 297-306. Add the following References in alphabetical order at appropriate page.

Backster, C. (1969). Technique fundamentals of the Tri-Zone Polygraph Test. New York: *Backster Research Foundation.*

Bongard, S., Pfeiffer, J. S., Al'Absi, M., Hodapp, V., and Linnemkemper, G. (1997). Cardiovascular responses during effortful active coping and acute experience of anger in women. *Psychophysiology*, 34: 459-466.

Hunter, F. L. (1974). Anger and the Polygraph Technique. *Polygraph*, 8(4): 381-385.

Matte, J. A. (1980). *The Art and Science of the Polygraph Technique.* Springfield, Illinois: Charles C. Thomas – Publisher.

Matte, J. A., Reuss, R. M. (1989). A field validation study of the Quadri-Zone Comparison Technique. *Polygraph*, 18(4): 187-202.

Matte, J. A., Reuss, R. M. (1989). Validation study on the Quadri-Zone Comparison Technique. *Research Abstract*, LD 01452, Vol. 1502, University Microfilm International.

Matte, J. A. (1998). An analysis of the psychodynamics of the directed lie control question in the control question technique. *Polygraph*, 27(1): 56-67.

Matte, J. A., Reuss, R. M. (1999). Validation of potential response elements in the directed-lie control question. *Polygraph*, 28(2): 124-142.

CHAPTER 9

THE NUMERICAL APPROACH AND ZONE COMPARISON TESTS: METHODOLOGY CAPABLE OF ADDRESSING IDENTIFIED IMPEDING VARIABLES.

Page 268. Add the following Reference following (Lee 1953; Matte 1993) at c. Mental exercise.
F. Boiten 1993; S. Bongard, J. S. Pfeiffer, M. Al'Absi, V. Hodapp, and G. Linnenkemper 1997; D. S. Fokkema 1999; A. Winzer, C. Ring, D. Carroll, G. Willemsen, M. Drayson, M. Kendall, 1999; C. Ring, D. Carroll, G. Willemsen, J. Cooke, A. Ferraro, and M. Drayson, 1999)

Page 275. Add the following quote from Cleve Backster regarding Confirmatory Examinations following the second paragraph ending with "on the same test."

Confirmatory Examinations

The following quote from Cleve Backster regarding the *Confirmatory* type of PV examination designed to verify the statements of victims or confirm the veracity of confessions, which expectedly elicits affirmative answers from aforesaid examinees to the relevant test questions, is set forth below:

"When considering the validity and reliability of the polygraph technique as related to confirmatory type cases, we must take into consideration the following information:

It would at first seem necessary to review that which we feel is important regarding the 'Pre-examination Reliability Estimate' for any direct question (that which we call 'YOU' phase) polygraph examination. In the Zone Comparison Technique we do an estimate as to (1) *the adequacy of the case information*, (2) *the intensity of the issue under consideration*, and (34) *the distinctness of the issue under consideration*. Utilizing a five position scale in compiling an estimate in each of these three factors, a total score is then established in an effort to numerically estimate the clarity of the target being considered for polygraph coverage.

With the 'confirmatory' type of examination there appears to be a serious deficiency with regard to each of the three factors above-mentioned. As related to the adequacy of information, in a substantial number of confirmatory cases we are dependent upon the person being tested as a primary source of information. This would involve a very low score as to the estimated adequacy of such information. In addition, target intensity also is likely to be deficient because target intensity involves that which is at stake for the individual. Were he detected as being deceptive as a result of the polygraph examination, it would seem that very little is at stake with regard to false or partially false accusations. It is true that there do exist in some states significant penalties for such misrepresentation. Even so, we must be practical in estimating the number of such offenses which actually are brought to trial, and also the degree of severity of resulting punishment, should the person be found guilty. All in all it would seem that far too often the target intensity is extremely weak. The third factor considered is 'distinctness of issue'. Because we are not actually certain that there is a valid issue in the first place, it is difficult to estimate distinctness. Here also a low numerical rating seems likely.

Far too often the total obtained by combining the three ratings above-mentioned indicates a need for extreme caution against over-estimating the accuracy of the examination results, no matter how productive the charts appear to be.

It is also our opinion that a degree of caution should be exercised in attempting to conduct confirmatory polygraph examinations immediately following the obtaining of a so-called confession on the part of the subject. If polygraph testing is attempted too soon after a 'confession' is obtained, it should be noted that additional emotional factors are injected into what would ordinarily be considered a well-structured polygraph testing situation.

In the properly designed polygraph test structure the only variety of emotion which should be allowed to remain part of the format is that of fear. Still further, within the structure, the only variety of fear that should be allowed to remain part of the format is the 'fear of detection' to the relevant question being asked. When a confirmatory test is conducted too soon after obtaining a confession, it is our opinion that additional emotional factors are injected. Such factors as fear of consequence, reflected anger for having given the confession, or resentment, are distinct possibilities, in addition to any possible fear because of the detection of giving inaccurate information as directly related to the alleged confession. These variables make such a test structure risky at best.

Although individual circumstances might provide otherwise, we are of the opinion that the test structure involved in the average 'confirmatory' polygraph examination could not be properly defended, were it to proceed to the courtroom stage of presentation. On the other hand, we feel that the 'specific incident' polygraph technique has now proceeded to a sufficient degree of validity and reliability where results can be tenaciously defended. 'Confirmatory' polygraph examinations do not fall in the area of such confidence."

NOTE BY AUTHOR: There are basically three types of 'confirmatory' examinations. (1) The Trauma Confirmatory PV Examination, i.e. Rape (2) The Non-Trauma Confirmatory PV Examination, i.e. Business Dispute, Fraud, and (3) The Confession Confirmatory PV Examination. Type (1) Confirmatory examination can present the biggest problem due to the probable trauma suffered by the legitimate victim. However, the type of offense does not necessarily dictate the degree of trauma, if any, suffered by the legitimate victim, inasmuch as the victim could be a tough-minded individual seeking justice and justifiable compensation rather than emotional closure. Of course the traumatic content of relevant questions will not be problematic to the *false* trauma victim/complainant. A method of avoiding the traditional 'confirmatory' examination format on trauma victims is to formulate the relevant test questions so that they elicit negative answers, i.e. "<u>Did you lie</u> when you reported to the Police that you had been raped by two police officers on 1 January 1999?" In that instance, the emphasis on telling the truth, and 'lie' controls are used for comparison.

However, the potential for false positive results can still be present, inasmuch as the genuine victim may relive the traumatic event contained in the relevant test questions. Hence, a *short statement* as to the alleged incident can *itself* be tested for its veracity, thus avoiding relevant test questions specifically descriptive of the traumatic event. Nevertheless, traditional, non-confirmatory PV examinations involving sex offenses such as rape and child molestation, have proved to be valid and reliable when the proper type of control (comparison) questions are used to compete with the relevant questions which admittedly do not contain victim trauma elements but which do contain elements of severe societal stigma, condemnation and punishment that can have a traumatizing effect on the innocent suspect. Type (2) Confirmatory examination subjects have not usually suffered a trauma, hence the traditional PV examination format can be used, but Backster's caution regarding adequate case information and distinctness of issue as well as case intensity should meet minimum requirements. Type (3) Confirmatory examinations regarding the reliability of confessions must take into account all of the factors delineated by Backster that can cause false positive results, such as: "fear of consequence, reflected anger for having given the confession, or resentment." Of the three types of Confirmatory examinations, Type 2 appears to be the least problematic. However, all of the aforementioned Confirmatory Examinations require extreme caution for the possibility of false positive/negative results and an expected increase in the rate of inconclusive findings.

Pages 298-308. Add the following References in alphabetical order on appropriate page.

Backster, C. (2001, December 5-10). 44th Annual Polygraph Examiner Work Conference. The Backster School of Lie Detection, San Diego, California.

Boiten, F. (1993). Component analysis of task-related respiratory patterns. International Journal of *Psychophysiology*, 15: 91-104.

Bongard, S., Pfeiffer, J. S. Al' Absi, M., Hodapp, V., and Linnenkemper, G. (1997). Cardiovascular responses during effortful active coping and acute experience of anger in women. *Psychophysiology*, 34: 459-466.

Fokkema, D. S. (1999). The psychobiology of strained breathing and its cardiovascular implications: A functional system review. *Psychophysiology*, 36(2): 164-175.

Winzer, A., Ring, C., Carroll, D., Willemsen, G., Drayson, M., and Kendall, M. (1999). Secretory immunoglobulin A and cardiovascular reactions to mental arithmetic, cold pressor, and exercise: Effects of beta-adrenergic blockade. *Psychophysiology*, 36(5): 591-601.

CHAPTER 11

THE NUMERICAL APPROACH

Page 339. Delete the following at bottom of Figure XI-6:

48   DURING THE FIRST (   ) YEARS OF YOUR LIFE – DO YOU REMEMBER:
_____
32
_____

Page 351. Add the "Tri-Zone" Reaction Combinations as Figure XI-10A (following Figure XI-10).

Consists of 9 pages.

"TRI-ZONE" REACTION COMBINATIONS
(Backster Zone Comparison Test)

COMBINATION			INDICATION		REMEDY	
A (r) dd	r	A1	PRESENCE OF RESPONSE TO ONE OR BOTH RED ZONE QUESTIONS INDICATES DECEPTION REGARDING TARGET ISSUE	A2	NO REMEDY NECESSARY; RED ZONE QUESTIONS HAVE BEEN FORMULATED AS IDEALLY AS POSSIBLE; RED ZONE QUESTIONS FUNCTIONING AS DESIGNED	r
	g	A3	LACK OF RESPONSE TO BOTH GREEN ZONE QUESTIONS BECAUSE OF DAMPENING BY RED ZONE QUESTION RESPONSES INDICATES DECEPTION REGARDING TARGET ISSUE	A4	NO REMEDY NECESSARY; NO REASON TO BELIEVE GREEN ZONE QUESTION STRUCTURE INADEQUATE; GREEN ZONE QUESTIONS FUNCTIONING AS DESIGNED	g
	b	A5	LACK OF RESPONSE TO BOTH BLACK ZONE QUESTIONS INDICATES THAT NO OUTSIDE ISSUE BOTHERING SUBJECT DUE TO MISTRUST OF EXAMINER	A6	NO REMEDY NECESSARY; EXAMINER HAS SUBJECT'S CONFIDENCE REGARDING AVOIDANCE OF UNREVIEWED QUESTIONS EMBRACING OUTSIDE ISSUE	b
B (g) ††	r	B1	LACK OF RESPONSE TO BOTH RED ZONE QUESTIONS INDICATES TRUTHFULNESS REGARDING TARGET ISSUE	B2	NO REMEDY NECESSARY; RED ZONE QUESTIONS HAVE BEEN FORMULATED AS IDEALLY AS POSSIBLE; RED ZONE QUESTIONS FUNCTIONING AS DESIGNED	r
	g	B3	PRESENCE OF RESPONSE TO ONE OR BOTH GREEN ZONE QUESTIONS INDICATES TRUTHFULNESS REGARDING TARGET ISSUE, AS NO OTHER ZONE IS DAMPENING OUT GREEN ZONE	B4	NO REMEDY NECESSARY; NO REASON TO BELIEVE GREEN ZONE QUESTION STRUCTURE INADEQUATE; GREEN ZONE QUESTIONS FUNCTIONING AS DESIGNED	g
	b	B5	LACK OF RESPONSE TO BOTH BLACK ZONE QUESTIONS INDICATES THAT NO OUTSIDE ISSUE BOTHERING SUBJECT DUE TO MISTRUST OF EXAMINER	B6	NO REMEDY NECESSARY; EXAMINER HAS SUBJECT'S CONFIDENCE REGARDING AVOIDANCE OF UNREVIEWED QUESTIONS EMBRACING OUTSIDE ISSUE	b
C (b) ?	r	C1	LACK OF RESPONSE TO BOTH RED ZONE QUESTIONS USUALLY INDICATES TRUTHFULNESS REGARDING TARGET ISSUE; THIS RULE NULLIFIED BY BLACK ZONE QUESTION RESPONSE	C2	NO REMEDY NECESSARY; RED ZONE QUESTIONS WILL BE FUNCTIONING AS DESIGNED AFTER BLACK ZONE QUESTION RESPONSE SUBSIDES	r
	g	C3	LACK OF RESPONSE TO BOTH GREEN ZONE QUESTIONS USUALLY INDICATES DECEPTION REGARDING TARGET ISSUE. THIS RULE NULLIFIED BY BLACK ZONE QUESTION RESPONSE	C4	NO REMEDY NECESSARY; NO CAUSE TO BELIEVE GREEN ZONE QUESTION STRUCTURE INADEQUATE; RECHECK AFTER RESPONSE TO BLACK ZONE QUESTION SUBSIDES	g
	b	C5	PRESENCE OF RESPONSE TO ONE OR BOTH BLACK ZONE QUESTIONS INDICATES OUTSIDE ISSUE BOTHERING SUBJECT DUE TO MISTRUST OF EXAMINER	C6	EXAMINER MUST GAIN SUBJECT'S CONFIDENCE REGARDING AVOIDANCE OF UNREVIEWED QUESTIONS EMBRACING OUTSIDE ISSUE	b
D (r)(g) ?d	r	D1	PRESENCE OF RESPONSE TO ONE OR BOTH RED ZONE QUESTIONS INDICATES DECEPTION REGARDING TARGET ISSUE	D2	NO REMEDY NECESSARY; RED ZONE QUESTIONS HAVE BEEN FORMULATED AS IDEALLY AS POSSIBLE; RED ZONE QUESTIONS FUNCTIONING AS DESIGNED	r
	g	D3	PRESENCE OF RESPONSE TO ONE OR BOTH GREEN ZONE QUESTIONS IN ADDITION TO RED ZONE QUESTION INDICATES SERIOUS GREEN ZONE QUESTION DEFECT	D4	REDUCE INTENSITY OF GREEN ZONE QUESTIONS BY ALTERING SUBJECT AGE CATEGORIES OR CHANGING SCOPE OF GREEN ZONE QUESTIONS	g
	b	D5	LACK OF RESPONSE TO BOTH BLACK ZONE QUESTIONS INDICATES NO OUTSIDE ISSUE BOTHERING SUBJECT DUE TO MISTRUST OF EXAMINER	D6	NO REMEDY NECESSARY; EXAMINER HAS SUBJECT'S CONFIDENCE REGARDING AVOIDANCE OF UNREVIEWED QUESTIONS EMBRACING OUTSIDE ISSUE	b

© 1962 by Cleve Backster

(1 of 2 parts)

"TRI-ZONE" REACTION COMBINATIONS
(Backster Zone Comparison Test)

COMBINATION			INDICATION		REMEDY	
E (r)(b) d	r	E1	PRESENCE OF RESPONSE TO ONE OR BOTH RED ZONE QUESTIONS INDICATES DECEPTION REGARDING TARGET ISSUE	E2	NO REMEDY NECESSARY; RED ZONE QUESTIONS HAVE BEEN FORMULATED AS IDEALLY AS POSSIBLE; RED ZONE QUESTIONS FUNCTIONING AS DESIGNED	r
	g	E3	LACK OF RESPONSE TO BOTH GREEN ZONE QUESTIONS BECAUSE OF DAMPENING BY RED ZONE QUESTION RESPONSE; INDICATES DECEPTION REGARDING TARGET ISSUE	E4	NO REMEDY NECESSARY; NO REASON TO BELIEVE GREEN ZONE QUESTION STRUCTURE INADEQUATE; GREEN ZONE QUESTIONS FUNCTIONING AS DESIGNED	g
	b	E5	PRESENCE OF RESPONSE TO ONE OR BOTH BLACK ZONE QUESTIONS INDICATES OUTSIDE ISSUE BOTHERING SUBJECT DUE TO MISTRUST OF EXAMINER	E6	EXAMINER MUST GAIN SUBJECT'S CONFIDENCE REGARDING AVOIDANCE OF UNREVIEWED QUESTIONS EMBRACING OUTSIDE ISSUE	b
F (r)(g)(b) ?d	r	F1	PRESENCE OF RESPONSE TO ONE OR BOTH RED ZONE QUESTIONS INDICATES DECEPTION REGARDING TARGET ISSUE	F2	NO REMEDY NECESSARY; RED ZONE QUESTIONS HAVE BEEN FORMULATED AS IDEALLY AS POSSIBLE; RED ZONE QUESTIONS FUNCTIONING AS DESIGNED	r
	g	F3	PRESENCE OF RESPONSE TO ONE OR BOTH GREEN ZONE QUESTIONS IN ADDITION TO RED ZONE RESPONSE INDICATES SERIOUS QUESTION DEFECT IN GREEN ZONE QUESTIONS	F4	REDUCE INTENSITY OF GREEN ZONE QUESTIONS BY ALTERING AGE CATEGORIES OR CHANGING SCOPE OF GREEN ZONE QUESTIONS	g
	b	F5	PRESENCE OF RESPONSE TO ONE OR BOTH BLACK ZONE QUESTIONS INDICATES OUTSIDE ISSUE BOTHERING SUBJECT DUE TO MISTRUST OF EXAMINER	F6	EXAMINER MUST GAIN SUBJECT'S CONFIDENCE REGARDING AVOIDANCE OF UNREVIEWED QUESTIONS EMBRACING AN OUTSIDE ISSUE	b
G (g)(b) †	r	G1	LACK OF RESPONSE TO BOTH RED ZONE QUESTIONS INDICATES TRUTHFULNESS REGARDING TARGET ISSUE	G2	NO REMEDY NECESSARY; RED ZONE QUESTIONS HAVE BEEN FORMULATED AS IDEALLY AS POSSIBLE; RED ZONE QUESTIONS FUNCTIONING AS DESIGNED	r
	g	G3	PRESENCE OF RESPONSE TO ONE OR BOTH GREEN ZONE QUESTIONS INDICATES TRUTHFULNESS REGARDING TARGET ISSUE; NO OTHER ZONE IS DAMPENING OUT GREEN ZONE	G4	NO REMEDY NECESSARY; NO CAUSE TO BELIEVE GREEN ZONE QUESTION STRUCTURE INADEQUATE; GREEN ZONE QUESTIONS FUNCTIONING AS DESIGNED	g
	b	G5	PRESENCE OF RESPONSE TO ONE OR BOTH BLACK ZONE QUESTIONS INDICATES OUTSIDE ISSUE BOTHERING SUBJECT DUE TO MISTRUST OF EXAMINER	G6	EXAMINER MUST GAIN SUBJECT'S CONFIDENCE REGARDING AVOIDANCE OF UNREVIEWED QUESTIONS EMBRACING AN OUTSIDE ISSUE	b
H !?	r	H1	LACK OF RESPONSE TO BOTH RED ZONE QUESTIONS STILL INDICATES TRUTH REGARDING TARGET ISSUE; THIS SYSTEM BASED ON SUBJECT CAPABILITY OF RESPONSE	H2	NO REMEDY NECESSARY; RED ZONE QUESTIONS HAVE BEEN FORMULATED AS IDEALLY AS POSSIBLE; RED ZONE QUESTIONS FUNCTIONING AS DESIGNED	r
	g	H3	LACK OF RESPONSE TO BOTH GREEN ZONE QUESTIONS IN ADDITION TO LACK OF RESPONSE TO RED ZONE QUESTIONS INDICATES SERIOUS GREEN ZONE QUESTION DEFECT	H4	INCREASE INTENSITY OF GREEN ZONE QUESTIONS BY ALTERING AGE CATEGORIES OR CHANGING SCOPE OF GREEN ZONE QUESTIONS	g
	b	H5	LACK OF RESPONSE TO BOTH BLACK ZONE QUESTIONS INDICATES NO OUTSIDE ISSUE BOTHERING SUBJECT DUE TO MISTRUST OF EXAMINER	H6	NO REMEDY NECESSARY; EXAMINER HAS SUBJECT'S CONFIDENCE REGARDING AVOIDANCE OF UNREVIEWED QUESTIONS EMBRACING OUTSIDE ISSUE	b

© 1962 by Cleve Backster

Backster Zone Comparison Test
"Tri-zone" Reaction Combination "A"

r	Truth		Indefinite			Deception		
−	tt	t	t?	?	?d	d	dd	
−							↑	

Orderly flow of psychological set
dd = Ideal Deception

	INDICATION		REMEDY
r	A1 Presence of response to one or both red zone questions indicates deception regarding target issue.	r	A2 No remedy is necessary; red zone questions have been formulated as ideally as possible; red zone questions functioning as designed.
g	A3 Lack of response to both green zone questions because of dampening by red zone question responses indicates deception regarding target issue.	g	A4 No remedy necessary; no reason to believe green zone question structure inadequate; green zone questions functioning as designed.
b	A5 Lack of response to both black zone questions indicates that no outside issue is bothering subject.	b	A6 No remedy necessary; examiner has subject's confidence regarding avoidance of unreviewed questions embracing outside issue.

Backster Zone Comparison Test
"Tri-zone" Reaction Combination "B"

−	Truth		Indefinite			Deception		
g	tt	t	t?	?	?d	d	dd	
−	↑							

Orderly flow of psychological set
tt=Ideal Truth

	INDICATION		REMEDY
r	B1 Lack of response to both red zone questions indicates truthfulness regarding target issue.	r	B2 No remedy necessary; red zone questions have been formulated as ideally as possible; red zone questions functioning as designed.
g	B3 Presence of response to one or both green zone questions indicates truthfulness regarding target issue, as no other zone is dampening out green zone.	g	B4 No remedy necessary; no reason to believe green zone question structure inadequate; green zone questions functioning as designed.
b	B5 Lack of response to both black zone questions indicates that no outside issue is bothering subject.	b	B6 No remedy necessary; examiner has subject's confidence regarding avoidance of unreviewed questions embracing outside issue.

Backster Zone Comparison Test
"Tri-zone" Reaction Combination "C"

_	Truth	Indefinite	Deception
_	tt	t	t?	?	?d	d	dd
ⓑ			↑				

Disorderly flow of psychological set
No "lean"* toward truth or deception
?

	INDICATION		REMEDY
r	C1 Lack of response to both red zone questions usually indicates truthfulness regarding target issue; this rule nullified by black zone question response.	r	C2 No remedy necessary; red zone questions will be functioning as designed after black zone question response subsides.
g	C3 Lack of response to green zone and to red zone usually indicates serious green zone question defect. This is nullified by black zone response.	g	C4 No remedy necessary; no cause to believe green zone question structure inadequate; recheck after response to black zone question subsides.
b	C5 Presence of response to one or both black zone questions indicates outside issue bothering subject.	b	C6 Examiner must gain subject's confidence regarding avoidance of unreviewed questions embracing outside issue.

*The Term "Lean": Allowed only in "tri-zone" assessment--not allowed in "spot analysis" final determination.

Backster Zone Comparison Test
"Tri-zone" Reaction Combination "D"

ⓡ	Truth	Indefinite	Deception
ⓖ	tt	t	t?	?	?d	d	dd
_			↑				

Disorderly flow of psychological set
"lean"* toward deception
?d

	INDICATION		REMEDY
r	D1 Presence of response to one or both red zone questions indicates deception regarding target issue.	r	D2 No remedy necessary; red zone questions have been formulated as ideally as possible; red zone questions functioning as designed.
g	D3 Presence of response to one or both green zone questions in addition to red zone question indicates serious green zone question defect.	g	D4 Reduce intensity of green zone questions by altering subject age categories or changing scope of green zone questions.
b	D5 Lack of response to both black zone questions indicates no outside issue bothering subject.	b	D6 No remedy necessary; examiner has subject's confidence regarding avoidance of unreviewed questions embracing outside issue.

*The Term "Lean": Allowed only in "tri-zone" assessment--not allowed in "spot analysis" final determination.

Backster Zone Comparison Test
"Tri-zone" Reaction Combination "E"

r	Truth		Indefinite			Deception	
−	tt	t	t?	?	?d	d	dd
b				↑			

Semi-orderly flow of psychological set
d = Adequate Deception

	INDICATION		REMEDY
r	E1 Presence of response to one or both red zone questions indicates deception regarding target issue.	r	E2 No remedy necessary; red zone questions have been formulated as ideally as possible; red zone questions functioning as designed.
g	E3 Lack of response to both green zone questions because of dampening by red zone question response; indicates deception regarding target issue.	g	E4 No remedy necessary; no reason to believe green zone question structure inadequate; green zone questions functioning as designed.
b	E5 Presence of response to one or both black zone questions indicates outside issue bothering subject.	b	E6 Examiner must gain subject's confidence regarding avoidance of unreviewed questions embracing outside issue.

Backster Zone Comparison Test
"Tri-zone" Reaction Combination "F"

r	Truth		Indefinite			Deception	
g	tt	t	t?	?	?d	d	dd
b				↑			

Disorderly flow of psychological set
"lean"* toward deception
?d

	INDICATION		REMEDY
r	F1 Presence of response to one or both red zone questions indicates deception regarding target issue.	r	F2 No remedy necessary; red zone questions have been formulated as ideally as possible; red zone questions functioning as designed.
g	F3 Presence of response to one or both green zone questions in addition to red zone response indicates serious question defect in green zone questions.	g	F4 Reduce intensity of green zone questions by altering age categories or changing scope of green zone questions.
b	F5 Presence of response to one or both black zone questions indicates outside issue bothering subject.	b	F6 Examiner must gain subject's confidence regarding avoidance of unreviewed questions embracing outside issue.

*The Term "Lean": Allowed only in "tri-zone" assessment--not allowed in "spot analysis"

Backster Zone Comparison Test
"Tri-zone" Reaction Combination "G"

_	Truth		Indefinite			Deception	
	tt	t	t?	?	?d	d	dd

g
b

↑

Semi-orderly flow of psychological set
t = Adequate Truth

	INDICATION		REMEDY
r	G1 Lack of response to both red zone questions indicates truthfulness regarding target issue.	r	G2 No remedy necessary; red zone questions have been formulated as ideally as possible; red zone questions functioning as designed.
g	G3 Presence of response to one or both green zone questions indicates truthfulness regarding target issue; No other zone is dampening out green zone.	g	G4 No remedy necessary; no cause to believe green zone question structure inadequate; green zone questions functioning as designed.
b	G5 Presence of response to one or both black zone questions indicates outside issue bothering subject.	b	G6 Examiner must gain subject's confidence regarding avoidance of unreviewed questions embracing outside issue.

Backster Zone Comparison Test
"Tri-zone" Reaction Combination "H"

_	Truth		Indefinite			Deception	
	tt	t	t?	?	?d	d	dd

_
_

↑

Disorderly flow of psychological set
"lean"* toward truth
t?

	INDICATION		REMEDY
r	H1 Lack of response to both red zone questions still indicates truth regarding target issue; this system based on subject capability of response.	r	H2 No remedy necessary; red zone questions have been formulated as ideally as possible; red zone questions functioning as designed.
g	H3 Lack of response to both green zone questions in addition to lack of response to red zone questions indicates serious green zone question defect.	g	H4 Increase intensity of green zone questions by altering age categories or changing scope of green zone questions.
b	H5 Lack of response to both black zone questions indicates no outside issue bothering subject.	b	H6 No remedy necessary; examiner has subject's confidence regarding avoidance of unreviewed questions embracing outside issue.

*The Term "Lean": Allowed only in "tri-zone" assessment--not allowed in "spot analysis"
final determination.

Page 351. Add the following regarding the ZCT intra-examination discussion of control (comparison) questions with the examinee, after Figure XI-10A.

After formulation and discussion of control (comparison) questions during the pre-test interview, further routine discussion of these questions will be avoided except as dictated by principles outlined in our Zone Comparison Indication-Remedy table.

1. Should the examinee be reacting to relevant questions only (Combination A), there is no need for further stimulation on the control (comparison) questions. through between-charts discussion. The adequacy of these questions can be verified by obtaining additional admissions following the last chart collected on that same target issue and prior to seeking target issue admissions due to the examinee's reactions to the relevant questions.

2. Should the examinee be reacting to the control (comparison) questions only (Combination B) there is no need for further "between charts" discussion of these questions.

3. Should the examinee be reacting to both the relevant questions and the control (comparisont) questions further direct discussion of these questions could be counter-productive. In a more subtle fashion the examiner should reduce the intensity of these questions through a more indirect approach.

4. Should the examinee show no reaction to any of the questions (Combination H) it would then be proper to attempt to stimulate reaction to the control (comparison) questions by directly discussing these questions between charts. (Backster 1998)

NOTE: In item 3 above, the subtle approach used is to first discuss with the examinee a cosmetic change to the irrelevant (neutral) question or even the symptomatic question(s). Then the relevant questions are reviewed followed by the changed control question(s). In that manner, the control questions are not singled out. (Backster 1998)

Page 354. Add the following after the last paragraph of the Integrated Zone Comparison Technique which ends with "(Gordon 1996)"

The Academy for Scientific Investigative Training developed software in 2001, which allows examiners to utilize their Horizontal Scoring System in conjunction with the Academy's Algorithm for Manual Scoring. What is unique about this software is that it can be used by examiners working with any computerized system, or analog system.

The software allows the examiner to utilize the Integrated Zone Comparison formats, the Matte Quadri-Track Zone Comparison format, any of the Backster Zone Formats, MZCT, MGQT, AFMGQT, Reid GQT and score a Peak of Tension Test.

The examiner makes measurements of their data as instructed and enters it on a single page. The software than automatically gives a Chart by Chart breakdown, as well as an overall question and examination analysis with determinations. The software also allows the examiner to use the Academy's Forensic Assessment Interview, which has drop down menus for the examiner to note verbal and nonverbal behavior, as well as score it.

Total scores for the interview are automatically performed by the software and inserted into the final examination analysis to warn the examiner of extreme differences between the examinee's interview performance and polygraph chart performance. These extreme differences may be due to improperly formulated questions or countermeasures employed by the examinee. (Gordon 2001)

Page 366. Add the following after the last sentence on that page which ends with "(c) Anything else is *inconclusive*."

NOTE: Blackwell's (1999) field study found "the PDD examiners mean level of accuracy was 75.7% and 66.3% for the 7- and 3- position scoring scales, respectively." Blackwell stated that "without exception, the overall level of accuracy generated by the examiners when using the 7-position scoring scale was higher than when using the 3-position scoring scale. The same was true when looking at the overall percentages for either the innocent examinations or the guilty examinations." Krapohl (1998) found that the 3-position scale with a cutoff (threshold) of +/-4 was statistically equivalent to the widely accepted 7-position scale with the +/- 6 cutoff score (threshold). However, Krapohl also found that "the highly experienced raters in this study rarely used the full range of available values in the 7-position scale, employing the narrower range of the 3-position scale for about 90% of the question comparisons." Capps and Ansley (1992) and Van Herk (1991), like Krapohl, found that the accuracy of the 7- and 3-position scales depended on the threshold used. The Backster and Matte Zone Comparison Techniques use an increasing threshold, whereas other Zone Comparison Technique modifications (DoDPI, Utah) employ a fixed threshold. (Matte, Backster 2000)

Pages 369-370. Add the following References in alphabetical order at appropriate pages.

Backster, C. (1998, September 18). Personal correspondence with J. A. Matte.
Backster, C. (1962). Tri-Zone Reaction Combinations: Backster Zone Comparison Test. Backster School of Lie Detection, New York, NY.
Blackwell, N. J. (1999). PolyScore 3.3 and psychophysiological detection of deception examiner rates of accuracy when scoring examinations from actual criminal investigations. *Polygraph*, 28(2): 149-175.
Gordon, N. (2001, December 10). Facsimile to J. A. Matte.
Matte, J. A., Backster C. (2000). A critical analysis of Amsel's comparative study of the exclusive v. nonexclusive comparison question. *Polygraph*, 29(3): 261-266.

CHAPTER 13

COMPUTERIZED POLYGRAPH SYSTEMS

Page 428. Add the following change to second paragraph on aforesaid page.

Replace "Weinstein 1997, 1998; Backster 1997, 1998; Keifer 1997, 1998)" with the following change "Weinstein 1997, 1998, 2000, 2001; Backster 1997, 1998, 2000, 2001; Keifer 1997, 1998, 2000; Shull 1999; Lewis 2001)"

Pages 429-430. Add the following References in alphabetical order at appropriate pages.

Backster, C. (2000-2001). Personal communication with J. A. Matte.
Keifer, R. W. (2000, July 13). Personal communication with J. A. Matte.
Lewis, T. (2001, Aug 24). Personal communication with J. A. Matte.
Shull, K. W. (1999, October 7). Personal communication with J. A. Matte.
Weinstein, D. A. (2000 and 2001, Aug 24). Personal communication with J. A. Matte.

CHAPTER 23

LEGAL ASPECTS OF THE PSYCHOPHYSIOLOGICIAL VERACITY EXAMINATION

Page 566. Make the following changes to legal citation contained at end of first paragraph.

(Johnson v. State, 208 Ga.App. 87, 429 S.E.2d690 [Ga.App.1993]; State v. Craig, 262 Mont. 240; 864 P.2d 1240; 1993 Mont. LEXIS 398; 50 Mont. St. Rep. 1533; Amyot v. Her Majesty the Queen, Province of Quebec, District of Montreal, Nos. 500-10-000015-837, and [705-01-000137-8353]; State of Wisconsin v. Cary Johnson, 193 Wis.2d 382, 535 N.W.2d 441[1995].)

Page 566. Add the following paragraph after the above legal citation.

In the State of Wisconsin v. Cary Johnson cited above, the Court of Appeals held that "Here, we conclude that the actual polygraph examination and the subsequent interview were sufficiently separate events as to both time and content. Johnson's inculpatory statements were made after the completion of the actual mechanical polygraph portion of the examination while he was not attached to the mechanical polygraph apparatus. Additionally, the post-polygraph examination took place in an adjacent room. From the hearing testimony, it is evident that the police officer questioning Johnson after the polygraph examination did not refer to polygraph charts or tell Johnson he had failed the polygraph test to elicit inculpatory statements. Although the post-polygraph interview was temporally proximate to the actual test, neither Barrera nor Schlise proscribe a bright-line rule of timing, but look to the totality of the circumstances. (See Barrera, 99 Wis. 2d at 288, 298N.W.2d at 828-29.) We conclude that where there is a distinct break between the two events and the post-polygraph interview does not specifically relate back to the actual mechanical polygraph test, the events are sufficiently attenuated; therefore, general rules of admissibility apply to the post-polygraph interview."

Page 595. Add the following paragraph after Table 5.

A 41-illustrations presentation that includes the above five tables is set forth in companion textbook titled "*Examination and Cross-Examination of Experts in Forensic Psychophysiology Using The*

Polygraph" by this author published in December 2000. This aforementioned presentation is designed to be used to lay the foundation for the admissibility of the results of a PV examination. (Matte, 2000)

Pages 595-595B. Add the following reference in alphabetical order.

Matte, J. A. (2000). *Examination and Cross-Examination of Experts in Forensic Psychophysiology Using The Polygraph.* Williamsville, New York: J. A. M. Publications.

CHAPTER 24

PSYCHOPHYSIOLOGICAL VERACITY EXAMINATIONS USING THE POLYGRAPH IN SEX OFFENSES

Page 596. Change first paragraph which starts with "In Part I of this chapter" to read as follows:

Part I of this chapter describes the origin and evolutionary process of post-conviction sex offender polygraph testing to its current state of operation, with some caveats and recommendations for improved methodology. Part II introduces new methods in the use of the polygraph in the treatment and monitoring of convicted sex offenders on parole or probation developed as a result of the experience gained during its formative period. Part III discusses the role of PV examinations in the investigation of sex offenses and the positive and negative aspects of its application to sex offense victims. The use of PV examinations in the private sector to resolve fidelity issues is also covered.

Page 622. Add the following paragraphs following the second paragraph which ends with "treatment of the offender."

Part II. - New Methods for Management and Polygraph Testing of Sex Offenders.

Since publication of this book in 1996, much has been learned about the application of psychophysiological veracity (PV) examinations in the assessment, treatment and supervision of post-conviction sex offenders. The benefits of PV examinations with this population, identified by Dr. Stan Abrams and Charles Edson, were soon realized by others across the country searching for new methods to manage sex offenders on probation or parole. The value of PV examinations specifically in this new role lies in the new information derived from offenders during PV examinations, and the ability to determine the veracity of an offender's self report, both of which are seen as crucial elements in providing the most effective specialized treatment and supervision. Similar to a substance abuser who may be asked to participate in urinalysis by a court to verify abstinence from illegal drugs, the use of PV examinations with sex offenders not only works as a tool to deter further criminal activities, but it also emphasizes the importance of being truthful (a strong element of sex offender treatment since most offenders use secrecy and lies as an avenue to commit deviant acts), and provides an opportunity to monitor the sex offender's compliance to specialized conditions of probation or parole. (Bullens, ed. 2002)

The Emergence of the Containment Approach Model (English, Pullen and Jones, 1996)

The role of post-conviction PV examinations was given national attention in 1996, following the conclusion of a national study of probation and parole agencies' management of adult felony sex offenders funded by the U. S. National Institute of Justice. In this study, researchers with the Colorado Division of Criminal Justice sought to define, "How are the nation's probation and parole agencies managing adult sex offenders?" by various research methods: Telephone surveys, a review of research and documents, and field research. (English, Pullen and Jones, 1996). It was in this research, that field practitioners identified PV examinations as an essential element in the management of sex offenders. This study resulted in the identification of a model process in the management of sex offenders, termed "The Containment Approach." (English, Pullen, Jones 1996; Bullens, ed 2002)

The containment approach is defined as "a particular method of individual case processing and case management of sex offenders in the criminal justice system. It rests on the dual premise that sex offenders are one hundred percent responsible for the damage they inflict on others and that they must constantly and consistently be held accountable for their inappropriate thoughts and feelings as well as for their illegal actions. In the containment approach, offenders are caught in a tight web of surveillance, monitoring and treatment." (English, Pullen, Jones 1996; Bullens, ed 2002) (See illustration on Page 61).

Three central elements exist within the context of the containment approach model identified by the research. They are the development of *internal control, external control* and the use of *PV examinations.* Collaboration and the frequent access and exchange of information between the supervision officer, treatment provider and polygraphist are essential to the execution of the aforesaid elements of the model. (Bullens, ed. 2002)

Internal Control: Developing an offender's internal control to cope with inappropriate sexual impulses, fantasies and behaviors is often achieved through specific sex offender treatment and psycho-educational or behavioral modification techniques. Essentially, the sex offender learns to identify and avoid high-risk situations and behaviors. Specialized treatment focussed on the identification of an offenders' offense cycle and relapse prevention become key components of building an offender's internal control. To be effective, the offender must truthfully report all past and present sexual paraphilias.

External Control: The justice system (court) must identify and implement limitations or barriers to foreseeable high-risk behavior in order to provide the highest level of public safety and offender accountability. This is accomplished with the use, monitoring and enforcement of specialized conditions of supervision. To be effective, external control, probation and parole agencies must develop strategies of supervision that appropriately address risks specific to the offender that protect known, unknown and potential victims. Goals and restrictions should be well defined. Progress toward or away from court expectations should be well documented by the probation or parole officer. Compliance enforcement should be consistent and timely.

PV Examination: The goal of the PV examination is to obtain information necessary for offender risk management and treatment, and to reduce the offender's denial mechanisms. Deceptive results flag areas of concern that the treatment provider and supervising officer need to investigate further. Every effort is made to assist the offender in obtaining a positive evaluation so that treatment and supervision can be informed and relevant. To this end, polygraph data should be used in conjunction with other verified information when making decisions about case management of sex offenders.

English, Jones, Pasini-Hill, Patrick and Cooley-Towell, 2000, used with permission.

The containment approach is one of the few published "models" for the management of sex offenders. Many jurisdictions, such as San Diego County, California, Tarrant Count, Texas, and Spokane, Washington, have identified this model as the basis for which sex offender management policies and practices evolve. In some cases, statewide policy, such as in the State of Colorado and Tennessee, support this model as an effective model for sex offender management. Other jurisdictions, such as New Haven, Connecticut, have modified this model to include a fourth central element: *victim advocacy*. In New Haven, a victim advocate works in concert with the supervision officer, treatment provider and polygraphist to assist offenders in developing victim empathy, as well as provide information and assistance to those within both the victim and offender's circle of support. (Bullens, ed. 2002)

Four Categories of PV Examinations for Sex Offender Management.

Different types of PV examinations are used in post-conviction sex offender testing which are classified as follows: (1) The Disclosure Test over the Instant Offense, previously referred to as the Conviction Verification Examination (See Page 597, Matte 1996), (2) The Disclosure Test over the Sexual History, formerly referred to as the Complete Disclosure Examination (See Page 597, Matte 1996), (3) The Monitoring PV Examination, and (4) The Maintenance PV Examination. These tests have become integral tools in the management of sex offenders' probation and parole requirements. Each type of test is distinctly different from the other, especially in terms of time frame (time of reference) and focus (frame of reference). (Holden, 2000). The Disclosure PV examinations focus on activities and behaviors that are historical in nature and are designed primarily for clinical or treatment use. Maintenance and Monitoring PV examinations focus on activities and behaviors while under court supervision. These tests allow the sex offender an opportunity to verify his or her self-report and compliance with supervision conditions and treatment rules. (Bullens, ed. 2002)

The Disclosure Test over the Instant Offense (Previously referred to as the Conviction Verification Examination. P. 597).

This examination is requested when the offender denies all or part of the accusations for which he/she is under court supervision. This test is used primarily in the clinical setting to promote progress in sex offender specific treatment. Clinicians report that the utility of this test lies in reinforcing honesty among group treatment members (sex offenders), and from the need to have accurate information in order to develop the most effective treatment plans. These missions can best be accomplished by understanding the nature and extent of the offender's behavior and actions that led to his/her arrest and conviction. (See Cycle of Abuse diagram by Bays and Freeman-Longo 1989 on P. 601). This PV examination is typically conducted when the offender has denied, post-conviction, all or some part of the allegations (i.e. denies offense, admits touching but denies penetration, etc) for which the offender is currently under court supervision. Research suggests that victims often under-report the extent of victimization, therefore this PV examination is useful in determining the extent and range of victimization involved in the Instant Offense. (Scheve III, 2001). *The time of reference* for the test is that defined by the investigation. The *frame of reference* for the test is the complainant's and/or victim's statement, investigative reports, arrest reports, etc. (Holden, 2000)

For the polygraphist conducting a Disclosure Test over the Instant Offense, the testing format is generally single-issue, making it much like the administration of a pre-conviction PV examination conducted during the investigation stages; however, to the offender the consequences are notably different, in that the offender who now admits his/her offense does not face further punshment, but benchmarks progress in overcoming denial within the treatment setting; thus, beginning the process of full accountability and taking responsibility. Additional information, such as the extent or duration of the abuse to the victim can also be shared with the victim's treatment provider in an effort to aid in the victim's recovery process. Deceptive results with continued denial (even on subsequent PV examinations) generally lead to sanctions within the treatment program, or ultimately unsuccessful termination from the sex offender treatment program. (Bullens, ed. 2002)

The Disclosure Test over the Sexual History (Formerly referred to as the Complete Disclosure Examination on P. 597)

This examination is usually requested by a treatment provider and is conducted to obtain a complete and truthful disclosure of the offender's sexual history as possible, again to assist the treatment provider in developing an effective treatment plan for the offender. The *frame of reference* is the completed Sexual History Questionnaire provided by the treatment provider. The *time of reference* is the individuals' lifetime prior to the date of conviction, excluding the instant offense. (Bullens, ed 2002)

This type of PV examination has come under the most debate since its development. In most cases, sex offenders are asked to complete a Sexual History Questionnaire (Salter & Holden, 2000) that identifies victims previous to the Instant Offense by age, gender and description of abuse and sexual paraphilias. A different approach to obtaining a sexual autobiography is having the sex offender complete a structured narrative, much like the one identified on pages 605-610, with some notable exceptions: prior victims are not always identified by name and the sexual history covers all sexual inappropriate or deviant activities from the offender's first sexual encounter, up until, but not including, the offense for which the offender is on probation or parole. Regardless of the manner in which this information is elicited, these questionnaires are continuously being revised to capture more information, such as emerging sex crimes that are technological based – for example, child pornography on the Internet, depicting oneself as a minor and entering youth based chat rooms. An accurate and complete sexual history document is an important part of the sex offender treatment program as it relates specifically and individually to an offender's risks to the community (by identifying potential victims) and often assists in determining effective treatment and behavioral modification techniques. (Bullens, ed. 2002)

It is important that the offender have ample time to prepare for the sexual history examination prior to the date of the PV examination. The PV examination should not be conducted without the required preparation and investment by the offender with the treatment provider into its accuracy (Edson, 1991; Janes, 1993; Blasingame, 1994), as it is not the role of the Polygraphist   to spend hours with the offender to collect the history. The role of this specific PV examination is to verify that the offender is not lying or withholding important information from the document, specifically as it relates to victims. For the polygraphist, the administration of a sexual history examination is similar to the use of PV examinations in applicant screening, such as the use of a police applicant booklet. It is common for the examinee, in this case the offender, to add information at the last minute when the polygraphist   reviews the completed document with him/her during the pretest phase of the PV examination. A non-deceptive test, even with significant disclosures during the pretest phase of the PV examination, is seen as a measurement of success for the offender who can demonstrate truthfulness about his/her sexual history. Deceptive results generally result in treatment sanctions until such time that the offender retests with non-deceptive results. (Bullens, ed. 2002)

Legal and ethical issues are at the heart of the debate around Sex History Disclosure PV examinations. (English, Jones, Pasini-Hill, Patrick, Cooley-Towell 2000). Courts continue to be challenged on self-incrimination issues that arise when sex offenders are ordered to undergo PV examinations by either a direct condition of release, or a component of Court ordered sex offender treatment. The identification of previous (prior to the Instant Offense for which the offender is under current supervision), unreported sex crimes and victims has led some jurisdictions to adopt limited immunity for offenders who remain in compliance with treatment and supervision orders. This limited immunity is based on the belief that the criminal justice system and treatment program can better manage the offender with clear knowledge of paraphilias and risks specific to the offender. Other jurisdictions instead make determinations of immunity or prosecution on a case-by-case basis or by simply asking the offender to not identify victims in their sexual history by name. (English, et al 2000). Legal challenges will continue to exist as stakes are increased for non-compliance with Sex History PV examinations. In states that have Civil Commitment, disclosing additional sex crimes as part of sex offender treatment may impede the offender's potential for release, however, not participating in the required PV examinations may lead to treatment or supervision sanctions. (Bullens, ed. 2002)

The Monitoring PV Examination

This examination is commonly ordered by the Court as a special condition of probation or parole, and is conducted to investigate re-offending while under supervision. These examinations and information obtained from these post-conviction tests have been addressed by several courts, and in general, have been supported. The *time of reference* is all or any defined part of the period under court supervision (from the date of conviction to present, or since the last non-deceptive polygraph while on probation or parole). The *frame of reference* is illegal sexual acts during the time of reference. Supervisory and treatment professionals, court officials, investigators, and others may require this test.

Examples of relevant questions on a Monitoring PV Examination include:

- *Since the start of your probation, have you touched the sexual parts of anyone under the age of eighteen?*

- *Since the start of your probation, have you illegally exposed your penis to anyone?*

- *Since the start of your probation, have you viewed any child pornography?*

The Maintenance PV Examination (Two Types)

This PV examination covers the same *time of reference* as the monitoring examination, however, its *frame of reference* is more broadly defined to include a variety of possible probation, parole or treatment rule violations. There are two types of maintenance PV examinations. A Maintenance examination can focus on either issues related to probation condition violations (i.e. alcohol/drug use, being alone with a child, travel violations, etc.) or treatment issues (i.e. masturbatory habits, fantasies and arousal logs, etc.). Each type of test is exclusive and cannot be combined. For instance, a maintenance test over treatment issues cannot also address probation violations, unless the treatment rule violation is also a violation of the written probation conditions. Supervisory and treatment professionals may request this test.

Examples of relevant questions on a Maintenance PV Examination include:

- *Since the start of your probation, have you been alone with anyone under the age of eighteen that you have not told me about today?*

- *Since the start of your probation, have you used any illegal drugs?*

- *Since the start of your probation, have you viewed any pornography?*

Special Considerations for PV Examination Implementation

It is recommended that agencies adopt specific policies and procedures around the use of PV examinations with sex offenders. These policies should address sanctions and rewards (i.e., increased or decreased supervision/treatment levels) for offenders based on demonstrated (implied, detected, and confirmed PV examination and other collateral information) progression toward, or regression from stated goals. *An offender's concern about being detected in a lie or engaging in violation behaviors is essential to the successful implementation of a supervision-based PV examination program.* Offenders who are deceptive on PV examinations should be required to retest on examinations until such time as they are deemed truthful to the relevant issues being tested. Understanding that overcoming denial is a multi-stage process for offenders, disclosure, even in sages, should be considered gradual progress. Similarly, a truthful opinion on a maintenance or monitoring PV examination supporting an offender's compliance with supervision and treatment conditions can provide documentation of an offender's success or progress. Alternatively, the identification of deception or admissions of high-risk behavior and violations of supervision and treatment terms during a maintenance/monitoring test should be the impetus for additional restrictions, intense investigations or possibly revocation and incarceration. Additionally, PV examination information and outcomes may focus the need for further treatment requirements. *Court action should never be sought solely on the results of a PV examination.* (Bullens, ed. 2002)

It should be expected that the use of PV examinations with a sex offender population will uncover activities and behaviors that would, in the absence of PV examinations, be virtually impossible to detect due to their private and secret nature. A Maintenance/Monitoring Checklist used by Bullens & Bullens Polygraph Services to elicit information in the pretest phase of both maintenance and monitoring PV examinations is depicted on Page 67 of this Supplement. (Bullens, ed. 2002)

A review of violation behaviors disclosed by sex offenders during the pretest phase of PV examinations provide supervision officials an indication of areas that need improved monitoring and new strategies for supervision. For example, a review of maintenance and monitoring PV examinations conducted on adult sex offenders on probation (not all in sex offender treatment) identified the following violation behaviors disclosed in the pretest alone. (see Violations Behaviors Identified during the Pretest Phase Maintenance/Monitoring Exams - July thru October 2001, on Page 68 of this Supplement). (Bullens, ed. 2002)

Collaboration between the supervision agent, treatment provider and polygraphist   is essential to determining goals and reactions to information obtained from a PV examination in the containment model. Information about non-compliance without action by supervision and treatment providers can lead to further violations and reduced fear of detection on subsequent PV examinations. Such necessary action by the containment team may include: increased supervision, drug testing, 4th waiver home and computer searches, electronic monitoring, or a return to sex offender treatment. More serious violations may require jail time, or even revocation. (Bullens, ed. 2002)

Quality Control and Standards

The effective use of PV examinations in sex offender management relies heavily upon an informed consumer and a competent polygraphist   , both having a commitment to proper polygraph use and quality control.   Both National and State Professional organizations have dedicated committees for the development of guidelines and standards in post-conviction sex offender PV examinations. These guidelines increase and improve the minimum qualifications of polygraphist s conducting post-conviction sex offender examinations, as well as define acceptable testing requirements with a method of quality control.   Such agencies as the American Polygraph Association (APA), the American Association of Police Polygraphist s (AAPP) and the American Society for Testing and Materials (ASTM) exist to provide information, professional standards and resources to the polygraph professionals and its consumers. (Bullens, ed. 2002)

BULLENS & BULLENS Polygraph Services

Maintenance/Monitoring Checklist

Since: _____

Criminal Law violations?

Driving while suspended/revoked?

Driving while intoxicated?

Sex registration violations?

Alcohol use-
　　　Last time?
　　　Frequency?
　　　How much?
　　　Type of drink?

Drug use-
　　　Last time?
　　　Frequency?
　　　How much?
　　　Type of drug?

Travel violations?

Contact with victim?
　　　Victim's family?

Contact with minors-
　　　Last time?
　　　Who?
　　　When?

Pornography-　　Child Porn-
　　　Print-
　　　Video-
　　　Television-
　　　Internet-
　　　Masturbate?

Internet use-
　　　E-mail address?
　　　Chat rooms?
　　　Transferred photos?
　　　Impersonation as a minor?
　　　Impersonation as member of opposite sex?

Visited Adult Bookstore?
　　　Purchase something?
　　　Sexual Contact?
　　　Masturbate?

Topless Bar/Adult Modeling Studio?
　　　Masturbate?
　　　Sexual contact?

Frequency?
Fantasy?
Involved minors?
Involved victim?
While exposing?
　In front of others?
　In vehicle?
　At work?
　While peeping on others?
　Other than at home?
　Used objects?

SEXUAL CONTACT/EXPERIENCES
　Paid for sex?
　Was paid for sex?
　Had sex with unconscious person?
　Had sex with sleeping person?
　Had sex with intoxicated person?
　Had group sex?
　Had sex in public place?
　Had sexual contact with animals?
　Used objects during sex?
　Had phone sex?　　　Masturbate?

　Approximate # of sexual relationships:
　　　Names
　　　Ages:
　　　Children?

　Affairs/Unfaithful?

Sexual contact with minors?

Indecent exposure?

Made obscene phone calls?　　Masturbate?

Cross dressed?　　Masturbate?

Taken nude photos of self?　　Others?

Bondage during sex/self?　　Others?

Homosexual contact?

Viewed or peeped on others?

Rubbed against others for sexual purposes?

Stalked or followed someone?

Stolen underwear or clothes?　　Masturbate?

Fondled adult w/o permission?

Became inappropriately aroused?

NOTES/OTHER AREAS OF CONCERN:

Other violations?
Treatment compliance?

Masturbation-
　　　Last time?

Margaret and Darryl Bullens
Polygraph Examiners

6540 Lusk Blvd, Suite C256
San Diego, CA 92121

858-622-1814 phone
858-622-9031 fax

Violation Behaviors Identified during the Pre-Test Phase Maintenance/Monitoring Exams July thru October 2001

Violation Behaviors	Totals # of offender's reporting (n=80)	Percentage of offenders engaging in behavior
Consuming alcohol	35	43.75%
Viewing pornographic magazines	26	32.50%
Fantasies of minors (including victims) during masturbation	22	27.50%
Viewing pornographic movies	19	23.75%
Viewing pornography on the Internet (including child pornography)	17	21.25%
Marijuana use	17	21.25%
Unsupervised contact with minors (including babysitting)	13	16.25%
Violating travel restrictions	13	16.25%
Frequenting adult bookstores	12	15.00%
Frequenting nude bars	10	12.50%
Masturbating in public	9	11.25%
Driving while license suspended	9	11.25%
Driving while intoxicated (including new charges)	7	8.75%
Paying for sex (prostitute)	5	6.25%
Disclosed sexual arousal in presence of minors (male and female)	5	6.25%
Methamphetamine use	4	5.00%
Indecent exposure	3	3.75%
Cocaine/Crank use	3	3.75%
Obscene phone calls (including 900)	2	2.50%
Stalking	2	2.50%
Voyeurism (peeping)	2	2.50%
Having sex in public	2	2.50%
Committing property theft	2	2.50%
Sexual arousal/contact with animals	2	2.50%
Misuse of prescription drugs	2	2.50%
Sexual contact with a child	1	1.25%
Taking nude photos of an adult without consent	1	1.25%
Domestic violence	1	1.25%
Engaging in sex with bondage	1	1.25%
Falsifying NA logs	1	1.25%
Ecstasy use	1	1.25%
Open container charge	1	1.25%

The violation behaviors identified above were *disclosed* by adult sex offenders on probation during the pre-test phase of post-conviction sex offender polygraphs. The majority of the examination noted above were referred for "Monitoring Exams" and focused exclusively on sexual re-offense issues as relevant questions.

Bullens & Bullens Polygraph Services
Margaret Bullens 2001

In Summary

The use of sex offender PV examinations continues to evolve due to its increasing application in sex offender management. Implementation of the post-conviction PV examination with the adult felony sex offender population has nearly doubled between 1994 and 1998. It has become an import asset for treatment and supervision, providing what many regard as an independent verification of compliance and progress. Progress or success is identified when an offender is deemed non-deceptive and compliant with Court ordered supervision and treatment rules. When an offender has engaged in non-compliant behavior, the polygraph often provides information that informs the case manager and assists in action to modify and manage risk, thus preventing relapse. The polygraphist is a key part of the containment team. (Bullens, ed. 2002)

The utility of sex offender PV examinations is in the valuable information it elicits. As courts recognize the value of these examinations, they too will see the benefits of PV examinations in the monitoring and treatment of other high-risk offender populations, such as stalkers, and domestic violence abusers. In sum, it will be increasingly important for polygraphists to adhere to the strictest standards, quality control and professionalism. (Bullens, ed. 2002)

Page 622. Change Part II, Use of PV Examinations on Victims of Sex Offenses to:

Part III – Use of PV Examinations on Victims of Sex Offenses.

Page 623. Add the following paragraph after first paragraph which ends with "American Psychological and Psychiatric Association."

As noted in part II of this Supplement, research results from Disclosure Instant Offense PV examinations indicate that victims often underreport the extent or duration of abuse, therefore, if conducting a PV examination on a victim's statement, one may conclude if the victim was found deceptive that it was a false statement and abuse did not occur, when in reality, the victim may have been sexually assaulted and minimized the abuse. Again, another reason why the subjects of these types of examinations should be the suspected perpetrator and not the victim. (M. Bullens, ed. 2002)

Page 625. Add the following paragraph after second paragraph which ends with "(Warner 1996)."

The testing of victims is classified into three types of Confirmatory Examinations. For a full discussion regarding these type of examinations and their inherent problems, see page 43-44, Chapter 9 of this Supplement.

Page 625. Add the following paragraph after the paragraph mentioned above concerning Fidelity Examinations.

Fidelity Examinations:

There has been a significant increase in the demand by the public for the administration of Psychophysiological Veracity (PV) examinations to resolve the matter of faithfulness or infidelity between spouses or couples in a serious relationship. Polygraphists in private practice have no doubt been contacted with numerous requests for such examinations. Inasmuch as the accuracy of PV examinations depends on the competency of the polygraphist and the polygraph technique used, errors may occur with unfavorable results and unintended consequences seriously impacting on the marriage or relationship of the parties involved. Hence, in order to provide a service to those wrongfully accused of infidelity, yet *cause no harm*, it becomes imperative that the examinee upon being informed of the results of the PV examination, be afforded the choice to decline or consent to the release of the results to the other party regardless of who pays for the examination, and that prior to the PV examination, both parties and the polygraphist execute an Agreement (see Appendix S) to that effect. The victim of a false positive can then declare their dissatisfaction with the examination process or the test result and request a re-examination by another polygraphist or an Independent Quality Control Review. The parties involved should also be advised that the results of the PV examination are not restricted to truth or deception but can also be inconclusive. In order for these type of PV examinations to be valid and reliable, they must meet the standards of the American Polygraph Association (APA) and the American Society for Testing and Material (ASTM). Therefore, the polygraphist should restrict the PV examination to single-issue tests that have been validated by published research (See Chapter 3). The issue(s) should be distinct as in any traditional examination. They usually deal with whether or not one spouse or partner has engaged in sexual intercourse (or sexual activity) with anyone other than their spouse or partner since the beginning of the marriage or partnership or since a particular date agreed to by both parties. Furthermore, both parties agree that should the polygraphist be required to testify at any hearing or judicial proceeding, the polygraphist will be compensated for their appearance in court. In addition, the polygraph release form executed by the examinee at the beginning and end of the PV examination (Appendix K), offers the examinee an opportunity upon receiving the results of their PV examination to decline or consent to the release of the results of their examination to a specific individual named by the examinee in the aforesaid release form. In this manner, all parties are protected and there is no reason to believe that this type of examination has any less validity and reliability than any other PV examination. (See ex-parte examinations P. 84, 111-112, 118, Forensic Psychophysiology Using The Polygraph, 1996). Published research (Matte, Reuss 1990; Matte, Armitage 2000; Raskin, Barland, Podlesny, 1978) indicate that PV examinations conducted under the umbrella of "Privileged Communication" (ex-parte) have no less autonomic arousal than PV examinations conducted without the privilege.

Pages 626-627. Add the following References in alphabetical order at appropriate pages.

Blasingame, G. (1994). *Sexual offender rehabilitative treatment: Program Manual.* Redding, CA: SORT Program.

Bullens, M. (2002, ed). Contribution of edited technical information pertaining to Post-Conviction Sex Offender testing to J. A. Matte for use in this Supplement.

Edson, C. (1991). Sex offender treatment. Medford, OR: Department of Corrections.

English, K., Pullen, S., Jones, L. (1996). *Managing adult sex offenders on probation and parole: a containment approach.* Lexington, KY: American Probation and Parole Association.

English, K., Jones, L., Pasini-Hill, D., Patrick, D., Cooley-Towell, S. (2000). *The Value of Polygraph testing in Sex Offender Management: Research Report Submitted to the National Institute of Justice.* Denver, CO: Colorado Division of Public Safety, Division of Criminal Justice, Office of Research & Statistics.

Holden, E. J. (2000). Pre- and Post-Conviction Polygraph: Building Blocks for the Future-Procedures, Principles and Practices. Special Edition, Post Conviction Sex Offender Testing. *Polygraph*, <u>29</u>(1): 69-115.

Janes, B. (1993).   Polygraph: A current perspective.   *Interchange.*   June. Denver, CO: National Adolescent Perpetrator Network.

Matte, J. A., Armitage, T. E. (2000).   Addendum to 1990 field study of the Friendly Polygrapher hypothesis. *Polygraph*, <u>29</u>(3): 267-270.

Matte, J. A., Reuss, R. M. (1990).   A field study of the 'Friendly Polygraphist   " concept. *Polygraph*, <u>19</u>(1): 1-9.

Raskin, D. C. Barland, G. H., Podlesny, J. A. (1978).   *Validity and reliability of detection of deception.* Washington, D.C.: National Institute of Law Enforcement and Criminal Justice.

Salter, A., Holden, E. J. (2000). Sex Offender Disclosure Questionnaire. *Polygraph*, <u>29</u>(1):

Scheve III, W. J. (2001). Making Complete Disclosure of the Instant Offense – What Wasn't Revealed. *Texas Resource,* <u>8</u>(2).

CHAPTER 25

APPLICATION OF THE EMPLOYEE POLYGRAPH PROTECTION ACT

Page 633. First line of top paragraph, add the following after (SCAN):

(Gordon & Fleisher 2002)

Page 633. Fourth line of top paragraph, add the following after (MITT):

(Gordon & Fleisher 2002)

Page 643. Add the following reference in alphabetical order:

REFERENCES

Gordon, N. J. & Fleisher, W. L. (2002). *Effective Interviewing & Interrogation Techniques*. San Diego, California: Academic Press.

APPENDIX P

AMERICAN POLYGRAPH ASSOCIATION (APA) ACCREDITED POLYGRAPH SCHOOLS.

Page 679. Replace the list of APA accredited polygraph school with the following list which is current as of April 2011.

Academy for Scientific Investigative Training
1704 Locust Street, 2nd Floor
Philadelphia, Pennsylvania 19103
Director: Nathan J. Gordon
Ph: (215) 732-3349
Fax: (215) 545-1773
E-mail: truthdoctor@polygraph-training.com
Webpage: www.polygraph-training.com

Academy of Polygraph Science
Nature Coast Office
5441 Emerald Drive
Ridge Manor, FL 33523
Director : Richard E. Poe
Ph: (727) 6426384 or (727) 420-0521
E-mail: acdypolyscience@tampabay.it.com
Webpage: www.drpoeandassoc.com

Academy of Polygraph Science Latinamerica
12945 Seminole Vlvd, Suite 15
Largo, FL 33778
Director: Arno Horvath – (727) 531-3782
E-mail: polygraphacademy@hotmail.com
Website: abhpolygraphscience.com

Backster School of Lie Detection
861 Sixth Avenue, Suite 403
San Diego, California 92101-6379
Director: Cleve Backster, Hon. Ph.D., D.Sc.
Ph. (619) 233-6669
Fax: (619) 233-3441
E-mail: clevebackster@cs.com
Webpage: www.backster.net

National Center for Credibility Assessment
7540 Pickens Avenue
Fort Jackson, SC 29207
Director: William F. Norris
Ph: (803) 751-9100
Fax: (803) 751-9125 or 37
Registrar e-mail: gatlins@daca.mil
Webpage: www.ncca.mil
Federal, State, and Local Law Enforcement

American Institute of Polygraph
908 Barton Street
Otsego, Michigan 49078-1583
Director: Lynn P. Marcy
Webpage: www.polygraphis.com
Ph: (262) 692-2413
Fax: (269) 694-4666

American International Institute of Polygraph
Morrow, GA 30260-0686
Director: Charles E. Slupski
Ph: (770) 960-1377
Fax: (770) 960-1355
E-mail: aiip@qpolygraph.com
Webpage: www.polygraphschool.com

Arizona School of Polygraph Science
3106 W. Thomas Road, Suite 1114
Phoenix, Arizona 85017
Director: Laura Wells de Perry
Ph: (602) 272-8123, (800) 464-7831
Fax: (602) 272-9735
E-mail: laurawellsperry@cox.net
Webpage: www.azpolygraphschool.com

Latin American Polygraph Institute
Transversal 17 No. 122-73
Bogota, Colombia
Director: Sidney Wise Arias
Ph: 57.1.4829421
Fax: 57.1.2148334
E-mail: swarias@bellsouth.net

Horowitz-Ginton Credibility Assessment Academy
11 Ben-Gurion, Vita Towers
Bnei-Brak 51260 Israel
Director: Dr. Avital Ginton
Ph: 972.3.616.1111
E-mail: ginton@zahav.net.il

International Academy of Polygraph
1835 South Perimeter Road, Suite 125
Fort Lauderdale, Florida 33309-3066
Director: Scott A. Walters
Ph: (954) 771-6900
Fax: (954) 776-7687
E-mail: dci@deception.com

Israeli Government Polygraph School
P. O. Box 17193
Tel—Aviv 61171 Israel
Director: Eyal Peled
E-mail: igpolyschool@012.net.il

Kentucky Institute of Polygraph Studies
EKU Funderburk Building
521 Lancaster Avenue
Richmond, KY 40475
Director: Pam Shaw
Ph: (859) 622-5944
E-mail: pam.shaw@ky.gov

Marston Polygraph Academy
390 Orange Show Lane
San Bernardino, CA 92408
Director: Thomas M. Kelly
Ph: (928) 257-0124
Fax: (410) 987-4808
Webpage: www.marstonpolygraphacademy.com

Maryland Institute of Criminal Justice
8424 Veterans Highway, Suite 3
Millersville, Maryland 21108-0458
Director: Billy H. Thompson
Ph: (410) 987-6665
Fax: (410) 987-4808
E-mail: MDMICJ@aol.com
Webpage: www.micj.com

Mexico Polygraph Studies Unit
Calle Cuauhtemoc #168
Colonia Tizapan de San Angel
Mexico D. F. 01059
Director: Luz Del Carmen Diaz
Ph: 011.52.55.5616.6273
E-mail: ldgalindo@entermas.net

Northeast Counterdrug Training Center Polygraph Program
c/o Dept. of Military & Veterans Affairs
Building 8-64 Fort Indiantown Gap
Annville, PA 17003-5002
Director: Elmer Criswell
Ph: (717) 861-9432
E-mail: lietestec@aol.com

Centro de Investigacion Forense Y Control de S. C.
Rodrigez Saro #523. Int. 501-A Col. Del Valle
Del. Benito Juarez
Mexico, DF. C.P. 03100
Director: Jaime Raul Dran Valle
Ph: 011.52.55.2455.4624

Texas Department of Public Safety Law Enforcement Polygraph School
P. O. Box 4087
Austin, Texas 78773-0001
Director: Walt Goodson
Ph: (512) 997-4093
Fax: (512) 424-5717
E-mail: Walt.goodson@txdps.state.tx.us
Local, State, and Federal agencies only.

Centro Mexicano de Analisis Poligrafico y Psicologico, S.C.
Arqueologos #53
Col. El Retono, C. P. 09440
Mexico, DF
Director: Maria Fernanda Gadeo Lucio
Ph: 011.52.55.5418.5464

Canadian Police College Polygraph Training School
P. O. Boxes (CP) 8900
Ottawa, Canada K1G 3J2
Director: Scott McCleod
Ph: (613) 998-0886
E-mail: scott.mcleod@rcmp-grc.gc.ca

Gazit International Polygraph School
29 Hamered, Industry Building
P. O. Box 50474
Tel Aviv 61500, Israel
Director: Mordechai (Mordi) Gazit
Ph: 972.3.575.2488
E-mail: mordi@gazitg-poly.co.il

International Polygraph Studies Center
Colima No. 385-2
Colonia Roma Norte
06700 Mexico D. F. Mexico
Director: Raymond Nelson
Ph: 303.587.0599
E-mail: international@poligrafia.com.mx

MINDEF Centre for Credibility Assessment
Block 13, Mandai Camp 2
Mandai Road
Singapore
Director: V. Cholan
Ph: (65) 67684147
E-mail: cholan@starnet.gov.sg

National Academy of Training and Investigations in Polygraph Analysis
Reforma #364, Colonia Juarez
Delegacion Cuauhtemoc
Mexico, DF. CP 0660
Director: Jesus Sandoval Escalante
Ph: 011.52.5.552.410313

New England Polygraph Institute
P. O. Box 825
Center Harbor, NH 03226
Director: David J. Crawford
Ph: 603.253.8002
E-mail: kacdc@worldpath.net

Orange County Polygraph Institute
27281 Las Ramblas, Suite 140
Mission Viejo, CA 92691
Director: Len Salcedo
Ph: 949.916.0111
E-mail: isalcedo@ocpica.com

Virginia School of Polygraph
7885 Coppermine Drive
Manassas, Virginia 20109
Director: Darryl Debow
Ph: 703.396.7657
Fax: 703.396.7660
E-mail: polygraph1@verizon.net
Web: www.virginiaschoolofpolygraph.com

Veridicus International Polygraph Academy
Domingo Gonzales #35 Bis, Col. San Antonio Culhuacan Del. Iztapalapa
Mexico DF. C.P. 09800
Director: Yasmin Rios
Ph: (01152) 15591033522
Web: www.veridicusinc.com

APPENDIX Q

PV EXAMINATION DOCUMENTS REQUIRED FOR INDEPENDENT REVIEW

Page 680. Replace existing Appendix Q with the following new Appendix Q:

PV EXAMINATION DOCUMENTS REQUIRED FOR INDEPENDENT QUALITY CONTROL REVIEW

1. Written report from polygraphist who conducted the psychophysiological veracity (PV) examination, which should describe the type/name of polygraph technique used in instant PV examination.

2. Continuous, actual size, polygraph charts containing the physiological data collected during the instant PV examination, including all sensitivity and other chart markings, to include all polygraph charts on all tests conducted, any acquaintance chart, stimulation test chart, silent answer test chart, and also any chart or test conducted but not used for the polygraphist's conclusions. Manufacturer's vertical and horizontal chart lines must be legible. (Charts should contain examinee's signature or identifying data from computerized polygraph systems).

3. Calibration test chart (for analog polygraph instrument) or functionality test chart (for computerized polygraph system) with required chart markings and examiner/examinee identification data including time and date of calibration/functionality test.

4. A copy of the polygraphist's worksheet which reflects the individual scores of each spot quantified for each tracing (pneumo, GSR/GSG, cardio, other channels) and the final tally of the scores, plus the scores threshold or cutoff used to reach conclusion and determination made from aforesaid scores.

5. A copy of the polygraphist's worksheet reflecting the background and other information provided by the examinee during the pretest interview, including recent use of prescribed/non-prescribed drugs/intoxicants, physical/mental health status, amount of sleep and food ingested before PV examination.

6. Type and model of polygraph instrument used in instant PV examination.

7. Type and model of any motion/movement detection sensor used in instant PV examination.

8. A complete list of all test questions used in each test, including all types of control/comparison questions. Whether the control/comparison questions were directed-lies or traditional non-directed lies.

9. The order in which the test questions were reviewed with the examinee and the order in which the test questions were asked during each test.

10. Any instructions, review, discussion and/or introduction of a question to the examinee between the conduct of any of the PV tests (charts).

11. Any written statement executed by the examinee or incriminating oral statement made by the examinee which the polygraphist reduced to writing, which was made by the examinee during any portion of the PV examination including pretest, actual test, post-test.

12. A copy of any video and/or audio recording of the PV examination which includes the pretest, actual test – collection of physiological data, and post-test.

APPENDIX S

FIDELITY TEST AGREEMENT

Page 680C. Add the following Appendix S to the Appendix Section of this book.

A-G-R-E-E-M-E-N-T

It is hereby agreed that for the sum of $_____.00 plus New York State Sales Tax, which includes case preparation fee of $_____.00, a polygraph examination will be conducted on (Name)_____ _____at Matte Polygraph Service, Inc., Williamsville, New York. The agreed time and date of said examination is_____hours, _____20___. The aforementioned fee is for the case preparation and conduct of the polygraph examination only, and said fee is payable prior to the scheduled polygraph test. A verbal report will be provided to the examinee and/or the person designated by the examinee in writing to receive the report. A written detailed report will be provided to the examinee and/or the person designated by the examinee in writing provided that the request for such report is made not later than the day that the polygraph examination was administered, and an additional fee of $150.00 will be paid prior to the issuance of aforesaid written report. An additional fee of $75.00 will be levied for a one-page letter report requested no later than the day the polygraph examination was administered and such fee will be paid prior to the issuance of such letter report. It is understood and agreed that such verbal and/or written report of the polygraph examination will be given only to the person indicated in writing by the examinee at the conclusion of the polygraph examination. It is understood that should the examinee upon conclusion of the polygraph examination, after being informed of the results of the polygraph examination, decline to sign an authorization to furnish the results to any person, said results will be held in confidence and will not be released to anyone, unless ordered by a court of law. Such declination by the examinee upon completion of the polygraph examination will be irrevocable. It is further understood that payment of aforementioned polygraph fee by a person other than the examinee does not entitle that person to the results of said polygraph examination, without the express written authorization of the examinee as mentioned in this agreement. It is further agreed and understood that cancellation of this polygraph examination at any time after it has been scheduled or this agreement has been signed by the parties to this agreement will result in forfeiture of the case preparation fee. Cancellation of this polygraph examination on the day prior to the schedule polygraph examination will further result in forfeiture of fifty percent of the polygraph examination fee in addition to the forfeiture of the case preparation fee. Cancellation of this polygraph examination on the day of the examination, or failure to appear for the scheduled examination or complete the polygraph examination for any reason will result in full forfeiture of the polygraph examination fee in addition to the case preparation fee. It is agreed and promised by all parties that the conduct and results of this polygraph examination will not be used in any news, entertainment, documentary or publicity media. It is further agreed that in the event any legal action ensues from this polygraph examination that requires testimony on the part of Matte Polygraph Service, Inc. (MPSI), and/or its polygraphist James Allan Matte, in any hearing or judicial proceeding, MPSI will be compensated by the person(s) requesting this polygraph examination or by the examinee if the requester defaults, in the minimum amount of $1900.00 per day plus all legal expenses incurred by MPSI and/or the Polygraphist   resulting from the hearing or judicial proceeding.

_____   _____
(Signature of Person Requesting Examination)   (Date)

_____   _____
(Signature of Examinee if other than Requester)   (Date)

_____   _____
(Signature of Polygraphist   )   (Date)

GLOSSARY OF TERMS

Page 682. Add the following term in alphabetical order:

Anticountermeasure: Any of various methods and systems employed by the polygraphist to deter and inhibit the use of countermeasures by a deceptive examinee. Anticountermeasures can be included in the methodology of the technique and also in the techniques' quantification system.

Page 685. Add the following term in alphabetical order:

Clinical Approach: This approach differs from the *numerical approach* to arrive at a determination of truth or deception in that it does not depend entirely upon the physiological data recorded on the polygraph charts in the decision-making process. The polygraphist employing the *clinical approach* evaluates the case facts (factual analysis) and the examinee's verbal and nonverbal behavior (behavior assessment) during the pretest interview, and uses these as adjuncts to the visual inspection, analysis, and in some cases quantification of the physiological data recorded on the polygraph charts, for a *global evaluation.*

Page 687. Add the following terms in alphabetical order:

Daubert Standard: The standard enunciated by the United States Supreme Court in William Daubert v. Merrell Dow Pharmaceuticals, Inc., 113 S.Ct 2786, 125 L.E.2d 469, 509 U.S. (1993), which superseded the Frye standard (see Frye) of "general acceptance" test, regarding admissibility of scientific evidence.

Directed-Lie Control (Comparison) Question: A question similar in structure to the traditional probable-lie control (comparison) question, which the examinee is instructed to answer untruthfully, rather than having the control question presented to the examinee in a manner that manipulates the examinee to deceive the polygraphist with an untruthful answer. Research (Fuse 1982; Abrams 1991; Barland 1998; Matte 1998; Matte, Reuss 1999) indicates that the directed-lie control question suffers several weaknesses and is prone to false negative results. See Chapter 5 of this book for further details and full citations of the above references.

Page 689. Add the following term in alphabetical order:

Fear of Error: A theory developed by James Allan Matte after extensive field experiments to resolve false positives which revealed that an innocent examinee may show a significant response to relevant test questions as a result of his fear that an error will be made on his test regarding the target issue. The Fear of Error question contains a suffix "regarding the target issue" and is treated as a control (comparison) question that is compared with its neighboring relevant question within the same track, namely the Hope of Error Question "regarding the target issue." The Fear and Hope of Error questions are contained in a Track labeled "Inside Track" within the Quadri-Track Zone Comparison Technique. The innocent examinee's Fear of Error was recognized by Dr. Paul Ekman (1985) who coined the concept as the "Othello Error." The National Research Council of the National Academies of Science's 2003 report (P.74, 127), cited the innocent examinee's fear of error as a potential for false positives.

Hope of Error: A relevant test question that is compared with the Fear of Error control question contained within the Inside Track of the Quadri-Track Zone Comparison Technique. Both the Fear of Error and the Hope of Error questions contain a suffix "regarding the target issue" so that the examinee whether innocent or guilty will associate these two test questions with the target issue for which the examine is being tested, not the two non-current exclusive control questions contained in separate tracks within the same test.

Page 692. Add the following term in alphabetical order:

Horizontal Scoring System: A system developed by Nathan J. Gordon and Philip M. Cochetti in 1984 that evaluated and ranked all of the responses in each channel recorded (pneumo, GSR/GSG, cardio) from the greatest response to the smallest response. Positive values were assigned to the control (comparison) questions and negative values were assigned to the relevant questions, with the greatest response receiving the greatest value.

Page 693. Add the following term in alphabetical order:

Judicial Notice: The Federal Evidence Rule 201(b) requires that a fact may receive judicial notice if it is "either (1) generally known within the territorial jurisdiction of the court or (2) capable of accurate and ready determination by resort to sources whose accuracy cannot reasonably be questioned." Inasmuch as PV examination results have not yet received judicial notice of acceptance in United States courts, a legal foundation for PV examination admissibility must be laid before the court in each case.

Page 695. Add the following term in alphabetical order:

Outside Track: One of four tracks in the Quadri-Track Zone Comparison Technique. It contains two *symptomatic questions*, developed by Cleve Backster, that are designed to elicit a response from the examinee who is fearful that an unreviewed question embracing an outside issue will be asked on the test, thus dampening out potential responses to the other test questions. The other three tracks are the primary track, the secondary track, and the inside track.

Page 697. Add the following terms in alphabetical order:

Primary Track: One of four tracks in the Quadri-Track Zone Comparison Technique. It contains a *non-current exclusive control question* and a *relevant question* for comparison and quantification. The other three tracks are the secondary track, the inside track, and the outside track.

Probable-Lie Control (Comparison) Question: A question that is inserted into a PV test for the purpose of eliciting the psychological set and thus a response from the innocent examinee. This probable-lie control question is used for comparison against the neighboring *relevant questions* contained in the same PV test. Consistently significant autonomic responses to the probable-lie control questions with a comparative absence of response to the relevant questions is an indication of truthfulness to the target issue represented by the relevant test questions. The probable-lie control question is usually formulated to be in the same category as the relevant questions(s) and is either *separated in time* from the relevant issue with the use of a *time bar*, thus is considered an earlier-in-life *non-current exclusive control question*, or *includes the time* period covered by the relevant issue, thus is considered a *non-exclusive* control question. The exclusive control question is also known as a *Backster control question*, and the non-exclusive control question is also known as the *Reid control question*.

Page 699. Add the following terms in alphabetical order:

Quadri-Track Zone Comparison Technique. (see Matte Quadri-Track Zone Comparison Technique).

Quality Control Review: An independent reconstruction of an entire psychophysiological veracity (PV) examination for an objective analysis, critique, quantification and evaluation by a qualified polygraphist to determine the validity and reliability of the results of the original PV examination.

Sacrifice/Preparatory Relevant Question: Presented during the test as the first relevant question, it is formulated as a preparatory relevant question to the introduction of the two or three relevant questions that follow it. Due to its position as the first relevant question, it is expected to elicit a response from both the innocent and the guilty examinee; thus it is treated as a sacrifice relevant question that is not evaluated or used in the decision-making process.

Page 700. Add the following term in alphabetical order:

Secondary Track: One of four tracks in the Quadri-Track Zone Comparison Technique. It contains a *non-current exclusive control question* and a *relevant question* for comparison and quantification. The other three tracks are the primary track, the inside track and the outside track.

SECTION II

Contents of 2012 Supplement

CHAPTER 23. Legal Aspects of the Psychophysiological Veracity (PV) Examination.   **131**

Part I – Legal status of PV examinations.

CHAPTER 3

RESEARCH AND THE SCIENTIFIC STATUS OF PV EXAMINATIONS

Page 146. Insert Summary: "Guiding Principles and Benchmarks for the Conduct of Validity Studies of Psychophysiological Veracity Examinations Using the Polygraph" by James Allan Matte, published in *European Polygraph*, Vol. 4, Nr. 4(14), 2010.

This thesis sets forth guiding principles and benchmarks for the conduct of validity studies of psychophysiological veracity (PV) examinations using the polygraph, some of which challenge research methods traditionally accepted by the academic and scientific community. The use of field studies is deemed mandatory for validating PV examinations such as Zone Comparison Techniques which have been classified as *lie tests*. Laboratory studies are limited to *recognition tests* such as the Concealed Information Test. The argument for this division in the use of field versus laboratory studies is based on published research that identifies autonomic responses from field studies as *defensive* responses due to the fear of detection by the guilty, fear of error by the innocent and anger by either examinee. Whereas responses elicited from role playing examinees in a mock crime paradigm used in laboratory studies are identified as *orienting* non-emotional responses due to their lack of aforementioned fears and serious consequences for failure. The results of laboratory studies are based on responses caused by a set of stimuli that are significantly different from those set of stimuli present in field studies. The authors challenge the traditional view that inconclusive results are *errors* inasmuch as it is based on insufficient physiological data from which a positive or negative decision can be made. A criterion for establishing ground truth is set forth that includes confessions, confirmed judicial convictions and confirmed judicial acquittals. Rules are established for the selection of confirmed PV examinations used in validity studies. For further details, visit www.mattepolygraph.com.

Page 147, Insert Summary of article "Influence of Case Facts on Blind Scorers of Polygraph Tests" by Tuvia Shurany. Published in *European Polygraph*, Vol. 3, Nr. 3-4 (9-10), 2009.

SUMMARY: Three groups of polygraph examiners were selected for this study totaling 82 Polygraphist from Mexico (n=35, United States (n=34), Bulgaria (n=13). They were instructed to evaluate and score the polygraph charts presented to them by PowerPoint slides in the manner in which they were trained using the 3-position scale. The charts were selected from cases that used the Backster Zone Comparison Technique. All Polygraphists were presented with eight separate examinations each containing four charts. The first and last polygraph examination consisted of the same confirmed No Deception Indicated (NDI) charts. The second through the seventh examination consisted of unconfirmed DI (Deception Indicated) and NDI results which were used as a buffer to prevent recognition of examination number eight as being the same as examination number one. Before presentation of examination number one, no case facts were given to the Polygraphist. However, immediately prior to the presentation of examination number two through seven, the polygraphists were given fictitious facts of the case. Hence they knew these facts prior to their evaluation and scoring of the charts. At examination number eight, the polygraphists were presented with fictitious case facts and information supposedly provided by the police that fingerprints of the examinee were found at the crime scene matched the examinee with 90% probability. The results of this study showed a significant decrease in chart scores following prior knowledge resulting in 9 (11%) false positives as compared to one false positive (1.2%) with no prior knowledge. In conclusion, the results of this study indicate that knowledge of case facts does have an influence on the polygraphist's evaluation and scoring of the physiological data recorded on polygraph charts. The study recommends that a Quality Control Review be conducted in three stages:

1. Blind scoring should be conducted without any knowledge of the cased facts, examiner's impression, and results of the polygraph examination.

2. After blind scoring has been completed, the polygraphist should review the case facts for adequacy of test question formulation.

3. Review the audio-video recording for assurance that no procedural violations were committed by the original polygraphist.

Page 148. Insert unabridged thesis entitled "Critique of Horvath-Palmatier Laboratory Study on the Effectiveness of Exclusive vs. Non-Exclusive Control Questions in Polygraph Examinations" by James Allan Matte. The abridged version of this thesis was published as a Commentary in a Letter-to-the-Editor, Journal of Forensic Sciences, Volume 56, Number 6, November 2011, available at: http:// *onlinelibrary.wiley.com/journal/10.1111/(ISSN)1556-4029*

Critique of Horvath-Palmatier Laboratory Study on Effectiveness of Exclusive vs. Non-Exclusive Control Questions in Polygraph Examinations.

James Allan Matte

ABSTRACT: The Horvath-Palmatier laboratory study (JFS 2008: 53-4) concluded that the accuracy of the Exclusive Control Question and Non-Exclusive Control Question in the identification of guilty examinees were not statistically significant (80% and 85% respectively). However, the difference in accuracy between Exclusive and Non-exclusive control questions in the identification of innocent examinees was statistically significant (45% and 91% respectively). A critical analysis of the Horvath-Palmatier study reveals a serious lack of understanding regarding the psychological structure and theoretical concept of the Backster Zone Comparison Technique. This is reflected by the test structure and question format of the Zone Comparison test used in the Horvath-Palmatier study and their failure to employ Backster's "Either-Or" rule which comprises the nucleus of the Backster ZCT for which the Exclusive Control Question was designed to enable. Recent published research revealed that the Backster ZCT's overall accuracy was significantly reduced when its "Either-Or" rule was excluded.

KEYWORDS: Forensic science, polygraph, exclusive control question, non-exclusive control question, Backster Zone Comparison Technique, Reid Control Question Technique, Modified General Question Test, Either-Or rule, psychological set, non-current exclusive control question, current exclusive control question.

BACKGROUND:

In order to understand the reasons for the failure of the Horvath-Palmatier [23] study to accurately evaluate the effectiveness of the Exclusive and Non-Exclusive Control Questions, it is imperative that the significant differences in the psychological structure and theoretical concept of the polygraph techniques for which these two types of control questions were designed to be used be fully explained.

The non-exclusive control question was first introduced in a publication [45] authored by John E. Reid for use in what became known as the Reid Control Question Technique. It was considered a major breakthrough in the field of forensic psychophysiology[1]. The Reid Technique used two reviewed control questions for comparison with usually four relevant questions dealing with the same crime but not the same issue. The crime questions included direct involvement, indirect involvement and guilty knowledge, hence a multiple-issue test. The reviewed control questions were in the same crime or offense category as the crime or matter for which the examinee was being tested. Reid's reviewed control questions were all-encompassing in that they included the period in which the crime was committed, i. e. "Did you ever steal anything in your life"

In 1960, Cleve Backster, former Director of the Keeler Polygraph Institute, developed the Backster Zone Comparison Technique. Backster's technique was a significant departure from the Keeler and Reid techniques for several reasons. Backster introduced reviewed probable-lie questions that used time bars to exclude the period in which the crime generating the test was committed. Hence Backster's control questions were named Exclusive control questions versus Reid's control questions which were labeled non-exclusive control questions. By design, the time bars created control questions structurally less intense than the relevant (crime) questions against which they were to be compared, although they are presented to the examinee as being of equal importance to the outcome of the test. Backster also used only two relevant questions, which dealt with the same relevant act of the crime, but were worded differently. Hence if the examinee was lying to one of the relevant questions, he would also be lying to the second relevant question. These two relevant questions were flanked by three exclusive control questions for comparison. These control questions would each encompass a different age category and would start with different wording so that the examinee would not be

---

1 The American Society for Testing and Materials (ASTM) established the controlling standards for Forensic Psychophysiology, a title which it enacted for the discipline of psychophysiological veracity examinations using the polygraph.

startled by the apparent repetition of a question (Figure 1). Furthermore, these differences in each of the three exclusive control questions are intended to inhibit or delay habituation and retain the strength of their stimuli which are designed to be structurally less intense than the relevant questions in order to avoid inconclusive results from guilty examinees. It should be noted that the exclusive control questions which

Figure 1
BACKSTER ZCT STRUCTURE

14	Neutral, Irrelevant Question
25	Symptomatic Question
39	Preparatory/Sacrifice Relevant Question
46	Non-Current Exclusive Control Question
33	Relevant Question
47	Non-Current Exclusive Control Question
35	Relevant Question
48	Non-Current Exclusive Control Question
26	Symptomatic Question

Backster labeled as the Green Zone are separated in time from the relevant questions labeled as the Red Zone by at least one to as many as seven years, depending on the age of the examinee. However some polygraphists/agencies have modified the exclusive control question by eliminating the time separation and excluding only the offense in question, i.e. "Not connected with this case..." This modification hampers the clear separation of the control and relevant test questions because it includes other crimes up to the day of the polygraph examination and renders the control questions of equal if not greater strength and threat than the relevant questions, in violation of the psychological structure of the Backster ZCT. Therefore in order to differentiate between the traditional Backster exclusive control questions and its modified version, this author [31] labeled the former as a Non-Current Exclusive Control Question, and the latter as Current Exclusive Control Question.

Backster also introduced a Sacrifice Relevant Question which acts as a safeguard in that it allows for dissipation of excessive general nervous tension or undue anxiety prior to the asking of the primary relevant questions. It is structured as an orienting relevant question specifically related to the single issue covered by the two relevant questions. Therefore it serves as both a sacrifice relevant question which may elicit an emotionally induced sympathetic response and as a preparatory question for the introduction of the two direct relevant questions, hence a dual-purpose question. Backster further developed and introduced two Symptomatic questions into his test structure to determine if an outside issue was bothering the examinee and interfering with the examinee's *psychological set*[2] [8, 36] also known as *selective attention*. The Backster Zone Comparison test structure as shown in Figure 2, places a control question on both sides of the two relevant questions. No other test question is inserted between the control and relevant questions in order not to disrupt the flow of the examinee's *psychological set* on the relevant questions if guilty which would enable dampening

---

2 Psychological set: Also known as *selective attention*, it is an adaptive psychophysiological response to fears, anxieties, and apprehensions with a selective focus on the particular issue or situation that presents the greatest threat to the legitimate security of the examinee while filtering out lesser threats. (Matte, 2000).

of neighboring control questions or the exclusive control questions if innocent which would enable dampening of neighboring relevant questions. The two Symptomatic questions as seen in Figure 1 are positioned in a manner that encases and frames the control and relevant questions, with the first symptomatic question preceding the first comparison question and the second Symptomatic question serving as the last test question with orienting value. This allows those examinees who relieve on the last test question to relieve on the Symptomatic question rather than the preceding control or relevant question that are used for a determination of truth or deception.

However, the Exclusive Control Question serves another important role in that it enables the "Either-Or" rule that forms the nucleus of the Backster Zone Comparison Technique.[3]

The "Either-Or" rule must be applied in the evaluation, interpretation and scoring of the physiological data collected from the examinee. According to the "Either-Or" rule, a significant reaction should be present in either the red zone or the green zone but not to both. If the red zone indicated a lack of reaction, it should be compared with the neighboring green zone containing the larger timely reaction. If the red zone indicates a timely and significant reaction it should be compared with the neighboring green zone containing no reaction or the least reaction. A timely and significant reaction to both the red and green zone questions being intercompared indicates a serious question defect in green zone question. In effect, that green zone question is deemed to be defective, therefore the significantly reactive relevant question is then compared to the other neighboring green zone question that should have little or no reaction if functioning as designed.

Unlike other polygraph techniques that use a fixed scoring threshold to arrive at a determination of truth or deception, the Backster ZCT[4] uses an increasing threshold with the conduct of each polygraph chart. Furthermore, the score threshold for the truthful is significantly lower than the threshold for the guilty due to its less intense structure, e.g.. Truthful: +3 for 1 chart; +5 for 2 charts; +7 for 3 charts, versus Guilty: -5 for 1 chart; -9 for 2 charts, -13 for 3 charts. A minimum of 2 charts must be collected to make a determination of truth or deception.

During the past three decades, several modifications have been made to the Backster ZCT, most notably by the Federal government that resulted in a Federal Zone Comparison Technique [12, 28, 52] , and the Utah Zone Comparison Technique developed at the University of Utah [10, 44] that bears little resemblance to the Backster ZCT. Unfortunately, a hybrid of the Federal and Utah ZCT rather than the Backster ZCT was used by Horvath & Palmatier[5] to test the effectiveness and accuracy of the Exclusive control question versus the Non-Exclusive control question. This is unfortunate because the Exclusive control question developed and designed by Backster as a Non-Current Exclusive Control question was specifically intended to enable the "Either-Or" rule which was not implemented in the Horvath & Palmatier study. Furthermore, other departures from the Backster ZCT's psychological test structure were noted which would have an adverse impact on the effectiveness of the

---

3 The Quadri-Track Zone Comparison Technique, a derivative of the Backster ZCT, also uses non-current exclusive control questions and the "Either-Or" rule on a non-selective basis.

4 The Quadri-Track Zone Comparison Technique also uses an increasing score threshold with a comparatively lower threshold for the truthful than the deceptive examinee [27].

5 Dr. Frank Horvath is a former staff member of John E. Reid and Associates, Chicago, Illinois.

Exclusive control questions and the accuracy of the Zone Comparison test used in the Horvath-Palmatier study, which are discussed below.

Horvath & Palmatier Lab Study:

1. Horvath-Palmatier failed to implement the "Either-Or" rule in the evaluation, interpretation and scoring of the physiological data collected in Zone Comparison Tests.

Field Research by Meiron, Krapohl, Ashkenazi [41] revealed that the overall accuracy of the Backster Zone Comparison Technique employing its "Either-Or" rule and non-current exclusive control questions attained an accuracy of 80% with 17% inconclusives and 3% errors. However when the "Either-Or" rule was not applied, the accuracy of decisions for deceptive cases was only 55%, and the overall accuracy was significantly decreased to 70% and its inconclusives increased to 27% with 3% errors

2. Horvath-Palmatier used the same introduction wording and age category for each of the exclusive control questions. The Backster ZCT uses different age category and introductory wording to retain anxiety level and delay habituation to the exclusive control questions.

3. Horvath-Palmatier used excessive time bars that seriously weakened the exclusive control question, e.g. "if a subject were 20 years old an Exclusive control question would begin as 'Before the age of 17…'"

The younger the examinee, the less time separation between the relevant and control questions is available, hence in the above scenario, the proper time frame for the exclusive control question would be "Before the age of 19…" which would have the effect of a stronger non-current exclusive control question.

4. Horvath-Palmatier used a "mixed question" test as the last test, in violation of the Backster ZCT test format and protocol. The Backster ZCT rotates the position of the two relevant questions with each succeeding chart conducted for comparison with each of the non-current exclusive control questions. However there is no random mixing of the test questions.

5. Horvath-Palmatier used an Irrelevant question between a Relevant and Control question, thus interrupting the flow of the examinee's psychological set, in violation of the Backster ZCT test format and protocol.

6. Horvath-Palmatier used a fixed scoring threshold of +- 6 in the scoring of the physiological data to arrive at a determination of truth or deception. The Backster ZCT uses an increasing score threshold with the conduct of each addition charts. Furthermore, the Backster ZCT uses a lower threshold for the Truthful (+3, +5, +7) versus the Deceptive examinee (-5, -7, -9), in recognition of the structurally less intense non-current exclusive control questions.

7. Horvath-Palmatier used a relevant test question as the last question on the test, in violation of the Backster ZCT test format and protocol. The last test question must not be used for a determination of truth or deception inasmuch as the examinee may relieve on the last test question. Therefore, Backster ZCT uses a second Symptomatic question having orienting value as the last test question.

8. Horvath-Palmatier used a sacrifice relevant question that was broad and lacked specificity as required by the Backster ZCT format and protocol. Should have been worded: Regarding whether

or not you stole the envelope containing $3.00 from Dr. Horvath's mail slot in Baker Hall: Do you intend to answer truthfully each question about that?

9. Horvath-Palmatier used three relevant questions in violation of the Backster ZCT format and protocol. A third relevant question has the effect of distributing the reactivity of the relevant questions amongst the three of them thereby reducing their individual responsivity [29], rather than a stronger focus on two relevant questions of similar content. Furthermore, in the Backster ZCT format, the three structurally less intense exclusive control questions are better able to cope with two rather than three strong relevant questions. In addition, the "Either-Or" rule requires that the two relevant questions be flanked by non-current exclusive control questions on either side in order to provide a second neighboring non-current exclusive control question to compare with in the event that the first non-current exclusive control question is deemed defective.

10. Horvath-Palmatier used a cuff pressure between 40 mm/Hg and 55 mm/Hg which produces cardiograph responses significantly weaker than cuff pressure of 70mm/Hg and higher. Barland [11] reported that a cuff pressure at 90mm/Hg, and a mean arterial blood pressure of 100 mm/Hg before reaction which increases to 120 mm/Hg during reaction will show a difference in pulse amplitude of 200% whereas a cuff pressure at 60 mm/Hg and a mean arterial blood pressure of 100 mm/Hg during reaction will show a difference in pulse amplitude of only 50%.

Furthermore, cuff pressure of 70 mm/Hg or more may divert the examinee's attention from his or her breathing to the cuff pressure. The redirected attention away from one's breathing could produce potentially truer, uncontrolled respiratory patterns. In several field studies, respiration was shown to have equal diagnostic value, and in some field studies greater diagnostic value than its neighboring parameters [13, 16, 17, 38, 42, 48]. An experimental scoring technique proposed and tested by Jayne [26] also supported the pneumograph as providing the most diagnostic information. Furthermore, a study by Elaad, Bonwitt, Eisenberg, Meytes [18] revealed that respiration was the only one of the three parameters not affected by beta blockers. Elaad, et al, concluded that "respiration seemed to improve the overall detection rate especially because skin resistance responses have the quality of rapid habituation."

11. Horvath-Palmatier had both the testing examiner and blind evaluator "scored and accumulated in their total scores, the values assigned to each of the two pneumograph tracings." Averaging the scores from the two pneumograph tracings diminishes the contribution of scores to the overall tally of scores from the other tracings. This procedure is contrary to Backster Zone Comparison Technique procedure. The Backster ZCT employs the most productive pneumograph tracing, and its scores are added to the overall tally.

12. Horvath-Palmatier used a Modified General Question Test (MGQT) format to test the effectiveness of two (2) Non-Exclusive control questions against five (5) relevant questions. Within this format that originated from the Reid Technique, a Stimulation Test was administered as the second chart after the first relevant test had been conducted. It is well known and documented [21, 22, 43] that in spite of the claim that both relevant and control questions are reviewed with the examinee between charts, the emphasis is clearly on the non-exclusive control questions. This is a manipulation of the examinee's psychological set towards the non-exclusive control questions, which has been severely criticized by Abrams [1, 2, 3], Matte [31, 32] and Matte & Reuss [39]. This also devalues the scientific comparison of the two types of control questions. The collection of the data must not

be interrupted with any language that would influence the examinee's psychological set towards the control or relevant questions [34].

Amsel Field Study (Cited by Horvath-Palmatier):

Horvath-Palmatier cited Amsel's [5] field study to support their findings that the non-exclusive control questions were more effective than the exclusive control questions. However they failed to mention a critical analysis of Amsels' comparative study by Matte & Backster [35] which nullifies the results of his study. The following discrepancies were noted:

1. Amsel failed to implement the "Either-Or" rule in the evaluation, interpretation and scoring of the physiological data collected in Zone Comparison tests.

2. Amsel used the three-position scale rather than the seven-position scale in scoring the physiological data collected. Use of the three-position scale does not differentiate between a subtle reaction and a dramatic reaction. Blackwell's [12] field study found "the PDD examiners mean level of accuracy was 75.7% and 66.3% for the 7- and 3- position scoring scales, respectively." Blackwell stated that "without exception, the overall level of accuracy generated by the examinee when using the 7-position scoring scale was higher than when using the 3-position scoring scale. The same was true when looking at the overall percentages for either the innocent examinations or the guilty examinations."

Furthermore, Capps and Ansley [14], van Herk [49], and Krapohl [27] found that the accuracy of the 7- and 3- position scales depended on the threshold used. The Backster and Matte Zone Comparison Techniques use an increasing threshold, whereas other Zone Comparison Technique modifications (DACA, Utah) employ a fixed threshold. Amsel used a fixed score threshold.

3. Amsel used current exclusive comparison questions that excluded only the specific instant crime, but not other crimes committed during that same period.

4. Amsel used a Sacrifice Relevant Question (SRQ) that violated the Backster concept and purpose of the Sacrifice Relevant question in that it covered both the control and relevant test questions. The Backster ZCT is designed to identify with preciseness the specific issue covered by all of the relevant questions included in its single-issue test, and those relevant questions must cover only one and the same act. Hence the examinee, whether guilty or innocent of the instant offense, will perceive the Sacrifice Relevant question as the first relevant test question dealing with the specific issue under investigation. The SRQ used by Amsel does not act as the first relevant question dealing with the specific issue under investigation, hence the innocent examinee is only afforded the first relevant question to vent his or her possible anxiety regarding the instant offense. Furthermore, the Backster SRQ also acts as a preparatory question for the introduction of the relevant questions, to direct the guilty examinee's psychological set onto the relevant questions.

5. The test structure used by Amsel in his field study used a control question as the last question in its test sequence, whereas the Backster ZCT uses a Symptomatic question. The danger of employing a test question that is used for comparison as the last test question is that the examinee may relieve on the last test question regardless of its nature. This could have the effect of degrading the effectiveness of that control question.

6. Amsel's research methodology did not attempt to determine the error rate. Furthermore he selected only the first three charts for evaluation, although some tests had as many as five charts, which may have created an artificial inconclusive rate. Without an error rate for each type of test, it is impossible to determine which technique or control question used within the technique is superior. It could be argued that the technique that employed the non-current exclusive control question with an inconclusive rate of 10% had no errors while the technique that employed the non-exclusive control question with an inconclusive rate of only 5% could have had an error rate of 15%. Amsel admitted that by using only the first three charts "I created a new situation in where the scoring of the tests that had 4 – 5 charts now totaled a figure that moved the outcome from a conclusive results to an inconclusive result." I submit that it could also have had an opposite effect.

7. Amsel failed to use Symptomatic questions as required in the Backster Zone Comparison Technique that are designed to identify the presence of an outside issue that may be interfering with the examinee's psychological set on the relevant or control questions.

8. Amsel administered a Stimulation Test as the second test, following the first relevant test. This procedure historically used in the Reid and Arther Techniques, can produce adverse effects on the innocent examinee who may wonder why this test presented as a sensitivity test is now being administered after the first relevant test. This procedure can raise the examinee's suspicion that he did not do well on his first test, thus redirecting his psychological set onto the relevant questions. The Backster ZCT and Matte Quadri-Track ZCT [30, 33, 37] administer the Stimulation Test as the first test or chart so that each succeeding test will have been subjected to the same influence.

Conclusion:

The Horvath & Palmatier laboratory study fails to present a persuasive scientific argument on the merits of the non-exclusive versus the exclusive control questions. Aside from the significant discrepancies found in the Horvath & Palmatier laboratory study and the Amsel field study cited by them in support of their conclusions, the Horvath & Palmatier study suffers from a very basic defect in that it is a laboratory study that employs mock paradigms that suffer the absence of serious consequences to the deceptive examinee and a total absence of the fear of error by the innocent examinee which in real-life can result in a false positive (an innocent examinee misdiagnosed as deceptive). Furthermore, laboratory studies are based on non-emotional responses generated by the offer of a reward such as additional college credits or a small sum of money, usually about twenty dollars, and/or by a desire for increased self-esteem if they can defeat the test. Responses in laboratory studies have thus been classified as orienting responses. [15, 19, 20, 49, 51]

Additionally, the potential for anger is absent due to the fact that the examinee is a volunteer in a mock crime paradigm. Furthermore guilty examinees are not motivated to employ countermeasures. For the non-truthful examinee in the analog study, the potential for embarrassment or punishment if found deceptive to the relevant questions is nonexistent. The subject sample is not representative of the diverse population that includes the criminal element present in field cases. Therefore, laboratory studies which are based on non-emotional orienting responses absolutely fail to replicate the field conditions that elicit emotional defensive responses wherein both the guilty and innocent examinee's primary emotion is "fear" of the consequences [4], if found deceptive which in criminal cases could result in imprisonment. The argument that laboratory studies offer complete control over subjects used in their study such as the assignment to deceptive and non-deceptive groups and the holding of variables constant in order to study the variable of interest, is useful in supporting the results of examinations involving non-emotional subjects role playing in a mock crime. However its results cannot be applied to field situations nor can they be used to validate the use of a polygraph technique or its various components on real suspects of crimes whose results pose a serious threat to the security of the examinee. [40]

Interestingly, Horvath [24] in a previously published laboratory study discussed the merits of laboratory studies which he stated "must be interpreted with some caution. These data were collected in a laboratory environment where motivational and other differences may make it unlikely that the results can be generalized to real-life testing situations. Of course, this caveat would apply to all laboratory studies and indeed there are some who maintain that results in that environment should not ever be extended to actual testing situations."

A recently published study authored by Matte & Reuss [40] presents convincing evidence that psychophysiological veracity examinations using the polygraph to detect lies and verify the truth, which include its psychological test structure components, should be validated by field research studies, and laboratory studies should be confined to recognition tests such as the Concealed Information Test or the Guilty Knowledge Test.

A research review published by the American Polygraph Association [47] regarding the Horvath-Palmatier laboratory study concluded that "we should now abandon the now outdated idea of time bars and use nonexclusive control/comparison questions whenever we run a test using a ZCT or MGQT format." This statement and conclusion based on a seriously flawed laboratory study that cited a field study with similar fatal flaws is not only misleading but can have serious consequences for polygraphists in the field. Hopefully, this critique will enlighten and educate polygraphists and researchers regarding the different psychological aspects of the exclusive and non-exclusive control (comparison) questions and their individual usefulness within the techniques in which they were designed to be implemented..

ACKNOWLEDGEMENT: The author wishes to express his gratitude to Cleve Backster, Director of the Backster School of Lie Detection, San Diego, California, and his Deputy Director Gregory C. Adams for their critical review of this article.

REFERENCES:

1. Abrams, S. The directed lie control question. Polygraph 1991; 20(1): 26-31.
2. Abrams, S. A response to Honts on the issue of the discussion of questions between charts. Polygraph 1999; 28(3): 223-228.
3. Abrams, S. Statistics and other lies. Polygraph 2001; 30(1): 29-36.
4. Amsel, T. T. (1997). Fear of Consequences and Motivation as Influencing Factors on Psychophysiological Detection of Deception. *Polygraph,* 26(4), 255-267.
5. Amsel, T. Exclusive or non-exclusive comparison questions: a comparative field study. Polygraph 1999; 28(4): 273-283.
6. Backster, C. Standardized Polygraph Notepack and Technique Guide. Backster Zone Comparison Technique. Backster School of Lie Detection, New York, N. Y.; 1963/1979.
7. Backster, C. Technique Fundamentals of the Tri-Zone Polygraph Test. New York: Backster Research Foundation; 1969.
8. Backster, C. Anticlimax Dampening Concept. Polygraph 1974; 3(1): 48-50.
9. Backster, C. Selection of Two Most Productive "You-Phase" Charts. Revision of the Backster Zone Comparison Test Numerical Cutoff Table. Backster School of Lie Detection, San Diego, CA; 1983.
10. Barland, G. H., Raskin, D. C. Detection of deception, In: Prokasy, W. F., Raskin, D.C., editors. Electrodermal activity in psychological research. New York; Academic Press 1975: 417-477.
11. Barland, G. H. The cardio channel: A primer. Paper presented at the Florida Polygraph Association seminar 1984, June 1-2: 15 pages.
12. Blackwell, N. J. PolyScore 3.3 and psychophysiological detection of deception examiner rates of accuracy when scoring examinations from actual criminal investigations. DTIC AD Numer A355504/PAA. Department of Defense Polygraph Institute, Ft. McClellan, AL, printed in Polygraph, 1998; 28(2): 149-175
13. Buckley, J. P., Senese, L. C. The influence of race and gender on blind polygraph chart analysis. Polygraph 1991; 20(4): 247-258.
14. Capps, M. H., Ansley, N. Comparison of two scoring scales. Polygraph 1992; 21(1): 39-43
15. Cook, E.W., III & Turpin, G. Differentiating orienting, startle, and defense responses: The role of affect and its implications for psychopathology. In P. Lang, R. Simons, M. Balaban (eds.). Attention and orienting: Sensory and motivational processes. (pp. 197-164). Hillsdale, NJ: Eribaum; 1997.
16. Elaad, E. Validity of the control question test in criminal cases. Unpublished manuscript. Scientific Interrogation Unit, Criminal Investigation Division, Israel National Police Headquarters, Jerusalem, Israel, 1985.
17. Elaad, E., Kleiner, M. Effects of polygraph chart interpreter experience on psychophysiological detection of deception. Journal of Police Science and Administration 1990; 17(2): 155-123.
18. Elaad, E., Bonwitt, G., Eisenberg, O, Meytes, I. Effects of beta blocking drugs on the polygraph detection rate: A pilot study. Polygraph 1982; 11(3): 225-233.

19. Graham, F. K. Distinguishing among orienting, defense and startle reflex. In H. D. Kimmel, E. H. van Olst, & J. H. Orlebeke (Eds.). The orienting reflex in humans. (pp. 137-167). Hillsdale, NJ: P Eribaum; 1979.

20. Graham, F. K., Clifton, R. K. Heart rate change as a component of the orienting response. Psychological Bulletin 1966; 65: 305-320.

21. Honts, C. R. The discussion of questions between list repetitions (charts) is associated with increased test accuracy. Polygraph 1999; 28(2): 117-123.

22. Honts, C. R., Raskin, D. C. A field study of the validity of the directed lie control question. Journal of Police Science and Administration 1988; 16: 56-61.

23. Horvath, F. , Palmatier, J. J. Effect of two types of control questions and two question formats on the outcomes of polygraph examinations. J. Forensic Science 2008; 53(4): 889-899.

24. Horvath, F. The value and effectiveness of the Sacrifice Relevant Question: An empirical assessment. Polygraph 1994, 23(4): 261-279.

25. Iacono, W. G., Lykken, D. T. The scientific status of research on polygraph techniques; the case against polygraph tests, In: Faigman, D. L., Kaye, D. H. Saks, M.J., Sanders, J. editors. Modern scientific evidence; the new law and science of expert testimony. St. Paul, MN: West Law, 2002:2: 483-538.

26. Jayne, B. C. Contributions of physiological recordings in the polygraph technique. Polygraph 1990; 19(2): 105-117.

27. Krapohl, D. J. A comparison of 3- and 7- position scoring scale with laboratory data. Polygraph 1998; 27(3): 210-218.

28. Krapohl, D. J. Polygraph decision rules for evidentiary and paired-testing (Marin Protocol) applications. Polygraph, 2005; 34(3): 184-192.

29, Krapohl, D. J. Pilot study on third evidentiary relevant question's influence on the salience of responses to neighboring relevant questions. Electronic communication with Cleve Backster; courtesy copy to J. A. Matte. 2001, October 11.

30. Mangan, D. J., Armitage, T. E., Adams, G. C. A field study on the validity of the Quadri-Track Zone Comparison Technique. Physiology & Behavior 2008; 95(1-2): 17-23.

31. Matte, J. A. An analysis of the psychodynamics of the directed lie control question in the control question technique. Polygraph 1998; 27(1): 56-67.

32. Matte, J. A. A critical analysis of Honts' study: The discussion (stimulation) of comparison questions. Polygraph 2000; 29(2): 146-150.

33. Matte, J. A. Forensic Psychophysiology Using The Polygraph: Scientific Truth Verification – Lie Detection. Williamsville, New York: J.A.M. Publications; 1996.

34. Matte, J. A. Psychological structure and theoretical concept of the Backster Zone Comparison Technique and the Quadri-Track Zone Comparison Technique. Polygraph 2007; 36(2): 84-90.

35. Matte, J. A., Backster, C. A critical analysis of Amsel's comparative study of the exclusive v. nonexclusive comparison question. Polygraph 2000; 29(3): 261-268.

36. Matte, J. A., Grove, R. N. Psychological set: Its Origin, Theory and Application. Polygraph 2001; 30(3): 196-202.

37. Matte, J. A., Reuss, R. M. A field validation study of the Quadri-Zone Comparison Technique. Polygraph 1989; 18(4): 187-202.

38. Matte, J. A., Reuss, R. M. A study of the relative effectiveness of physiological data in field polygraph examinations. Polygraph 1992; 21(1): 1-22.

39. Matte, J. A., Reuss, R. M. Validation of potential response elements in the directed- lie control question. *Polygraph* 1999; 28(2): 124-142.

40. Matte, J. A. Guiding principles and benchmarks for the conduct of validity studies of psychophysiological veracity examinations using the polygraph. *European Polygraph*, 2010; 4(14).

41. Meiron, E., Krapohl. D. J., Ashkenazi, T. An assessment of the Backster "Either-Or" rule in polygraph scoring. *Polygraph* 2009; 37(4):

42. Nakayama, M., Yamamura, T. Changes in respiration pattern to the critical question on Guilty Knowledge Technique. *Polygraph* 1990; 19(3): 188-198.

43. Polina, D. A., Dollins, A. B., Senter, S. M., Krapohl, D. J., Ryan, A. H. Comparison of polygraph data obtained from individuals involved in mock crimes and actual criminal investigations. *Journal of Applied Psychology* 2004; 89(6): 1099-1105.

44. Raskin, D. C., Barland, G. H., Podlesny, J. A. *Validity and reliability of detection of deception.* Washington, D. C.: National Institute of Law Enforcement and Criminal Justice; 1978.

45. Reid, J. A revised questioning technique in lie detection tests. *J. Crim Law and Criminology* 1947: 37:342-347.

46. Reid, J., Inbau, F. *Truth and deception: the polygraph (lie-detector) technique*, Baltimore, MD: Williams & Wilkins, 1977.

47. Rovner, L. Nonexclusive comparison questions lead to higher accuracy. Research Review, *APA Magazine*, 2008, Sep-Oct; 41,5.

48. Slowik, S., Buckley, J. Relative accuracy of polygraph examiner diagnosis of respiration, blood pressure, and GSR recordings. *Journal of Police Science and Administration* 1975; 3(3): 305-310.

49. Sokolov, E., Cacioppo, J. *Orienting and defensive reflexes: Vector coding the cardiac response.* In P. Lang, R. Simons, & M. Balaban (eds.). *Attention and orienting: Sensory and motivational processes*: 1-22. Mahwah, NJ: Eribaum; 1997.

50. Van Herk, M. Numerical evaluations: Seven point scale +-6 and possible alternatives; A discussion. *Polygraph* 1991; 20(2): 70-79.

51. Verschuere, B., Crombez, G., De Clercq, A., Koster, E.H.W. Autonomic and behavioral responding in concealed information: Differentiating orienting and defensive responses. *Psychophysiology* 2004; 41(3): 461-466.

52. Yankee, W. J., Powell, J. M., III, & Newland, R. An investigation of the accuracy and consistency of polygraph chart interpretation by inexperienced and experienced examiners. *Polygraph*, 1985; 14(2): 108-117.

Page 161. Insert: Matte Rebuttal to Response by F. Horvath to J. Matte's Critique of the Horvath-Palmatier Laboratory Study on Effectiveness of Exclusive v. Non-Exclusive Control Questions in Polygraph Examination, published in *Journal of Forensic Sciences*, Vol. 53, Nr. 4, 2008. The Matte Rebuttal set forth below incorporates the salient points of Horvath's response to Matte's critique of the Horvath-Palmatier laboratory study cited above. The unabridged response by Horvath was published along with Matte's Letter-to-the-Editor Critique in the *Journal of Forensic Sciences*, Volume 56, Issue Number 6, November 2011 available at: http://onlinelibrary.wiley.com/journal/10.1111/(ISSN)1556-4029. The original unabridge critique and rebuttal by Matte is available at: www.mattepolygraph. com/pdf/CritiqueRebuttal-HorvathPalmatier.pdf It must be noted that the rules of the *Journal of Forensic Sciences* do not permit the acceptance and publication of a rebuttal to a response from the original authors to a critique of their study, hence its publication in this supplement.

The first author (Horvath) begins his response by noting for the record that he is not nor has ever claimed to be a graduate of the Reid College, nor is he now or has ever been a staff member of that college. He further noted for the record that he "was however employed in various positions not related to that 'college' at John E. Reid and Associates, Chicago." A review of John E. Reid and Fred E. Inbau's 1966 textbook titled "Truth and Deception: The Polygraph ("Lie-Detector") Technique [26], which was used at the Reid College, revealed on Page 266 and again on Page 278 photographs of Frank S. Horvath, identified as a polygraph examiner on the staff of John E. Reid and Associates. It is a reasonable assumption that as a polygraph examiner for Reid and Associates, Horvath would have employed a polygraph technique that used the Reid non-exclusive control question, which has been the focus of some of his research. (Horvath 1988 [5], 1991[6] and 2008 [8]).

Horvath states that "this method (BacksterZCT) is merely one of many variations of the most frequently administered polygraph testing procedure in the U. S., what is generically known as the Comparison ("control") Question Technique (CQT). While it is common to find that variations in the CQT are identified by the name of a person who made an alteration in the testing protocol, in principle, they all function in roughly the same way." This statement suggests that the Backster ZCT is a derative of some other technique when in fact it is the first technique that employed non-current exclusive control questions, symptomatic questions and a standardized numerical scoring system of chart interpretation from which other techniques were developed with various modifications, some of which significantly altered the psychological structure of the Backster ZCT which relies on its "Either-Or" rule supported by the non-current exclusive control questions. Horvath dismisses the importance of the "Either-0r" rule stating that "This rule has never been reported to be of value in any peer-reviewed scientific journal. In the paper on that topic to which Matte refers, the only published assessment available, the findings showed something quite different from what he reports. In that paper, the BZCT testing that was carried out using the "either-or" rule did not produce an outcome that was significantly different from what was obtained by a different testing method that didn't employ that rule. Matte's statement about what was reported in that paper is misleading."

Quite the contrary, there were two field studies published in peer-reviewed journals regarding the effectiveness of the "Either-Or" rule, namely "A field Study of the Backster Zone Comparison

Technique's Either-Or Rule and Scoring System Versus two other Scoring Systems When Relevant Question Elicits Strong Response," Matte, 2010 [11], *European Polygraph*. The results of this field study comprising 123 cases representing 270 polygraph charts averaged 2.2 charts per case. Two false negatives would have occurred using the Greatest Reaction Control (GRC) and the GRC produced the greatest number of Inconclusives at 35.3%. The comparison of the relevant questions with the control question that elicited the least or no reaction in accordance with the "Either-Or" rule produced the least number of Inconclusives (12.1%) and with no errors. The results of this field research study supports Backster's "Either-Or" Rule of comparison of the relevant question that elicits a strong reaction with the control question that elicits the least or no reaction, and refutes the contention that its practice makes the Backster Zone Comparison Technique biased against the innocent examinee.

The second field study cited in Matte's critique is "An Assessment of the Backster "Either-Or" Rule in Polygraph Scoring" by Eldad Meiron, Dolnald J. Krapohl and Tzachi Ashkenazi. *Polygraph*, 2008 [23]. In referring to this study, Horvath stated that "the BZCT testing that was carried out using the "either-or" rule did not produce an outcome that was significantly different from what was obtained by a different testing method that didn't employ that rule. Matte' statement about what was reported in that paper is misleading." Horvath misses the point, which is that when the Backster ZCT is administered **without** the "Either'Or" rule, the results show a significant decrease in accuracy. Page 244 of cited study reflects: "It can be seen at the above figure that the percentage of cases in which all three examiners correctly decided was lower in the Backster (no EOR) method (59%) and higher both in the Backster (EOR) (70%) and the Federal method (73%) who achieved similar results. It can be seen that the Backster (No EOR) method has a relatively high percentage of cases in which none of the three examiners correctly decided (16%)." "Analysis showed the following: Backster (EOR) scoring method is significantly more accurate than Backster (no EOR) method (p<0.05 in Binomial distribution." "Focusing only in the deceptive cases one can see larger differences between the scoring methods. In contrast to a relatively lower percentage of cases in which all three examiners decided correctly using Backster (no EOR) method (42%), one can see a relatively high percent of cases in which all three examiners decided correctly using Backster (EOR) method (68%)." This data is consistent with the data from the aforesaid (Matte 2010 [11]) field study. The Meiron, et al study conducted a significance analysis "using either Sign Test or the Binomial distribution (in cases of small N or many ties). Analysis showed the following: (1) Backster (EOR) scoring method is significantly more accurate than Backster (No EOR) method (P<0.05 in Binomial distrubution); (2) The Federal scoring method is significantly more accurate than Backster (No EOR) method (p<0.05 in Binomial distribution), and: (3) The federal scoring method is not significantly different in accuracy than Backster (EOR) method (p<0.05 in Binomial distribution).

The above two field research studies leave no doubt about the significant difference the "Either-Or" Rule makes when it is omitted from the Backster ZCT. Horvath makes the point that there is no significant difference between the Backster method with its Either-Or Rule and the Federal Method, but ignores the most important issue of this debate which is the fact that his laboratory study tested the effectiveness of Backster's non-current exclusive control question without its related "Either-Or" rule in formats (CQT and MGQT) that were not designed to accommodate its effective use, as indicated in paragraphs numbered 1 thru 12 of the Matte Critique which Horvath failed to specifically address. Horvath stated that he chose not to employ the Backster ZCT format because "there isn't a single empirical study in the scientific literature in which that procedure has been used as Matte described it." In fact the two aforesaid field studies (Matte 2010 [11]; Meiron, et al 2008 [23]) used the Backster ZCT format as I described it, inasmuch as the Backster ZCT is standardized and deviations are not permitted. Nonetheless, whether there are empirical studies in the scientific literature or not is not relevant inasmuch as the Horvath-Palmatier laboratory study was suppose to test the effectiveness of the exclusive v. the non-exclusive control questions, hence the exclusive control questions should have been tested in the format in which it was designed to be used by its developer (Backster) in concert with the utilization of its related "Either-Or" Rule. Instead, the exclusive control question was tested under conditions that violated standard Backster ZCT procedures listed in the 12 points set forth in the Matte Critique.

Horvath states that the point made in the critique about the review and emphasis on the control questions between charts has no relevance to what was reported in his Horvath-Palmatier lab study. He states that "Like the other points made in the Matte critique it is simply a personal comment, in this case, made up out of thin air and without any foundation in regard to our study." Horvath fails to understand that this author (Matte) was only allowed to submit his critique as a letter to the editor which limited his critique and precluded lengthy references. Nevertheless, in response to Horvath's comment, Stanley Abrams authored "A Response to Honts on the Issue of the Discussion of Questions Between Charts" published in *Polygraph*, 1999 [1]; and "The Directed Lie Control Question" published in *Polygraph*, 1991 [2]. Also Matte, J. A. & Reuss, R. M., "Validation of Potential Response Elements in the Directed-Lie Control Question" published in *Polygraph*, 1999 [22]. Matte, J. A., "An Analysis of the Psychodynamics of the Directed Lie Control Question in the Control Question Technique. *Polygraph*, 1998 [17]. All of the aforementioned publications indicate that the review of control questions between charts is a recipe for false negatives. The review of the control questions between the collection of the polygraph charts stimulates the examinee towards the control questions, thus depriving the examinee the choice of self-directing his psychological set [13] towards the questions (control or relevant) that present the greatest threat to his well-being which is determined from the analysis of the physiological data collected from the examinee. The Backster ZCT rules mandate that once the test questions have been reviewed with the examinee, the collection of the data must not be interrupted with any language that would influence the examinee's psychological set towards the control or relevant questions. The sole exception is when there is no response to either the relevant or the control questions. Then the control questions only are reviewed with the examinee in accordance with Backster's Eight-Reaction Combination Guide (Backster 1963 & 1979 [4], 1969 [3]) or Matte's 23 Reaction Combination Guide (Matte, 1981 [18], 1996 [14]). See also "Psychological Structure and Theoretical Concept of the Backster Zone Comparison Technique and the Quadri-Track Zone Comparison Technique. *Polygraph*, 2007 [15].

Horvath mentions the use of the MGQT (Modified General Question Technique) in his laboratory study which he states generally makes use of the non-exclusive control question. The exclusive as well as the non-exclusive control questions were tested using the MGQT format and found that the exclusive control question did not perform as well as the non-exclusive control question, which is of no surprise to this author (Matte) inasmuch as the format included five relevant questions and only two exclusive control questions. This failure to use the proper format for each type of control question was previously discussed on pages 116-117 of 1996 textbook [14] "Forensic Psychophysiology Using The Polygraph."

The Utah Study (Raskin, Barland, Podlesny, 1978 [24]), evaluated the psychostructural validity of the Reid non-exclusive control question as used in the Reid Technique and format, versus the Backster exclusive control question as used in the Backster Technique and format. The rate of accuracy of decisions using Backster exclusive control questions was 94%, and 83% with the Reid non-exclusive control questions. In the comparison of Backster exclusive control questions and the Reid non-exclusive control questions, the tests using exclusive control questions which employed a time bar to exclude the period of the crime from the period encompassed by the control question, produced significant identification of innocent subjects (mean score = +13) and guilty subjects (mean score = -11.7), but the results with Reid non-exclusive control questions which included the period of the crime encompassed by the control question, were significant for innocent subjects (mean score = +14.2) but not guilty subjects (mean score = -6.3). A quantitative analysis of physiological responses also produced some results which indicated a superiority for test utilizing exclusive control questions. Measures of skin conductance response recovery times and amplitude of negative skin potential responses showed strong reactions to relevant questions by guilty subjects and to control questions by innocent subjects only with exclusive control questions. The test which used non-exclusive control questions showed no discrimination for either of those measures. The study concluded that control questions which are separated from the relevant issue by age or time of occurrence have some advantages over control questions which do not have those exclusionary characteristics. Had the Horvath-Palmatier study used the psychostructural format for which the exclusive and non-exclusive control questions were designed to be used, the outcome of their study would most likely mirror that of the Raskin, et al 1978 study [24].

In addition it should be noted that in the Horvath-Palmatier laboratory study, a stimulation test was administered after the first relevant chart was collected, in violation of the Backster ZCT protocol. The accuracy of aforesaid MGQT was reported by D. Krapohl in *Polygraph*, 2006 [9], which listed two field studies and one laboratory study as the basis for his findings which are as follows:

MGQT accuracy for Deceptive cases: 97% correct, 7% inconclusives.

MGQT accuracy for Truthful cases: 25% correct, 35% inconclusives.

Overall accuracy, 61% correct without inconclusives, 21% inconclusives.

The dismal performance of the MGQT in aforesaid studies used non-exclusive control questions.

Horvath stated that of all the polygraph schools accredited by the American Polygraph Association, only one of them, the Backster School of Lie Detection focusses primarily on the approach described by this author (Matte), which is the Backster ZCT. However, Horvath failed to recognize that the Quadri-Track Zone Comparison Technique also uses non-current exclusive control questions and the "Either-Or" rule on a non-selective basis. Three field studies (Matte, Reuss, 1989 [20,21]; Mangan, Armitage, Adams, 2008 [10]; Shurany, Stein, Brant, 2009 [25]) published in peer-reviewed journals (*Polygraph, Physiology & Behavior, European Polygraph*) respectively, have validated the technique with an overall accuracy of 98.8% and a 2.4% Inconclusive rate.

Horvath attempts to justify the use of a laboratory study as being a viable alternative to a field study in spite of his comments in a previous laboratory study (Horvath, *Polygraph,* 1994 [7]) where he stated that laboratory studies "must be interpreted with some caution. These data were collected in a laboratory environment where motivational and other differences may make it unlikely that the results can be generalized to real-life testing situation. Of course, this caveat would apply to all laboratory studies and indeed there are some who maintain that results in this environment should not ever be extended to actual testing situations."

A recently published paper by this author (Matte) entitled "Guiding Principles and Benchmarks for the Conduct of Validity Studies of Psychophysiological Veracity Examinations Using the Polygraph" in *European Polygraph*, 2010 [12], clearly and persuasively argues against the use of laboratory studies to validate control question techniques and their related components. This thesis sets forth guidelines for acceptable scientific conduct of field validity studies of control question techniques.

A current research paper entitled "Psychological Aspects of the Quadri-Track Zone Comparison Technique and Attendant Benefits of its Inside Track" by Matte published in *European Polygraph*, 2011 [19], discusses at length each component of the Quadri-Track ZCT test structure with supporting research, and addresses challenges against the use of symptomatic questions, the sacrifice relevant question, exclusive control question and other issues relevant to the application of this technique and the Backster ZCT.

In summation, Horvath apparently failed to understand that the non-current exclusive control question was designed by Cleve Backster to enable the Backster Zone Comparison Techniques's "Either-Or" rule, hence is not designed to be used in a MGQT or other control question technique format that does not use the "Either-Or" rule and related Backster technique protocol. The Horvath-Palmatier laboratory study's failure to duplicate the psychostructural format and protocol in which the non-current exclusive control question is designed to be used resulted in an invalid assessment of the effectiveness of the non-current exclusive control question. The fact that the aforesaid study was conducted under laboratory conditions further precludes its findings from being applied to real-life testing situations.

REFERENCES:

1. Abrams, S. A response to Honts on the issue of the discussion of questions between charts. Polygraph 1999; 28-3:

2. Abrams, S. The directed lie control question. Polygraph 1991; 20-1:

3 Backster, C. *Technique fundamentals of the Tri-Zone Polygraph Test*. New York, NY: Backster Research Foundation; 1969.

4. Backster, C. Standardized polygraph notepack and technique guide: Backster zone comparison technique. 1963-1979; New York, NY: Backster School of Lie Detection.

5. Horvath, F. The utilility of control questions and the effects of two control question types in field polygraph techniques. *J. of Police Science and Administration* 1988; 16-3: 198-209.

6. Horvath, F. The utility of control questions and the effects of two control questions tests on field polygraph techniques. *Polygraph* 1991; 20-1: 7-25.

7. Horvath, F. The value and effectiveness of the sacrifice relevant question: an empirical assessment. *Polygraph* 1994; 23-4: 261-279.

8. Horvath, F., Palmatier, J. Effect of two types of control questions and two question formats on the outcomes of polygraph examinations. *J. Forensic Science* 2008; 53-4: 889-899.

9. Krapohl, D. Validated polygraph techniques. *Polygraph* 2006; 35-3: 149-155.

10. Mangan, D. J., Armitage, T. E., Adams, G. C. A field study on the validity of the Quadri-Track Zone Comparison Technique. *Physiology & Behavior* 2008; 95: 17-23.

11. Matte, J. A. A field study of the Backster Zone Comparison Technique's Either-Or Rule and scoring system when relevant question elilcitgs strong response. *European Polygraph* 2010; 4-2(12); 53-70.

12. Matte, J. A. Guiding principles and benchmarks for the conduct of validity studies of psychophysiological veracity examinations using the polygraph. European Polygraph 2010; 4-4(14): 173-198.

13. Matte, J. A., Grove, R. N. Psychological set: its origin, theory and application. *Polygraph* 2001; 30-3: 196-203.

14. Matte, J. A. *Forensic psychophysiology using the polygraph: scientific truth verification – lie detection*. Williamsville, New York: J.A.M. Publications; 1996.

15. Matte, J. A. Psychological structure and theoretical concept of the Backster Zone Comparison Technique and the Quadri-Track Zone Comparison Technique. *Polygraph* 2007; 36-2: 84-90.

16. Matte, J. A. Critique of Horvath-Palmatier laboratory study on effectiveness of exclusive v. non-exclusive control questions in polygraph examinations, plus response to critique by F. Horvath. *Journal of Forensic Sciences*, Vol. 56, Nr. 6, 2011; 1664-1670.

17. Matte, J. A. An analysis of the psychodynamics of the directed lie control question in the control question technique. *Polygraph* 1998; 27-1:

18. Matte, J. A. Polygraph Quadri-Zone Reaction Combination Guide. Polygraph 1981; 10-3: 186-193.

19. Matte, J. A. Pschological aspects of the Quadri-Track Zone Comparison Technique and attendant benefits of its Inside Track. *European Polygraph* 2011; 5-4(17):_____

20. Matte, J. A., Reuss, R. M. A field validation study of the Quadri-Track Zone Comparison Technique. *Polygraph* 1989; 18-4: 187-202.

21. Matte, J. A., Reuss, R. M. *Validation study on the polygraph Quadri-Zone Comparison Technique.* Research Asbtract LD 01452, Vol. 1502, 1989 University Microfilm International (UMI), Ann Arbor, MI.

22. Matte, J. A., Reuss, R. M. Validation of potential response elements in the directed-lie control question. *Polygraph* 1999; 28-2:

23. Meiron, E., Krapohl, D. J., Ashkenazi, T. An assessment of the Backster "Either-Or" rule in polygraph scoring. *Polygraph* 2008; 37-4: 240-249.

24. Raskin, D. C., Barland, G. H., Podlesny, J. A. *Validity and reliability of detection of deception.* 1978. Washington, D. C., National Institute of Law Enforcement and Criminal Justice

25. Shurany, T., Stein, E., Brand, E. A field study on the validity of the Quadri-Track Zone Comparison Technique. *European Polygraph* 2009; 1-1(7): 5-24.

26. Reid, J. E., Inbau, F. E. *Truth and Deception: The Polygraph ("Lie-Detector") Technique.* Baltimore, MD: Williams & Wilkins 1966.

Page 166. Insert Summary of "A Field Study on the Validity of the Quadri-Track Zone Comparison Technique" by Daniel J. Mangan, Thomas E. Armitage and Gregory C. Adams, published in *Physiology & Behavior*, Volume 95: 17-23, 2008.

This field study tested and demonstrated the validity and reliability of the Quadri-Track Zone Comparison Technique designed for specific Single-Issue Psychophysiological Veracity (PV) examinations using the polygraph, using one hundred and forty confirmed real-life cases from a private polygraph firm under contract with a metropolitan police department. The Quadri-Track Zone Comparison Technique's unique Inside Track accurately increased the scores for the innocent by 43.6% and the guilty by 37.1% thereby reducing the overall inconclusive rate from 19.5% to 1.4% which effectively remedies the major cause (Fear/Hope of Error) of inconclusive results in Single-Issue tests. The Quadri-Track Zone Comparison Technique correctly identified 100% of the innocent as truthful with no inconclusives and no errors. It further correctly identified 97.8% of the guilty as deceptive and 2.2% as inconclusive, with no errors. Inconclusives excluded, the Quadri-Track Zone Comparison Technique was 100% accurate in the identification of the innocent and the guilty. Inconclusives included, the utility rate was 98.6 %. Blind scoring of polygraph charts showed extremely high correlations for the individual and total scores with a combined accuracy of 98.3 percent. For further details visit www.mattepolygraph.com.

Page 150. Insert Summary of "Rebuttal of Objections by Iacono and Verschuere, et al" by Daniel J. Mangan, Thomas E. Armitage and Gregory Adams, published in *Physiology & Behavior*, Volume 95: 29-31, 2008.

The arguments presented by Iacono and Verschuere, et al, against the publication of the Mangan, et al, field study of the Quadri-Track Zone Comparison Technique in *Physiology & Behavior*, are based largely on dated articles that examined control question polygraph tests whose psychological test structure and physiological analysis and scoring system was significantly different than the Quadri-Track ZCT. Iacono and Verschuere, et al, alleged that the Quadri-Track ZCT is biased against the innocent and can be defeated with the use of countermeasures without considering the technique's unique "remedial inside track" that quantifies the innocent examinees *fear of error* and the guilty examinee's *hope of error* which are factored into the overall score, thus avoiding false positive and false negative errors. Their objection to the use of confessions as the criterion for ground truth presumes that the polygraph examinations conducted in this field study were conducted in a vacuum. They ignored the various methods of post-test confirmation and research studies that support the use of confessions as ground truth. Verschuere, et al, cited the National Research Council's 2003 report to support their conviction that the accuracy of polygraph tests is well below perfection and errors often occur. However, they failed to mention that the accuracy range values of the seven field studies which met the National Research Council's scientific criteria was from 0.711 to 0.999 with a median value of 0.89, and that the field study with the highest accuracy (0.999) was from a published 1989 field study on the Quadri-Track Zone Comparison Technique. For further details, visit www.mattepolygraph.com.

Page 151. Insert Summary of "A Field Study on the Validity of the Quadri-Track Zone Comparison Technique" by Tuvia Shurany, Einat Stein and Eytan Brand, published in *European Polygraph,* Volume 1, Number 1(7), 2009.

This field research study comprises the third independent published field study on the validity of the Quadri-Track Zone Comparison Technique (ZCT) initially developed by James Allan Matte in 1977. This study tested and demonstrated the validity and reliability of the Quadri-Track ZC T designed for specific-issue Psychophysiological Veracity (PV) examinations using the polygraph, using fifty-seven confirmed real-life cases from the Liecatcher and Polygraph Center, Thailand, consisting of 26 men and 31 women. Four polygraphists, all formally trained in the use of the Quadri-Track ZCT participated in this field study that examined 4 Israelis, 42 Thais, 4 Chinese, 2 Columbians, 1 American, 1 Vietnamese, 1 Burmese, 1 Englishman, and 1 Australian, indicative of a multi-cultural application of the Quadri-Track ZCT. Lafayette LX 4000 computerized polygraph systems were used in this study. This study indicates that the Quadri-Track ZCT's unique *Inside Track* accurately identifies and remedies the major cause (Fear/Hope of Error) of false Positives/Negatives and Inconclusives in Single-Issue tests. The Inside Track's Fear/Hope of Error reduced the Inconclusives for the confirmed Deceptive cases by 71.5% and the confirmed Truthful cases by 31%. The Inside Track further accurately increased the scores for the Deceptive by 41% and the Truthful by 37%, thereby reducing the overall inconclusive rate from 50.8% to 0%. The Quadri-Track ZCT correctly identified 100% of the Innocent as Truthful with no Inconclusive and no errors. It further correctly identified 92.9% of the Guilty as Deceptive, with no Inconclusive and a 7.1% error rate. Overall, the Quadri-Track ZCT was 96.5% accurate in the identification of the Innocent and the Guilty. Furthermore, a comparison was made of the results of the Quadri-Track ZCT between the confirmed cases (n. 57) and the unconfirmed cases (n. 108) which revealed no significant difference in the frequency of the three decisions, nor was there any significant difference in the average score per chart for the confirmed and unconfirmed cases, with and without the inside track. Hence the data shows that there is no significant difference in the reactivity or responsiveness of the examinees in the confirmed versus the unconfirmed cases, thus the confirmed cases appear to be a representative sample of the total cases. For further details, visit www.mattepolygraph.com

Page 152. Insert Summary of "A Field Validity Study of the Integrated Zone Comparison Technique" by Nathan J. Gordon, William L. Fleisher, Hisham Morsie, Walid Habib and Khaled Salah, published in *Polygraph*, Volume 29, Number 3, 2000.

This field study tested the validity of the Integrated Zone Comparison Technique (IZCT) designed for specific issue tests, utilizing 309 confirmed field cases by examiners of the Egyptian Government. During 1998 and 1999 the IZCT correctly identified 100% of the innocent examinees and 99.5% of the guilty examinees, excluding Inconclusives, or 94.8% of innocent examinees and 90.5% of the deceptive examinees, including Inconclusives.

Page 152. Insert Summary of "A Study of Deception Utilizing fMRI, the Accuracy of Scoring Algorithms of the Polygraph Component" by Nathan J. Gordon, Feroze B. Mohamed, Scott H. Faro, Steven M. Platek, Harris ahmad and J. Michael Williams, published in *Physiology & Behavior*, Volume 87, 2006.

The data collected in the previously mentioned experiment was further analyzed with the PolyScore algorithm and Objective Scoring System (OSS-2), as compared to ASIT PolySuite. ASIT PolySuite had 1 Inconclusive and 10 correct decisions, both Polyscore and OSS-2 had 3 Inconclusives and 8 correct calls. All 3 algorithms had 100% accuracy excluding Inconclusives. Where Inconclusives were included ASIT PolySuite had 90% accuracy, and PolyScore and OSS-2 had 72% accuracy.

Page 153. Insert Summary of "Brain Mapping of Deception and Truth telling about an ecologically valid situation: An fMRI and polygraph investigation" by Feroze B. Mohamed †, Scott H. Faro †, Nathan J Gordon §, Steven M. Platek ‡, Harris Ahmad †, & J Michael Williams ‡ published in *Radialogy*, Volume 238, Number 2, February 2006.

Mock crime scenario was established for ground truth where half the group fired a blank gun in a hospital and deny firing the gun, and half were told someone had fired a gun that looked like them on a surveillance camera. All subjects were told they would receive a monetary reward if they were determined to be truthful after polygraph and fMRI testing. Therefore, all subjects were motivated to come out truthful, as occurs in actual real life examinations (both truthful and deceptive suspects want to come out truthful). All subjects were given pre-test FAINT (Forensic Assessment Interview Technique) interviews. Half the group were given polygraph examinations followed by fMRI examinations, and half were given fMRI examinations followed by polygraph examinations. The Lafayette LX-4000 computerized system was used with the ASIT PolySuite Algorithm scoring three charts of a single issue Integrated Zone Comparison Technique. The polygraph results were 1 Inconclusive, and 10 correct decisions (100% accuracy excluding the Inconclusive, and 90% accuracy with the Inconclusive counted as an error).

Page 154, Insert Summary of "Accuracy Demonstration of the Horizontal Scoring System Using Field Cases Conducted with the Federal Zone Comparison" By Donald Krapohl, Nathan Gordon & Christopher Lombardi. published in *Polygraph*, Volume 37, Number 4, 2008.

A hundred Federal Zone Comparison field examinations were scored using the Horizontal Scoring System (HSS) by a blind examiner trained in the procedure . This was the first study of the HSS using multi-faceted cases. Overall accuracy using cutoffs of a + or − 1.5 per relevant question per chart was 84%, which met the standard necessary for investigative examinations.

Page 155. Insert Summary of "An Assessment of the Backster "Either-Or" Rule in Polygraph Scoring" by Eldad Meiron, Donald Krapohl and Tzachi Ashkenazi, published in *Polygraph*, Volume 37, Number 4, 2008.

The Backster "Either-Or" Rule (EOR) was investigated using 100 Backster field cases which were blind scored by field examiners who used either the Backster scoring system or the US federal scoring system. The Backster scorers indicated those scores which were the product of the EOR. Without the EOR the Backster scorers made an average of 70% correct decisions, 3% errors, and 27% inconclusive results. With the EOR they rendered an average of 80% correct decisions, 3% errors, and 17% inconclusives. All of the increase in decision accuracy and reduction in inconclusive rate was attributable to improvement in classifying deceptive cases. There was no effect on truthful cases. The scores from the US federal system produced an average of 86% correct decisions, 5% errors, and 9% inconclusives. Decision accuracy, inconclusives and errors between the US federal and the Backster (with EOR) were not significantly different, though both performed better than the Backster method without EOR. The implications and limitations of these findings are discussed. For further details, visit www.mattepolygraph.com.

Page 156. Insert Summary of validity study on the Backster Zone Comparison Technique:

The following is a summary of Part I of laboratory study titled "Effects of physical countermeasures on the physiological detection of deception" by Honts, Hodes and Raskin, published in Volume 70, Number 1, 1985, *Journal of Applied Psychology* wherein the Backster Zone Comparison Technique was used.

In Experiment I of this laboratory study, 48 students were involved in a mock crime wherein 75 percent of the students were assigned to the guilty role and instructed in the use of physical countermeasures. In addition, between each presentation of the questions, the examiner reviewed the control questions with the subject in an effort to prevent habituation to the control questions. They were then administered a polygraph examination using the Backster Zone Comparison Technique. Excluding inconclusives, the original examiner was 80% correct. Independent evaluator's decisions using the Backster System, excluding inconclusives, was 83% correct. The use of physical countermeasures in this experiment had no significant effect on either the categorical decisions of the original examiner or on the semi-objective scores of the independent evaluator.

Page 157. Insert Summary of "Field Study of the Backster Zone Comparison Technique's Either-Or Rule and Scoring System Versus Two Other Scoring Systems When Relevant Question Elicits Strong Response" by James Allan Matte, published in *European Polygraph*, Vol. 4, Nr. 2(12), 2010.

The Backster Zone Comparison Technique has been criticized as being biased against the innocent examinee because it compares a strong relevant question reaction to the control question that elicited the least or no reaction while ignoring a strong reaction neighboring the same relevant question. Backster's anticlimax dampening concept forms the basis of his "Either Or" rule which dictates that when there is a significant reaction in one zone, there should be a comparative absence of reaction in the other zone against which it is being compared. Thus in the presence of a strong reaction to the relevant question, the neighboring control question that elicits little or no reaction is functioning as designed and in fact is the effective control question. However several research studies have been conducted to determine the effectiveness of comparing a strong relevant question to the control question that elicited the greatest response, the control question that elicited the weakest response, and the straight paired non-selective comparison where the relevant question was compared to the control question that preceded it. But none of those studies replicated the Backster Zone Comparison Technique to any degree that would render their results applicable to the validity of Backster's relevant/control comparison rules articulated in his Tri-Zone Reaction Combinations. This field study used 123 confirmed guilty cases that employed the Backster "You Phase" Zone Comparison Technique to determine the accuracy and effectiveness of each of the three methods of comparison to the relevant question that elicited a strong response, expectedly present only in confirmed guilty cases. The results of this field study comprising 123 cases representing 270 polygraph charts averaged 2.2 charts per case. Two false negatives would have occurred using the Greatest Reaction Control (GRC) and the GRC produced the greatest number of Inconclusives at 35.3%. The comparison of the relevant questions with the control question that elicited the least or no reaction produced the least number of Inconclusives and with no errors, followed by the comparison of the relevant questions with the control question that preceded the particular relevant question with no errors. The results of this field research study supports Backster's "Either-Or" Rule of comparison of the relevant question that elicits a strong reaction with the control question that elicits the least or no reaction, and refutes the contention that its practice makes the Backster Zone Comparison Technique biased against the innocent examinee. For further details, visit www.mattepolygraph.com.

Page 158. Insert Summary of "Field Study on Confirmed Mental Countermeasure Case in Costa Rica" by Tuvia Shurany. *European Polygraph*, Vol. 4, Nr. 1(11), 2010.

The author relates his unusual experience in the conduct of several psychophysiological veracity (PV) examinations using the multi-faceted Integrated Zone Comparison Technique with the 3-position scale and horizontal scoring system verified with the ASIT (Academy for Scientific Investigative Training) algorithm for chart interpretation. One of the examinees tested showed no signs of deception either during the pretest interview or the collected physiological data. In fact, the examinee's charts indicated NDI (No Deception Indicated) by ASIT, PolyScore version 6.3, and OSS (Objective Scoring System) version 3. However, the author observed several points that raised suspicion that the examinee had employed mental countermeasures in an attempt to manipulate the results of the PV examination. The responses in the cardio tracing to the control questions were too late and the responses in the pneumograph tracing to the control questions in the first and third charts were most unusual and strong, and thirdly, in two of the charts, the IZCT countermeasure question had a significant response. In view of these factors, the author rendered a No Opinion test results. The examinee was reinterviewed and advised that some responses existed which caused a noise in the test and he was asked to explain those responses. The examinee confessed to the crime and admitted that he had used countermeasures provided him by a friend who advised him to utter to himself three times "I am innocent" when asked the exclusive control questions, and in the third chart he had to try and inhale and exhale less, 4 times. The examinee stated he was very focused in identifying the exclusive control questions. The author noted that if he had used the conventional vertical scoring system and Matte's "Dual-Equal Strong Reaction:" Rule, it would had resulted in a minus one (-1) score at relevant question R-6 resulting in an Inconclusive finding.

Page 158. Insert: Validated Polygraph Techniques.

Techniques with a criterion accuracy of 90% or higher with an inconclusive rate of 20% or lower have been categorized as *Evidentiary Techniques* in the 2011 APA Meta-Analytic Survey of Criterion Accuracy of Validated Polygraph Techniques [Polygraph, 40(4), 2011]. Techniques that fail to meet that criteria but have a criterion accuracy of 86% or higher with an inconclusive rate of 20% or lower have been categorized as *Paired Testing Techniques*. Techniques that fail to meet the 86% criteria but have a criterion accuracy of 80% or higher with an inconclusive rate of 20% or lower have been categorized as *Investigative Techniques*. Five *Evidentiary Techniques* have emerged from the Meta-Analytic Survey which are listed below: The Matte Quadri-Track ZCT, the Integrated ZCT, the Federal ZCT, the Utah ZCT and the Event-Specific ZCT. The Backster ZCT is also listed in this Supplement due to ongoing research that is expected to raise it from *Paired Testing* to *Evidentiary Technique*.

Polygraph techniques that qualified as Validated Evidentiary Techniques:

Validation of Matte Quadri-Track Zone Comparison Technique.

- 1989 Field Study published in *Polygraph*, Vol. 18, Nr. 4.
  Accuracy: 100% without Inconclusives. 6% Inconclusives.
- 1989 Field Study Accepted by *National Academies of Science* in 2003.
- 2008 Field Study published in *Physiology & Behavior*, Vol. 95, 17-23.
  Accuracy: 100% without Inconclusives. 1.4% Inconclusives.
- 2008 Rebuttal to Objections published in *Physiology & Behavior*, Vol. 95, 29-31.
- 2009 Field Study published in *European Polygraph*, Vol. 1, Nr. 1(7).
  Accuracy: 96.5%, Zero 0% Inconclusives.
- 2011 APA Meta-Analytic Survey of Criterion Accuracy of MQTZCT:
  99.4% without Inconclusives. 2.9% Inconclusives.

Validation of Integrated Zone Comparison Technique.

- 2005 Field Study published in *Physiology & behavior*, Vol. 87.
  Accuracy: 100% without Inconclusives. 10% Inconclusives.
- 2010 Field Study published in *European Polygraph*, Vol. 4, Nr. 2(12).
  Accuracy: 98.8% without Inconclusives, 5.9% Inconclusives.
- 2011 Field Study published in *European Polygraph*, Vol. 5, Nr. 2(16).
  Accuracy: 100%. Zero Inconclusives
- 2011 APA Meta-Analytic Survey of Criterion Accuracy of IZCT:
  Accuracy: 99.4% without Inconclusives. 3.3% Inconclusives.

Validation of Federal Zone Comparison Technique.

- 1998 Field Study published in *Polygraph*, Vol. 28, Nr. 2: 149-175.
- 2005 Field Study published in *Polygraph*, Vol. 34, Nr. 3: 184-192.
- 1985 Field Study published in *Polygraph*, Vol. 14, Nr. 2: 108-117.
  Federal ZCT Overall Accuracy: 89% without Inconclusives. 16%
  Inconclusives.
  Source: *Polygraph*, Vol. 35, Nr. 3: 149-155, 2006.
- 2011 APA Meta-Analytic Survey of Criterion Accuracy of Federal ZCT:
  Accuracy: 90.4% without Inconclusives. 19.2% Inconclusives.

Validation of Utah Zone Comparison Technique.

- 1985 Laboratory Study published in Applied Psychology, Vol. 70, Nr. 1:177-187.
- 1987 Laboratory Study published in Psychophysiology, Vol. 1, Nr. 3: 421-247.
- 1994 Laboratory Study published in Applied Psychology, Vol. 79, Nr. 2: 252-259.
- 1988 Laboratory Study published in Applied Psychology, Vol. 73, Nr. 2: 291-302.
- 1978 Laboratory Study published in Psychophysiology, Vol. 15: 126-136.
- 1997 Laboratory Study published in Psychophysiology, Vol. 34, Nr. 1: 108-115.
- 1986 Laboratory Study published in Polygraph, Vol. 15, Nr. 1: 1-39.
  Utah ZCT Overall Accuracy: 90% without Inconclusives. 12%
  Inconclusives.
  Source: *Polygraph*, Vol. 35, Nr. 3: 149-155, 2006.
- 2011 APA Meta-Analytic Survey of Criterion Accuracy of Utah ZCT Combined:
  Accuracy: 93.0% without Inconclusives. 10.7% Inconclusives.

Validation of Event Specific Zone Comparison Technique (Empirical Scoring System).

- 2011 APA Meta-Analytic Survey of Criterion Accuracy of ESZCT (ESS):
  Accuracy: 92.1% without Inconclusives. 9.8% Inconclusives.

Validation of Backster Zone Comparison Technique.

- 2011 APA Meta-Analytic Survey of Criterion Accuracy of Backster ZCT:
  Accuracy: 86.2% without Inconclusives. 19.6% Inconclusives.
- Research studies on the Backster ZCT are in progress with an
  expected accuracy that will meet the *evidentiary technique* requirement.

The Army Modified General Question Technique (MGQT) is listed below as a caveat due to its wide usage in the public and private sectors in spite of its dismal record in the identification of Truthful cases (25% correct) and an overall accuracy of 61% correct decisions. The APA Meta-Analytic Survey of the Army MGQT/Seven-Position TDA revealed a criterion accuracy of 3.9% for truthful cases and an overall accuracy of 69.4% correct decisions.

Validation of Army Modified General Question Technique (MGQT).

- 1988 Field Study published in *Polygraph*, Vol. 28, Nr. 2: 149-175.
- 2000 Field Study published in *Polygraph*. Vol. 29, Nr. 2: 185-194.
- 1993 Laboratory Study published in *Journal of Applied Psychology*.
- Vol. 75, Nr. 5: 788-794. Reprinted in *Polygraph*, Vol. 23, Nr. 3, 195-218.
  MGQT accuracy for Deceptive cases: 97% correct. 7% Inconclusives.
  MGQT accuracy for Truthful cases: 25% correct. 35% Inconclusives.

Overall accuracy. 61% correct without Inconclusives. 21% Inconclusives. Source: *Polygraph*, Vol. 25, Nr. 3: 149-155, 2006.
- **2011 APA Meta-Analytic Survey of Criterion Accuracy of Army MGQT: Accuracy: 69.4% without Inconclusives. 13.3% Inconclusives.**

NOTE: Laboratory studies have been criticized as lacking the emotional involvement of real-life examinees whose fear of detection or error is proportionate to the dire consequences, usually imprisonment and its attendant perils. For a full discussion on the merits and pitfalls of laboratory studies versus field studies, you are invited to read *"Guiding Principles and Benchmarks for the Conduct of Validity Studies of Psychophysiological Veracity Examinations Using the Polygraph"* published in *European Polygraph*, Vol. 4, Nr. 4(14), 2010 at www.mattepolygraph.com

REFERENCES:

Abrams, S. (1973). Polygraph validity and reliability: A review. *Journal of Forensic Sciences, 18,* 313-326.

Abrams, S. (1977). *A Polygraph Handbook for Attorneys.* Lexington, MA: Lexington Books.

Abrams, S. (1989). *The Complete Polygraph Handbook.* Lexington, MA: Lexington Books.

Abrams, S. (1984). The question of the intent question. *Polygraph, 13,* 326-332.

Anderson, C. A., Lindsay, J. J., & Bushman, B. J. (1999). Research in the psychological laboratory: Truth or triviality? *Current Directions In Psychological Science, 8,* 3-9.

Ansley, N. (1983). A compendium on polygraph validity. *Polygraph, 12,* 53-61.

Ansley, N. (1989). *Accuracy and utility of RI screening by student examiners at DODPI.* Polygraph and Personnel Security Research. Office of Security. National Security Agency. Fort George G. Meade, MD.

Ansley, N. (1990). The validity and reliability of polygraph decisions in real cases. *Polygraph, 19,* 169-181.

Ansley, N. (1992). The history and accuracy of guilty knowledge and peak of tension tests. *Polygraph, 21,* 174-247.

Backster, C. (1963). *Standardized polygraph notepack and technique guide: Backster zone comparison technique.* Cleve Backster: New York.

Backster School of Lie Detection (2011). *Basic polygraph examiner's course chart interpretation notebook.* Backster School of Lie Detection: San Diego.

Barland, G. H., Honts, C. R., & Barger, S. D. (1989). Studies of the accuracy of security screening polygraph examinations. Department of Defense Polygraph Institute.

Barland, G. H. & Raskin, D. C. (1975). Psychopathy and detection of deception in criminal suspects. *Psychophysiology, 12,* 224.

Bell, B. G., Kircher, J. C., & Bernhardt, P. C. (2008). New measures improve the accuracy of the directed-lie test when detecting deception using a mock crime. *Physiology and Behavior, 94,* 331-340.

Bell, B. G., Raskin, D. C., Honts, C. R., & Kircher, J. C. (1999). The Utah numerical scoring system. *Polygraph, 28*(1), 1-9.

Blackstone, K. (2011). *Polygraph, Sex Offenders, and the Court: What Professionals Should Know About Polygraph..., and a Lot More.* Concord, MA: Emerson Books.

Blackwell, J. N. (1998). *PolyScore 33 and psychophysiological detection of deception examiner rates of accuracy when scoring examination from actual criminal investigations.* Available at the Defense Technical Information Center. DTIC AD Number A355504/PAA. Reprinted in *Polygraph, 28*(2) 149-175.

Blalock, B., Cushman, B., & Nelson, R. (2009). A replication and validation study on an empirically based manual scoring system. *Polygraph, 38,* 281-288.

Blalock, B., Nelson, R., Handler, M., & Shaw, P. (2011). A position paper on the use of directed lie comparison questions in diagnostic and screening polygraphs. *Police Polygraph Digest,* 2-5.

Capps, M. H. (1991). Predictive value of the sacrifice relevant. *Polygraph, 20*(1), 1-8.

Capps, M. H. & Ansley, N. (1992). Comparison of two scoring scales. *Polygraph, 21,* 39-43.

Capps, M. H., Knill, B. L., & Evans, R. K. (1993). Effectiveness of the symptomatic questions. *Polygraph, 22, 285-298.*

Correa, E. J. & Adams, H. E. (1981). The validity of the pre-employment polygraph examination and the effects of motivation. *Polygraph, 10,* 143-155.

Crewson, P. E. (2001). *A comparative analysis of polygraph with other screening and diagnostic tools.* Research Support Service. Report No. DoDPI01-R-0003. Reprinted in Polygraph 32, (57-85).

Department of Defense (2006). *Federal psychophysiological detection of deception examiner handbook.* Reprinted in *Polygraph, 40(1),* 2-66.

Driscoll, L. N., Honts, C. R., & Jones, D. (1987). The validity of the positive control physiological detection of deception technique. *Journal of Police Science and Administration, 15,* 46-50. Reprinted in *Polygraph, 16(3),* 218-225.

Forman, R. F. & McCauley, C. (1986). Validity of the positive control polygraph test using the field practice model. *Journal of Applied Psychology, 71,* 691-698. Reprinted in *Polygraph, 16(2),* 145-160.

Ganguly, A. K., Lahri, S. K., & Bhaseen, V. (1986). Detection of deception by conventional qualitative method and its confirmation by quantitative method - An experimental study in polygraphy. *Polygraph, 15,* 203-210.

Ginton, A., Daie, N., Elaad, E., & Ben-Shakhar, G. (1982). A method for evaluating the use of the polygraph in a real-life situation. *Journal of Applied Psychology, 67,* 131-137.

Gordon, N. J. (1999). The academy for scientific investigative training's horizontal scoring system and examiner's algorithm system for chart interpretation. *Polygraph, 28,* 56-64.

Gordon, N. J., Fleisher, W. L., Morsie, H., Habib, W., & Salah, K. (2000). A field validity study of the integrated zone comparison technique. *Polygraph, 29,* 220-225.

Gordon, N. J., Mohamed, F. B., Faro, S. H., Platek, S. M., Ahmad, H., & Williams, J. M. (2005). Integrated zone comparison polygraph technique accuracy with scoring algorithms. *Physiology & behavior, 87(2),* 251-254.

Gougler, M., Nelson, R., Handler, M., Krapohl, D., Shaw, P., Bierman, L. (2011). Meta-Analytic Survey of Criterion accuracy of Validated Polygraph Techniques. Polygraph, 40(4).

Handler, M. (2006). The Utah PLC. *Polygraph, 35,* 139-148.

Handler, M. & Nelson, R. (2008). Utah approach to comparison question polygraph testing. *European Polygraph, 2,* 83-119.

Handler, M. & Nelson, R. (In press 2012). Criterion validity of the United States Air Force Modified General Question Technique and three position scoring. *Polygraph.*

Handler, M., Nelson, R., Goodson, W., & Hicks, M. (2010). Empirical Scoring System: A cross-cultural replication and extension study of manual scoring and decision policies. *Polygraph, 39,* 200-215.

Harwell, E. M. (2000). A comparison of 3- and 7-position scoring scales with field examinations. *Polygraph, 29,* 195-197.

Hilliard, D. L. (1979). A cross analysis between relevant questions and a generalized intent to answer truthfully question. *Polygraph, 8,* 73-77.

Honts, C. R. (1996). Criterion development and validity of the CQT in field application. *The Journal of General Psychology, 123,* 309-324.

Honts, C. R., & Amato, S. L. (1999). *The automated polygraph examination:* Final report of U. S. Government Contract No. 110224-1998-MO. Boise State University.

Honts, C. R., Amato, S. & Gordon, A. (2004). Effects of outside issues on the comparison question test. *Journal of General Psychology, 131(1)*, 53-74.

Honts, C. R. & Driscoll, L. N. (1987). An evaluation of the reliability and validity of rank order and standard numerical scoring of polygraph charts. *Polygraph, 16*, 241-257.

Honts, C. R. & Hodes, R. L. (1983). The detection of physical countermeasures. *Polygraph, 12*, 7-17.

Honts, C. R., Hodes, R. L., & Raskin, D. C. (1985). Effects of physical countermeasures on the physiological detection of deception. *Journal of Applied Psychology, 70(1)*, 177-187.

Honts, C. R. & Raskin, D. (1988). A field study of the validity of the directed lie control question. *Journal of Police Science and Administration, 16(1)*, 56-61.

Honts, C. R., Raskin, D. C., & Kircher, J. C. (1987). Effects of physical countermeasures and their electromyographic detection during polygraph tests for deception. *Psychophysiology, 1*, 241-247.

Honts, C. R., & Reavy, R. (2009). *Effects of Comparison Question Type and Between Test Stimulation on the Validity of Comparison Question Test.* US Army Research Office: Grant Number W911NF-07-1-0670.

Horowitz, S. W., Kircher, J. C., Honts, C. R., & Raskin, D. C. (1997). The role of comparison questions in physiological detection of deception. *Psychophysiology, 34*, 108-115.

Horvath, F. S. (1977). The effect of selected variables on interpretation of polygraph records. *Journal of Applied Psychology, 62*, 127-136.

Horvath F. S. (1988). The utility of control questions and the effects of two control question types in field polygraph techniques. *Journal of Police Science and Administration, 16(3)*, 198-209. Reprinted in *Polygraph, 20*, 7-25.

Horvath, F. S. (1994). The value and effectiveness of the sacrifice relevant question: An empirical assessment. *Polygraph, 23*, 261-279.

Horvath, F. & Palmatier, J. (2008). Effect of two types of control questions and two question formats on the outcomes of polygraph examinations. *Journal of Forensic Sciences, 53(4)*, 1-11.

Horvath, F. S. & Reid, J. E. (1971). The reliability of polygraph examiner diagnosis of truth and deception. *Journal of Criminal Law, Criminology and Police Science, 62*, 276-281.

Hunter, F. L., & Ash, P. (1973). The accuracy and consistency of polygraph examiners' diagnosis. *Journal of Police Science and Administration, 1*, 370-375.

Iacono, W. G. (2008). Accuracy of polygraph techniques: Problems using confessions to determine ground truth. *Physiology & Behavior*, 95 (1-2), 24-26.

Jayne, B. (1989). A comparison between the predictive value of two common preemployment screening procedures. *The Investigator, 5(3)*.

Jayne, B. C. (1990). Contributions of physiological recordings in the polygraph technique. *Polygraph, 19*, 105-117.

Kircher, J. C., Kristjiansson, S. D., Gardner, M. K., & Webb, A. (2005). *Human and computer decision-making in the psychophysiological detection of deception.* University of Utah.

Kircher, J. C. & Raskin, D. C. (1988). Human versus computerized evaluations of polygraph data in a laboratory setting. *Journal of Applied Psychology, 73*, 291-302.

Kokish, R., Levenson, J. S., & Blasingame, G. D. (2005). Post-conviction sex offender polygraph examination: client-reported perceptions of utility and accuracy. *Sexual Abuse : A Journal of Research and Treatment, 17*, 211-21.

Krapohl, D. J. (1998). A comparison of 3- and 7- position scoring scales with laboratory data. *Polygraph, 27,* 210-218.

Krapohl, D. J. (2002). Short report: Update for the objective scoring system. *Polygraph, 31,* 298-302.

Krapohl, D. J. (2005). Polygraph decision rules for evidentiary and paired testing (Marin protocol) applications. *Polygraph, 34,* 184-192.

Krapohl, D. J. (2006). Validated polygraph techniques. *Polygraph, 35(3),* 149-155.

Krapohl, D. J. (2010). Short report: A test of the ESS with two-question field cases. *Polygraph, 39,* 124-126.

Krapohl, D. J. & Cushman, B. (2006). Comparison of evidentiary and investigative decision rules: A replication. *Polygraph, 35(1),* 55-63.

Krapohl, D. J., Dutton, D. W. & Ryan, A. H. (2001). The rank order scoring system: Replication and extension with field data. *Polygraph, 30,* 172-181.

Krapohl, D. J. & McManus, B. (1999). An objective method for manually scoring polygraph data. *Polygraph, 28,* 209-222.

Krapohl, D. J. & Norris, W. F. (2000). An exploratory study of traditional and objective scoring systems with MGQT field cases. *Polygraph, 29,* 185-194.

Krapohl, D. J. & Ryan, A. H. (2001). A belated look at symptomatic questions. *Polygraph, 30,* 206-212.

Krapohl, D. J., Senter, S. M., & Stern, B. A. (2005). An exploration of methods for the analysis of multiple-issue Relevant/Irrelevant screening data. *Polygraph, 34*(1), 47-62.

Lykken, D. T. (1959). The GSR in the detection of guilt. *Journal of Applied Psychology, 43,* 385-388.

MacLaren, V. V. (2001). A quantitative review of the guilty knowledge test. *The Journal of Applied Psychology, 86,* 674-683.

Mangan, D. J., Armitage, T. E., & Adams, G. C. (2008). A field study on the validity of the Quadri-Track Zone Comparison Technique. *Physiology and Behavior,* 95, 17-23.

Mangan, D. J., Armitage, T. E., & Adams, G. C. (2008). Rebuttal to objection by Iacono and Verschuere et al. *Physiology & Behavior,* 95, 29-31.

Matte, J. A. (1980). *The Art and Science of the Polygraph Technique.* Springfield, IL: Charles C. Thomas, Publisher.

Matte, J. A. (1990). *Validation study on the polygraph Quadri-Zone Comparison Technique.* Research Abstract LD 01452, Vol. 1502, 1989, University Microfilm International (UMI), Ann Arbor, MI.

Matte, J. A. (1996). *Forensic Psychophysiology Using The Polygraph: Scientific Truth Verification – Lie Detection.* Williamsville, NY: J.A.M. Publications.

Matte, J. A. (2000). *Examination and Cross-Examination of Experts in Forensic Psychophysiology Using The Polygraph.* Williamsville, NY: J.A.M. Publications.

Matte, J. A. (2002). *2002 Supplement to Forensic Psychophysiology Using The Polygraph.* Williamsville, NY: J.A.M. Publications.

Matte, J. A. (2010). A field study of the Backster Zone Comparison Technique's Either Or Rule and scoring system versus two other scoring systems when relevant question elicits strong response. *European Polygraph,* 4, 2(12), 53-69.

Matte, J. A. (2010). Guiding principles and benchmarks for the conduct of validity studies of psychophysiological veracity examinations using the polygraph. *European Polygraph,* 4, 2(14), 173-198.

Matte, J. A. (2011). Psychological Aspects of the Quadri-Track Zone Comparison Technique and attendant benefits of its Inside-Track. *European Polygraph*, 5, 2(16), 41-60.

Matte, J. A. & Reuss, R. M. (1989). A field validation study of the Quadri-Zone Comparison `Technique. *Polygraph*, 18(4), 187-202.

Meiron, E., Krapohl, D. J., & Ashkenazi, T. (2008). An assessment of the Backster "Either-Or" Rule in polygraph scoring. *Polygraph*, 37, 240-249.

Mohamed, F. B., Faro, S. H., Gordon, N. J., Platek, S. M., Ahmad, H., & Williams, J. M. (2006). Brain mapping of deception and truth telling about an ecologically valid situation: functional MR imaging and polygraph investigation--initial experience. *Radiology, 238*, 679-88.

National Research Council (2003). *The Polygraph and Lie Detection*. Washington, D.C.: National Academy of Sciences.

Nelson, R. (In press 2012). Monte Carlo study of criterion validity of Backster You-Phase examinations. *Polygraph*.

Nelson, R. (In press 2012). Monte Carlo study of criterion validity of the Directed Lie Screening Test using the seven-position, three-position and Empirical Scoring Systems. *Polygraph*.

Nelson, R. (2011). Monte Carlo study of criterion validity for two-question zone comparison tests with the Empirical Scoring System, seven-position, and three-position scoring models.
Polygraph, 40, 146-156.

Nelson, R. & Blalock, B. (In press 2012). Extended analysis of Senter, Waller and Krapohl's AFMGQT examination data with the Empirical Scoring System and the Objective Scoring System, version 3. *Polygraph*,

Nelson, R., Blalock, B., & Handler, M. (2011). Criterion validity of the Empirical Scoring System and the Objective Scoring System, version 3 with the USAF Modified General Question Technique. *Polygraph*, 40, 172-179.

Nelson, R., Blalock, B., Oelrich, M., & Cushman, B. (2011). Reliability of the Empirical Scoring System with expert examiners. *Polygraph*, 40, 131-139. Nelson, R. & Handler, M. (2010). *Empirical Scoring System*. Lafayette Instrument Company.

Nelson, R. & Handler, M. (In press). Monte Carlo study of the United States Air Force Modified General Question Technique with two three and four questions. *Polygraph*.

Nelson, R., Handler, M., Adams, G., & Backster, C. (In press 2012). Survey of reliability and criterion validity of Backster numerical scores of You-Phase exams from confirmed field investigations. *Polygraph*.

Nelson, R., Handler, M., Blalock, B., & Cushman, B. (In press 2012). Blind scoring of confirmed federal You-Phase examinations by experienced and inexperienced examiners: Criterion validity with the Empirical Scoring System and the seven-position model. *Polygraph*.

Nelson, R., Handler, M., Blalock, B., & Hernández, N. (In press 2012). Replication and extension study of Directed Lie Screening Tests: Criterion validity with the seven- and three-position models and the Empirical Scoring System. *Polygraph*.

Nelson, R., Handler, M., & Morgan, C. (In press 2012). Criterion validity of the Directed Lie Screening Test and the Empirical Scoring System with inexperienced examiners and non-naïve examinees in a laboratory setting. *Polygraph*.

Nelson, R., Handler, M., Morgan, C., & O'Burke, P. (In press 2012). Criterion validity of the United States Air Force Modified General Question Technique and Iraqi scorers. *Polygraph*.

Nelson, R., Handler, M., & Senter, S. (In press 2012). Monte Carlo study of criterion validity of the Directed Lie Screening Test using the Empirical Scoring System and the Objective Scoring System version 3. *Polygraph*.

Nelson, R., Handler, M., Shaw, P., Gougler, M., Blalock, B., Russell, C., Cushman, B., & Oelrich, M. (2011). Using the Empirical Scoring System. *Polygraph*, 40(2), 67-78.

Nelson, R. & Krapohl, D. (2011). Criterion validity of the Empirical Scoring System with experienced examiners: Comparison with the seven-position evidentiary model using the Federal Zone Comparison Technique. *Polygraph*, 40, 79-85.

Nelson, R., Krapohl, D., & Handler, M. (2008). Brute force comparison: A Monte Carlo study of the Objective Scoring System version 3 (OSS-3) and human polygraph scorers. *Polygraph*, 37, 185-215.

Office of Technology Assessment (1983). The validity of polygraph testing: A research review and evaluation. Washington, D.C.: U.S. Congress, Office of Technology Assessment.

Patrick, C. J. & Iacono, W. G. (1989). Psychopathy, threat and polygraph test accuracy. *Journal of Applied Psychology*, 74, 347-355.

Patrick, C. J. & Iacono, W. G. (1991). Validity of the control question polygraph test: The problem of sampling bias. *Journal of Applied Psychology*, 76, 229-238.

Podlesny, J. A. & Raskin, D. C. (1978). Effectiveness of techniques and physiological measures in the detection of deception. *Psychophysiology*, 15, 344-359.

Podlesny, J., Raskin, D., & Barland, G. (1976). *Effectiveness of Techniques and Physiological Measures in the Detection of Deception*. Report No. 76-5, Contract 75-N1-99-001 LEAA (available through Department of Psychology, University of Utah, Salt Lake City).

Podlesny, J. A. & Truslow, C. M. (1993). Validity of an expanded-issue (modified general question) polygraph technique in a simulated distributed-crime-roles context. *Journal of Applied Psychology*, 78, 788-797.

Pollina, D. A., Dollins, A. B., Senter, S. M., Krapohl, D. J. & Ryan, A. H. (2004). Comparison of polygraph data obtained from individuals involved in mock crimes and actual criminal investigations. *Journal of applied psychology*, 89, 1099-105.

Raskin, D. C. & Hare, R. D. (1978). Psychopathy and detection of deception in a prison population. *Psychophysiology*, 15, 126-136.

Raskin, D. C. & Honts, C. R. (2002). Handbook of polygraph testing. In M. Kleiner (Ed.), *Handbook of Polygraph Testing*. San Diego: Academic Press.

Raskin, D. C. & Podlesny, J. A. (1979). Truth and deception: A reply to Lykken. *Psychological Bulletin*, 86, 54-59.

Reid, J. E. (1947). A revised questioning technique in lie detection tests. *Journal of Criminal Law and Criminology*, 37, 542-547. Reprinted in *Polygraph 11*, 17-21.

Reid, J. E. & Inbau, F. E. (1977). *Truth and deception: The polygraph ('lie detector') technique* (2nd ed). Baltimore, MD: Williams & Wilkins.

Research Division Staff (1995a). *A comparison of psychophysiological detection of deception accuracy rates obtained using the counterintelligence scope Polygraph and the test for espionage and sabotage question formats.* DTIC AD Number A319333. Department of Defense Polygraph Institute. Fort Jackson, SC. Reprinted in *Polygraph, 26*(2), 79-106.

Research Division Staff (1995b). *Psychophysiological detection of deception accuracy rates obtained using the test for espionage and sabotage.* DTIC AD Number A330774. Department of Defense Polygraph Institute. Fort Jackson, SC. Reprinted in *Polygraph, 27*(3), 171-180.

Research Division Staff (2001). *Test of a mock theft scenario for use in the Psychophysiological Detection of Deception: IV.* Report No. DoDPI00-R-0002. Department of Defense Polygraph Institute. Reprinted in *Polygraph 30*(4) 244-253.

Rovner, L. I. (1986). Accuracy of physiological detection of deception for subjects with prior knowledge. *Polygraph, 15(1),* 1-39.

Senter, S. M. (2003). Modified general question test decision rule exploration. *Polygraph, 32,* 251-263.

Senter, S. M. & Dollins, A. B. (2002). *New Decision Rule Development: Exploration of a two-stage approach.* Report number DoDPI00-R-0001. Department of Defense Polygraph Institute Research Division, Fort Jackson, SC. Reprinted in *Polygraph 37,* 149-164.

Senter, S. & Dollins, A. B. (2004). Comparison of question series and decision rules: A replication. *Polygraph, 33,* 223-233.

Senter, S. M. & Dollins, A. B. (2008). Optimal decision rules for evaluating psychophysiological detection of deception data: an exploration. *Polygraph, 37*(2), 112-124.

Senter, S., Waller, J., & Krapohl, D. (2008). Air Force Modified General Question Test validation study. *Polygraph, 37*(3), 174-184.

Senter, S., Weatherman, D., Krapohl, D., & Horvath, F. (2010). Psychological set or differential salience: A proposal for reconciling theory and terminology in polygraph testing. Polygraph, 39 (2), 109-117.

Shurany, T. (2011). Polygraph verification test. *European Polygraph*, 5, 2(16), 61-70.

Shurany, T. & Chaves, F. (2010). Integrated Zone Comparison Technique and ASIT PolySuite algorithm: A field validity study. *European Polygraph*, 4(2), 71-80.

Shurany, T., Stein, E. & Brand, E. (2009). A Field Study on the Validity of the Quadri-Track Zone Comparison Technique. *European Polygraph*, 1, 5-24.

Slowik, S. M. & Buckley, J. P., III (1975). Relative accuracy of polygraph examiner diagnosis of respiration, blood pressure and GSR recordings. *Journal of Police Science and Administration, 3,* 305-309.

Van Herk, M. (1990). Numerical evaluation: Seven point scale +/-6 and possible alternatives: A discussion. *The Newsletter of the Canadian Association of Police Polygraphists, 7,* 28-47. Reprinted in *Polygraph, 20*(2), 70-79.

Verschuere, B., Meijer, E., & Merckelbach, H. (2008). The Quadri-Track Zone Comparison Technique: It's just not science. A critique to Mangan, Armitage, and Adams (2008). *Physiology and Behavior,* 1-2, 27-28.

Wicklander, D. E. & Hunter, F. L. (1975). The influence of auxiliary sources of information *in polygraph diagnosis.*

CHAPTER 8

FORMULATION, REVIEW, PRESENTATION, INTERPRETATION OF TEST QUESTIONS.
Review of the Error Question.

Page 255. Insert new paragraph:

When an examinee insists on giving an affirmative answer to the Fear of Error control question regarding the target issue, the examinee is reminded of the earlier declaration by the polygraphist, after listening to the examinee's version of the incident, of his *assumption* of the examinee's innocence until all of the charts have been collected, analyzed and scored for a determination of truth or deception. Hence the polygraphist now asks for the examinee to reciprocate with his *vote of confidence* in the accuracy of the polygraph instrument and the competency of the polygraphist until all of the charts have been collected and analyzed. This creates a conflict in that the examinee does not want to appear uncooperative which he is informed is expected of a deceptive examinee, hence will provide the desired negative answer.

CHAPTER 9

THE NUMERICAL APPROACH AND ZONE COMPARISON TESTS: METHODOLOGY CAPABLE OF ADDRESSING IDENTIFIED IMPEDING VARIABLES.

Page 260. Insert Summary of "Psychological Structure and Theoretical Concept of the Backster Zone Comparison Technique and the Quadri-Track Zone Comparison Technique" published in *Polygraph*, Vol. 36, Nr. 2: 84-90, 2007.

As the title of the article implies, the psychological structure and theoretical concept of the Backster and Quadri-Track Zone Comparison Techniques are fully described and discussed with a full explanation of the function of Backster's "Either-Or" rule and the role and importance of the non-current exclusive control questions that enable the aforesaid rule.   The article discusses the polygraph community's recent emphasis in combating the use of countermeasures, mental countermeasures in particular, which has resulted in some modifications to Zone Comparison Techniques that appear on the surface to address the mental countermeasure problem, but in fact these modifications create a significantly greater problem wherein the cure is worse than the disease. The article provides an understanding of the basic theory, principles and protocol related to the Backster and Quadri-Track Zone Comparison Techniques which should aid polygraphists in avoiding well-intentioned but misguided modifications to well-founded techniques or procedures that violate their established protocol.   This article should be required reading for all polygraphists who use the Backster or Quadri-Track Zone Comparison Technique.   For further details, visit www.mattepolygraph.com.

Page 263. Insert Summary of "Psychological Aspects of the Quadri-Track Zone Comparison Technique and Attendant Benefits of its Inside-Track" published in *European Polygraph*, Vol. 5, Nr. 3(17), 2011.

The Quadri-Track Zone Comparison Technique is a psychological test that *infers* deception or truthfulness to the target issue by the elimination of variables identified in Chapter 9, Forensic Psychophysiology Using The Polygraph (Matte 1996) that could have caused the autonomic responses other than a deliberate attempt at deception.   This thesis discusses those variables and how they are addressed by the various test questions within the Quadri-Track ZCT format.   The function of each of these test questions and their diagnostic value is discussed with supporting research studies that respond to some of the questions raised by B. Cushman and D. Krapohl in their presentation of technical questions at the 2010 APA seminar, which include the Sacrifice Relevant Question, the Symptomatic Questions and the Inside-Issue Questions. This thesis provides an in-depth explanation of the psychological aspects of the Quadri-Track Zone Comparison Technique. For further details. visit www.mattepolygraph.com.

Page 267. B2A which refers to *signal value*. Insert the following explanation:

Signal Value is the significance of stimulus for the examinee. Cognitive Awareness requires the examinee to differentiate between relevant and control questions. To the Guilty, the relevant question has greater signal value. To the Innocent, the control question has greater signal value. Anti-polygraph scientists attempt to discredit polygraph by claiming that external concept causes innocent people to respond to relevant question and be falsely accused. i.e. External "…this is the gun that murdered…" Internal "…this is the gun that I used to murder…" Conclusion: Polygraphist must make relevant and control questions equally (externally) significant to examinee. However, it must be said that control questions are structurally less intense than the relevant questions by virtue of the fact that they are separated from the relevant questions with time bars that removes them from the current period of the relevant questions dealing with the target issue. However, due to the construct of the control questions which embrace a substantial time period that is designed to elicit mental effort/that research has shown to produce an autonomic response that does not require a lie from the individual, it should elicit the innocent examinee's psychological set even though it is structurally less intense than the relevant questions which have greater signal value to the guilty examinee. Hence, the control and relevant questions should be presented in a manner that is equally significant to the examinee who must choose which of these questions offers the greatest threat to his well-being and this is determined from the physiological recording collected from the examinee.

Page 273. Add the following regarding mental effort and Anger:

Citation: Stephan Bongard, Jutta S. Pfeiffer, Mustafa Al'Absi, Volker Hodapp, and Gabi Linnenkemper (1997). Cardiovascular responses during effortful active coping and acute experience of anger in women. Psychophysiology, 34, 459-466, Cambridge University Press. The study revealed that active coping (mental arithmetic) elevated cardiovascular activity including increase in heart rate, systolic and diastolic blood pressure. The study further revealed that anger provocation also elevated cardiovascular activity, particularly the heart rate and diastolic blood pressure responses.

CHAPTER 11

THE NUMERICAL APPROACH TO PSYCHOPHYSIOLOGICAL VERACITY EXAMINATIONS.

Page 323. Insert at end of paragraph titled "Psychological Set" the following reference:

(Matte, J. A., & Grove, R. N., 2001).

Page 323. Insert after the paragraph titled "Psychological Set" the following paragraph:

In 1960, Cleve Backster used the term *psychological set* to explain anti-climax dampening, the basis for his Zone Comparison Technique. In an article authored by James Allan Matte and Robert Nelson Grove, titled "Psychological Set: Its Origin, Theory and Application" published in Polygraph, Volume 30, Nr. 3, 2001, the term psychological set was attributed to Backster who believed that he had acquired the term from a Psychology and Life textbook by Floyd L. Ruch published in 1948. However, subsequent research disclosed that the date of the aforesaid titled textbook was in fact 1953 which accurately reflected Backster's quote of Ruch's explanation of the selective attention process from which Backster developed the term *Psychological Set*.

An attempt was made (Handler & Nelson, 2007) to replace *Psychological Set* with the term *Salience* to be compatible with terminology used in other sciences. The authors described *salience* by quoting Wikipedia as "state or quality of standing out relative to neighboring items. *Salience* is considered to be a key attentional mechanism that facilitates learning and survival by enabling organisms to focus their limited perceptual and cognitive resources on the most pertinent subset of available sensory data." The Oxford Dictionary of Psychology defines salience as "The prominence, conspicuousness, or striking quality of a stimulus." (Colman, 2001). Handler & Nelson quoted C. Honts (2000) stating "The notion of 'psychological set' is a contrivance of the polygraph profession and has received little scientific validation. Moreover, 'psychological set' is not a term that is currently used much in mainstream psychological science." Handler & Nelson argue that laboratory studies on polygraph testing invite arousal from a number of sources including "guilt, fear, excitement or content complexity (Vrij, 2000). Thus Backster's definition of Psychological Set which they limit to his description that encompasses a person's fears, anxieties and apprehensions, fails to incorporate other sources of arousal such as guilt, excitement or content complexity. Some would argue that the Directed Lie Control Question fails to produce fear, hence cannot be explained by Psychological Set. This argument is quickly set aside by published studies (Matte, 1998; Matte, Reuss, 1999), the former providing the following analysis:

"The Directed Lie Control Question (DLCQ) may be perceived by the guilty examinee as a relevant exemplar of deception question, inasmuch as the guilty examine is led to believe or perceives that the DLCQ will provide the polygraphist with a physiological fingerprint of his/her lie pattern which will be compared with his/her response to the neighboring relevant test question. Even the subtle presentation of the DLCQ must raise the guilty examinee's suspicion that the acquisition of his/her known lie pattern is for the purpose of comparison with his/her physiological pattern to the relevant test questions. Hence the DLCQ may well be perceived by the guilty examinee as a deception exemplar question. The guilty examinee thus is likely to believe that without the DLCQ, identification of a lie to the relevant test question is significantly reduced or improbable. The focus of the guilty examinee will normally be on the test question that offers him/her the greatest threat to his/her immediate security. The DLCQ offers a new and immediate competing threat to the guilty examinee that may be equal or even greater than the threat offered by the relevant question because of its perceived capacity to identify his/her lie to the relevant question. The DLCQ further invites the guilty examinee to employ countermeasures to defeat the perceived purpose of the DLCQ which in turn elicits greater mental exercise and selective attention (psychological set) from the guilty examinee. In short, the DLCQ offers the guilty examinee a new, and immediate competing threat which may be equal or greater than that offered by the expected relevant test questions."

Others would argue that the Concealed Information Test also known as the Guilty Knowledge Test lacks the element of fear inasmuch as it is a recognition test rather than a lie test (Lykken, 1981, 1998), but fail to realize that the test questions are necessarily reviewed with the examinee prior to the administration of the test, hence the guilty examinee's *psychological set* will be focused on the presentation of the key item which will produce a *salient* response.

However, Backster's definition of Psychological Set was in the context of real-life cases wherein fear of the consequences and fear of detection are the primary cause for arousal or stimuli (Amsel, 1997; Matte, Reuss, 2009). Nevertheless, *Psychological Set* is applicable and can be used by simply defining it as "the examinee will focus on those test questions within a polygraph test format that hold the greatest *threat* or *interest* to the examinee's immediate or consequential well-being." Actually the term *salience* can be used in concert with *psychological set,* i.e. the examinee's psychological set was focused on those test questions that held the greatest salience.

Polygraph science now known as forensic psychophysiology has been around for more than half a century and thus need not apologize for its development and use of terminology that best describes theoretical concepts unique to its discipline. Nate Gordon, Director of the Academy for Scientific Investigative Training once said "I am sure many, many great minds had observed that when an apple breaks its connection with the tree, it invariably falls straight down to the ground; it took Newton to identify this 'force' and name it gravity. Backster should have that same honor and respect regarding 'psychological set.'"

An excellent illustration of *Psychological Set* and *Anti-Climax Dampening* is provided by an experiment conducted by Raul Hernandez-Peon, Harald Scherrer and Michel Jouvet (1956) that involved modification of electric activity in cochlear nucleus during *attention* in unanesthetized cats which revealed that "during presentation of visual stimuli (two mice in a closed bottle), the auditory responses in the cochlear nucleus were greatly reduced in comparison with the control responses; they were practically abolished as long as the visual stimuli elicited behavioral evidence of attention. When the mice were removed, the auditory responses returned to the same order of magnitude as the initial controls. An olfactory stimulus that attracted the animal's attention produced a similar blocking effect." This research and others (French, Verzeano and Magoun, 1953; Hagbarth and Kerr, 1954; Adrian, 1954;) support the theory of *Psychological Set* in PV examinations using the polygraph (Backster, 1974; Matte & Grove, 2001), also known as Selective Attention, which is an adaptive psychophysiological response to fears, anxieties, and apprehensions with a selective focus on the particular issue or situation which presents the greatest threat to the legitimate security of the examinee while filtering out lesser threats. (Matte, 1996). This phenomenon explains the reason for the primary dominating stimulus "Fear" of consequences (Amsel, 1997) inhibiting secondary stimuli such as guilt[6] and lie avoidance conflict, as well as orienting responses normally found in laboratory studies such as the promise of reward and increased self-esteem.

The following three figures by Shirley Sturm derived from text of study by Hernandez-Peon, Scherrer, and Jouvet (1956), illustrate the neurological pathway and results of the Hernandez-Peon, et al's experiment.

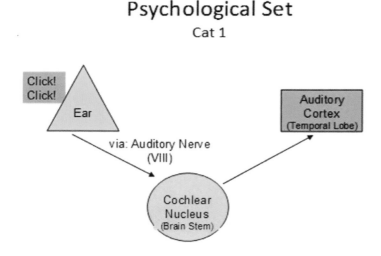

Hernandez-Peon, Scherrer, & Jouvet (1956)

---

6 Raskin, et al (1978) conducted a field study of PV examinations using the polygraph on convicted felons diagnosed psychopathic who lack a sense of guilt. Not a single guilty subject was able to produce a truthful result. In fact, there were indications that psychopaths may be somewhat easier to detect using PV examinations. However, psychopathic subjects are equally "fearful" of consequences as non-psychopaths.

Psychological Set

Cat 2

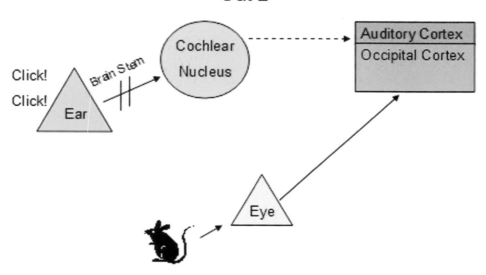

Hernandez-Peon, Scherrer, & Jouvet (1956)

Psychological Set

Cat 3

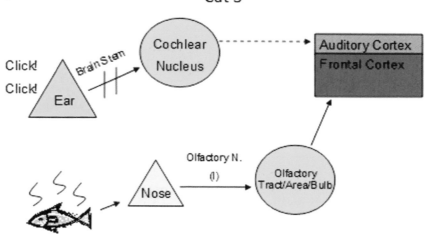

Hernandez-Peon, Scherrer, & Jouvet (1956)

Page 330. Add following diagram depicting psychological structure and format of the Quadri-Track Zone Comparison Technique.

Matte Quadri-Track Zone Comparison Technique

Applicable Testing Situation	TECHNIQUE FAMILY
• For single issue tests only	Zone Comparison Test
	AUTHOR
	James Allan Matte

Basic Format

- ☐ 14. Neutral Irrelevant
- ▢ 39. Preparatory/Sacrifice Relevant
- ■ 25. Symptomatic
- ☐ 46. Non-Current Exclusive Control
- ▨ 33. Relevant
- ☐ 47. Non-Current Exclusive Control
- ▨ 35. Relevant
- ▢ 23. Fear of Error Control
- ▢ 24. Hope of Error Relevant
- ■ 26. Symptomatic

Standard Rules

- **Applied as Single issue test.**
- **Minimum of two charts for decision of truth/deception.**
- **Rotate relevant questions with each chart.**
- **Acquire feedback in review of questions 23 and 24**
- **Always include suffix "regarding target issue" in question 23 and 24.**

Chart Evaluation & Scoring

- **There are three spots (Tracks) to score (33, 35, 24)**
- **Relevants are compared with preceding control questions (within same track).**
- **DI = Average of -5 or less (-6, -7, etc) per chart.**
- **NDI = Average of +3 or more (+4, +5, etc) per chart.**
- **Evaluation according to 7 position scale rules.**
- **Application of "Dual-Equal Strong Reaction" Rule.**

Respiration – EDA – Cardio scoring Rules

2:1 ratio equals ± 1

3:1 ratio equals ± 2

4:1 ratio equals ± 3

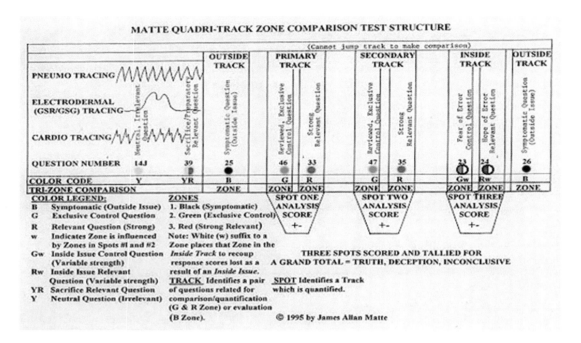

Page 332. Insert Summary of published field study "Effect of Habituation to Least Threatening Zone Questions on the Most Threatening Zone Comparison Questions in Psychophysiological Veracity Examinations." *European Polygraph,* Vol. 5, Nr. 2(16), 2011.

This study examines the raw data of a field study (Matte-Reuss, 1989) comprising 122 confirmed real-life cases that used the Quadri-Track Zone Comparison Technique where the scores for each chart collected were recorded and reported. The data for the deceptive cases indicated a lack of habituation to the relevant test question throughout the collection of the 4 charts with apparent habituation to the neighboring control questions. The data for the truthful cases indicated a lack of habituation of the control questions with apparent habituation to the neighboring relevant questions. The implication from this data is that polygraphists should be receptive to the collection of an additional chart beyond the customary three-charts when confronted with an inconclusive result, especially when using a single-issue polygraph technique that employs an increasing score threshold with each chart collected rather than a fixed score threshold that does not increase with each chart collected. Further details available at www.mattepolygraph.com.

Page 333. Insert Summary of published field study "Minimum Number of Polygraph Charts Required to Reach a Conclusion of Truth or Deception in Psychophysiological Veracity Examinations." *European Polygraph,* Vol. 5, Nr. 3(17), 2011.

This study examined the raw data of three field studies (Matte-Reuss, 1989; Mangan, Armitage, Adams, 2008; Shurany, Stein, Brand, 2009) to determine the minimum number of polygraph charts that provide an accurate and valid determination of truth and deception. The results of this study indicate that a minimum of two polygraph charts can provide an accurate and valid result of truth or deception. Interestingly, the American Society for Testing and Materials (ASTM) and the American Polygraph Association (APA) standards of practice both require a sufficient number of charts for evaluation in compliance with the technique used. At the present time, the Federal, Utah and Integrated Zone Comparison Techniques require a minimum of three polygraph charts to be collected while the Backster Zone Comparison Technique, the Quadri-Track Zone Comparison Technique and the Reid Technique require a minimum of two polygraph charts to be collected to reach a determination of truth or deception. Further details available at www.mattepolygraph.com.

Page 367. Insert revised version of the Air Force Modified General Question Test (AFMGQT), reported in *Polygraph*, Vol. 37, Nr. 3, 2008. In aforesaid journal, a laboratory validation study was conducted which produced the following results: 91.7 % accuracy in the identification of the Truthful participants, 75.8% accuracy for Deceptive participants, and 1.5% inconclusive.

Note: In order for a polygraph technique to be considered Validated, it must have been tested in two separate, independent studies (preferably field studies) published in peer-reviewed journals.

I1.   Irrelevant Question.
I2.   Irrelevant Question.
SR.   Sacrifice Relevant Question.
C1   Non-Exclusive Control Question.
R1   Relevant Question
C2   Non-Exclusive Control Question
R2   Relevant Question
C3   Non-Exclusive Control Question.

Page 368. The Utah Control Question Test as reported in *Polygraph*, Vol. 38, Nr. 1: 15-33 (2009, consists of a Three-Relevant Question Format and a Four-Relevant Question Format.

The Utah CQT Three-Relevant Question Format can be used as a single-issue examination or a multiple-facet examination. The following is an example of the single-issue format:
Introductory (Symptomatic)

Sacrifice Relevant
Neutral
Comparison (exclusive)
Relevant
Neutral
Comparison (exclusive)

Relevant
Neutral
Comparison (exclusive)
Relevant

The following is an example of the Four-Relevant Question Format:

Introductory (Symptomatic)
Sacrifice Relevant
Neutral
Comparison (exclusive)
Relevant
Relevant
Comparison (exclusive)
Neutral (optional)
Relevant
Relevant
Comparison (exclusive
Neutral

The Utah CQT allows the polygraphist to rotate the neutral, comparison and relevant questions during the second and subsequent presentation of test questions during the collection of the physiological data. It also allows the review and discussion of the control and relevant test questions with the examinee in between the collection of the polygraph charts.

Page 370. Insert the following references:

Adrian, E. D. (1954). *Brain Mechanism and Consciousness*, J. F. Delafresnaye, Ed. Oxford: Blackwell, p. 238.

Amsel, T. T. (1997). Fear of Consequences and Motivation as Influencing Factors on Psychophysiological Detection of Deception. *Polygraph*, 26(4): 255-267.

Bongard, S., Pfeiffer, J. S., Al'Absi, M., Hodapp, V., & Linnenkemper, G. (1997). Cardiovascular responses during effortful active coping and acute experience of anger in women. *Psychophysiology*: 34, 429-466.

Colman, A. L. (2001). *The Oxford Dictionary of Psychology*. New York, NY: Oxford University Press.

French, J. D., Verzeano, M., Magoun, H. W. (1953. *Arch.* Neutol. Psychiat. 69, 505.

Hagbarth, K. E., & Kerr, D. I. B. (1954). *Journal of Neurophysiology*, 17, 295.

Handler, M., & Nelson, R. (2007). Polygraph Terms for the 21st Century. *Polygraph*, 36(3): 157-164.

Hernandez-Peon, R., Scherrer, H., Jouvet, M. (24 Feb 1956). Modification of Electric Activity in Cochlear Nucleus during "Attention: in Unanesthetized Cats. *Science*, Vol. 25, P. 351-352.

Honts, C. R. (2000). A Brief Note on the Misleading and Inaccurate: A Rejoinder to Matte (2000) with Critical Comments on Matte and Reuss (1999). *Polygraph*, 29(4): 321-325.

Matte, J. A., & Grove, R. N. (2001). Psychological Set: Its Origin, Theory and Application. *Polygraph,* Vol. 30, Nr. 3: 196-202.

Matte, J. A., (2010). Guiding Principles and Benchmarks for the Conduct of Validity Studies of Psychophysiological Veracity Examinations Using the Polygraph. *European Polygraph*, Vol. 4, Nr. 4(14), P. 173-198.

Vrij, A.(2000). *Detecting Lies and Deceit.* Chichester, England: John Wiley & Sons.

CHAPTER 23

LEGAL ASPECTS OF THE PSYCHOPHYSIOLOGICAL VERACITY EXAMINATION

Page 564. Insert as separate paragraph under the paragraph titled Criteria for General Acceptance and Published Validation:

LEGAL ADMISSIBILITY OF POLYGRAPH TEST RESULTS

The results of polygraph tests known as psychophysiological veracity (PV) examinations are admissible in a court of law if the particular polygraph technique used in the proffered PV examination meets the *Daubert* standard to the satisfaction of the presiding judge who acts as the gatekeeper of the Federal Rules of Evidence. As of 1 May 2009, 18 states have adopted the Daubert standard of admissibility and the judicial door is open for other states to follow.

The federal courts and most state courts that adopted the *Frye* standard have since then, with rare exceptions except for the State of New Mexico, denied admissibility of psychophysiological veracity (PV) examination (polygraph) results in court. 19 States admit results of PV examinations under stipulation by the parties. The State of New Mexico permits the introduction of polygraph results into evidence without a stipulation, under strict evidentiary rules.

It was not until 1993 that the U.S. Supreme Court revisited the *Frye* standard in *Daubert v. Merrell Dow Pharmaceuticals, Inc.,* 113 S.Ct 2786, 125 L.E.2d 469, 509 U.S. (1993), and issued another landmark decision directly affecting the admissibility of expert testimony, including PV examinations results.

Under the standard enunciated by the United States Supreme Court in *Daubert*, which superseded the *Frye* standard of "general acceptance" test, the court ruled that:

> the trial judge, pursuant to Rule 104(a), must make a preliminary assessment of whether the testimony's underlying reasoning or methodology is scientifically valid and properly can be applied to the facts at issue. Many considerations will bear on the inquiry, including whether the theory or technique in question can be (and has been) tested, whether it has been subject to peer review and publication, its known or potential error rate, and the existence and maintenance of standards controlling its operation, and whether it has attracted widespread acceptance within a relevant scientific community.

The court also stated:

> Cross-examination, presentation of contrary evidence, and careful instruction on the burden of proof, rather than wholesale exclusion under an uncompromising "general acceptance" standard, is the appropriate means by which evidence based on valid principles may be challenged.

The Supreme Court in Daubert summarized that:

> "general acceptance" is not a necessary precondition to the admissibility of scientific evidence under the federal Rules of Evidence, but the rules of Evidence – especially Rule 702 – do assign to the trial judge the task of ensuring that an expert's testimony both rests on a reliable foundation and is relevant to the task at hand. Pertinent evidence based on scientifically valid principles will satisfy those demands.

Therefore lawyers must insure that the polygraphist they hire has been formally trained in a polygraph technique that has been validated by published peer-reviewed research.

Validation requires at least two independent research studies published in peer-reviewed journals. The preference is for field studies rather than laboratory studies, inasmuch as laboratory studies cannot generalize their results to real-world situations. For a detailed explanation of the value of field versus laboratory studies of polygraph techniques, please read *"Guiding Principles and Benchmarks for the Conduct of Validation Studies on Psychophysiological Veracity Examinations Using The Polygraph"* published in *European Polygraph*, Vol. 4, Nr. 4(14), 2010. Full text available at www.mattepolygraph.com.

As can be seen in the Validated Polygraph Techniques listed in this Supplement, some polygraph techniques have been validated by field studies, some by laboratory studies, and some by a combination of both types of studies.

Psychophysiological Veracity Examinations using the polygraph can be used in criminal and civil cases such Plea Bargaining, Motions to Suppress Evidence, Settlements, Sentencing, Supporting Evidence, Parole and Probation, Arbitration, and Civil Actions. Since the advent of the Daubert decision there has been an increased willingness to accept polygraph results into evidence by court judges without jury, and administrative and post-trial hearings.

The defense attorney who intends to introduce PV examination results as evidence in a court of law on behalf of his or her client must realize that the supersedence of the *Frye* standard in favor of the Federal Rules of Evidence by *William Daubert v. Merrill Dow Pharmaceuticals* is merely an invitation for forensic psychophysiology to show that it is worthy of acceptance by the court. It therefore behooves the attorney who has such an aspiration to present to the court a most competent and well-prepared polygraphist   formally trained in a validated polygraph technique, whose expert testimony is preferably preceded by the scientific testimony of a foundation expert, and whose results (of the PV examination) are confirmed by a qualified quality control reviewer.

The following case laws pertaining to the admissibility of polygraph results in court govern the countries of Canada, Belgium, Japan and England.

CANADA

Polygraph results not admissible as evidence in criminal courts, per R. V. Beland and Phillips (1987) 2 S.C.R. 398 Docket: 18856, which holds that polygraph results should not supersede the role of the jury to decide the credibility of a defendant or witness. However, results of polygraph examinations are admissible in civil and labor courts at the discretion of the judge. The following are court citations wherein polygraph results were admitted as evidence.

Lamothe v. General Accident Insurance Company, Court of Quebec, REJB 1998-10865.

Hotel Central Victoriaville Inc. V. Reliance Insurance Company, Quebec Court of Appeal, REJB 1998-06721.

Vetements Paul Allaire Inc. v. La Citadelle, compagnie d'assurances generales, Quebec Superior Court, REJB 2000-19632.

Fraternity des Policiers et Policieres de Longueuil, Inc. v. Ville de Longueuil, Province de Quebec, Canada, Quebec Labour Court. Griefs Nos: 98-05 et 99-03, 30 March 2001. Admitted polygraph evidence over objections.

BELGIUM

The Supreme Court on 15 February 2006, afforded polygraph results judicial notice of acceptance with certain requirements that assure the reliability of the test and protect the rights of the defendant/examinee.

Supreme Court of Belgium, February, 15th 2006. .05.1583.F/1, Nb P.05.1583.F M.F.J.F., accused, Plaintiff in appeal before the Supreme Court,

With Marc Kauten and Nathalie Lequeux, counsels at the Bar Association of Arlon,

Against S.N., D.J.L., D.M., E.M.M. Plaintififs claiming damages.

Supreme Court Proceedings: The appeal to the Supreme Court refers to an arrest of October, 27th 2005 by the Court of Appeal in Liège, Grand Jury.

The Supreme Court stated that "Even if these conclusions are an indication which directed the investigation and justified some investigation duties during the preliminary investigation, the conclusions of a polygraph test are left to the judge's appreciation, who in fact decides to follow them or not in order to measure the credibility he particularly gives to the interview. The judicial expert is skilled because of his knowledge and is appointed by the judge (he is not his proxy) in order to give him independently and impartially a technical opinion in view of the judge's mission. He gives his conclusions only after solemn oath of reporting in all honesty, honour and accuracy."

JAPAN

21 April 1982, Tokyo High Court. A written expert opinion of polygraph examination was admitted as evidence. The Polygraphist had used both Concealed Information Test (CIT) and the Control Question Technique (CQT). The judge decided that the result of the CIT was reliable enough. The CQT result was questioned not because the CQT method itself was unreliable, but because the questionnaire used in this case was not in standard format.

25 October 1989. Urawa District Court. The defendant demanded the conduct of polygraph examinations as to who was lying, he or the interrogator. His application was rejected because of two reasons. (a) the CIT, called "The peak of tension test) in the main text of the judgement, was inapplicable in that situation, and (b) the CQT was unreliable and not at all admissible.

Source for above information: Yukihisa Yokoi, Polygraphist , Aichi Pref. Police.

ENGLAND

The current legal position, with respect to the second *Bonython* requirement, is that, for expert evidence to be admissible in England and Wales, it must be "sufficiently well-established to pass the ordinary tests of relevance and reliability".2

That is to say, the expert witness's evidence must be sufficiently reliable to be fit for a jury to consider.
Convicted sex offenders on probation are required by law to submit to periodic polygraph examinations as a condition of their probation.

Page 595. Change that paragraph after Table 5 that starts with "A 41-Illustrations presentation" to read as follows:

A 50-illustrations presentation that includes the above five tables plus four figures illustrating a comparative analysis of polygraph with other screening and diagnostic tools in medicine and psychology. Hard copy and compact disk available at www.mattepolygraph.com.

Page 593. Add Part V – EXPERT ENGAGEMENT AGREEMENT.

The Expert Engagement Agreement set forth below includes the services of the polygraph expert in the conduct of a psychophysiological veracity (PV) examination, a quality control review (QCR), and testifying in a judicial proceeding. This expert engagement agreement should be filed in MS Word "Read Only" format that will serve as a template which will permit the deletion of those sections of the agreement that are not pertinent to the services requested by the lawyer/law firm. In addition to the agreement setting the terms and conditions under which the requested services will be rendered, it will insure that the polygraph expert will be adequately compensated in the event that upon being hired after executing the usual confidentiality agreement (Kovel Letter) his services are never used but the expert is effectively prevented from being hired by opposing counsel.

EXPERT ENGAGEMENT AGREEMENT

CASE RE: _____

THIS AGREEMENT, made by and between James Allan Matte, Polygraph Consultant/Expert at Matte Polygraph Service, Inc., (the consultant/expert) and _____Attorney at Law and the Law Firm of_____(lawyer/law firm).

It is hereby agreed by the above parties that in consideration for James Allan Matte's services as a polygraph consultant and expert, he will be compensated for the services described below in the amounts indicated.

It is understood by all parties that the consultant and expert service provided herein is (not) in the nature of privileged communication between attorney-client-expert.

POLYGRAPH EXAMINATION: A psychophysiological veracity (PV) examination using the polygraph will be administered to _____

on (date)_____ for the lawyer/law firm of _____.

The PV examination will be conducted at the office of Matte Polygraph Service, Inc., 43 Brookside, Williamsville, New York. A written report of the results of aforesaid PV examination will be provided to the aforementioned attorney/law firm within 36 hours of completion of examination. The lawyer/law firm will be responsible for providing the polygraph expert with all documents related to the issue to be tested including any previous polygraph tests administered to the client/examinee, any written statements made by, for and against the client/examinee, any investigative, psychiatric, medical reports pertaining to the client/examinee and other information deemed necessary by the polygraph expert in the conduct of his examination.

QUALITY CONTROL REVIEW (QCR): Includes review and analysis of all documents including polygraph charts and video/audio recording related to the polygraph examination administered to_____ on (date)_____.

All documents requested by the above polygraph consultant/expert that are required for the conduct of the QCR as determined by aforesaid expert will be provided by the lawyer/law firm for the conduct of the QCR. A verbal and written report of the expert's findings will be provided to the lawyer/law firm after full payment for this service has been made.

EXPERT TESTIMONY: It is understood that the expert will not testify as to the results of his Quality Control Review nor lay the foundation for its admissibility in court unless the results of his QCR are favorable to the lawyer/law firm's case. The exception is when the QCR and Expert Testimony regarding its findings are not covered under the privilege and the expert is subpoenaed or ordered by a court to testify.

The expert testimony requires and includes case preparation and a thorough review of the expert's testimony with the lawyer/law firm at least 36 hours prior to the expert's scheduled testimony.

Required Documents: All documents provided to the Quality Control Reviewer including copy of polygraph charts in compliance with the requirements of Appendix C, *Examination & Cross-Examination of Experts in Forensic Psychophysiology Using The Polygraph.*

By this agreement/contract, the lawyer/law firm is hereby informed that the Court and opposing counsel may request a copy of the polygraph charts and the video or audio recording for their independent review. It is herewith agreed that it is the responsibility of the lawyer/law firm to acquire such copies from the original polygraphist for availability to the court and opposing counsel.

The lawyer/law firm agrees to acquire or purchase the following items that will be required by the expert in laying the foundation for his expert testimony. These items may be purchased directly from J.A.M. Publications as a total package for $350.00 plus $30.00 for Priority shipping/handling. If lawyer/law firm is located in New York State, an 8.75 percent sales tax must be added to the cost of the aforesaid package.

1. Textbook (for the lawyer/law firm) titled *"Examination and Cross-Examination of Experts in Forensic Psychophysiology Using The Polygraph"* by James Allan Matte, 1996. ISBN: 0-9655794-25, published by J.A.M. Publications, Williamsville, NY 14221.

2. One copy of CD-ROM, PowerPoint Presentation: *Illustrations for Use in Laying the Foundation for the Admissibility of the Results of PV Examinations Using the Polygraph.* 2003-2005. ISBN: 0-9655794-41, published by J.A.M. Publications, Williamsville, NY. This is for use by the expert in a PowerPoint presentation to the court which is subsequently surrendered to the lawyer/law firm for his file.

3. Four copies of Booklet: *Illustrations for Use in Laying the Foundation for the Admissibility of the Results of PV Examinations Using the Polygraph.* 2003-2005. ISBN: 0-9655794-5X, published by J.A.M. Publications, Williamsville, NY. One copy is provided to the Court Judge, one copy is entered as an evidentiary exhibit, one copy is given to the opposing counsel and one copy is for the lawyer/law firm.

Payment of Retainer Fee: A non-refundable retainer fee of $1500.00 plus New York State Sales Tax of 8.75% ($131.25) will be paid to Matte Polygraph Service, Inc.,(MPSI) prior to the signing of a Kovel Letter or other instrument binding the polygraph expert to a confidentiality agreement. This retainer fee is levied in case of cancellation of services by the lawyer/law firm, or failure of the lawyer/law firm to employ the services contained in this agreement within 30 days of the signing of this agreement. Failure of the client/examinee to report to the office of Matte Polygraph Service, Inc., at the agreed time and date for the PV examination will result in forfeiture of the retainer fee or fee for the PV examination, whichever is available to MPSI. Rescheduling of the PV examination will require additional fee of $1000.00 plus the NYS Sales Tax of 8.75% ($87.50).

Payment for PV Examination: The fee for the conduct of above PV examination in the amount of $1500./00 plus New York State Sales Tax of 8.75% ($131.25) will be paid to Matte Polygraph Service, Inc., by the lawyer/law firm by check drawn on the attorney or law firm's account before any work is performed by the aforementioned polygraph expert.

Payment for QCR Services: The entire fee for above QCR in the amount of $1800.00 plus New York State Sales Tax of $157.50 (8.75%) will be paid by the lawyer/law firm by check drawn on the attorney or law firm's account before any work is performed by the aforementioned polygraph consultant/expert. The entire Quality Control Review will be performed by the polygraph consultant/expert at his place of business unless otherwise agreed upon by the consultant/expert.

Payment for Court Testimony: Court testimony within Erie and Niagara County, State of New York is $3000.00 for the first day and $2500.00 each day thereafter, regardless of the amount of time per day spent testifying. Court testimony outside of Erie and Niagara County but within two-hour drive from Buffalo, New York is $3500.00 for the first day and $2500.00 each day thereafter. Court testimony beyond a two-hour drive from Buffalo, will require lodging overnight for the day prior to scheduled testimony and the night of scheduled testimony, hence $3500.00 for one day testimony and

$1500.00 for each day traveling and away from office ($3000.00 for a total of $6500.00. Additional days of testimony are chargeable at the rate of $2500.00 per day. All fees are payable in advance on the assumption that only one day testimony will be required unless known otherwise. The fee for testimony within New York State is taxable at the rate of 8.75 percent.

If the aforementioned retainer fee and this signed agreement are not received by the consultant/expert within 10 working days following initial contact and submission of this agreement, the consultant/expert may cancel and terminate with written notification his verbal agreement and extract himself from the case.

Cancellation of Services: Cancellation of services by lawyer/law firm including PV examination, Quality Control Review, and Expert Testimony will result in forfeiture of the retainer fee. In addition, the lawyer/law firm will reimburse Matte Polygraph Service, Inc., for any travel and lodging arrangements made prior to cancellation of services pertaining to the services to be rendered that are not cancellable or without monetary penalty.

Payment of Expenses: When travel is required related to the research and conduct of the QCR, or the expert's testimony, all expenses including the cost of travel, meals and lodging will be paid by the lawyer/law firm upon receipt of invoice. Air travel in excess of one hour will be first class. Travel by automobile will be compensated at the rate of $____.00 per mile. Meals will be compensated at rates considered reasonable for that city/region.

Payment by Third Parties: The lawyer and the law firm he/she represents are responsible for the payment of all fees, including those fees incurred by the consultant/expert as a result of a subpoena by opposing counsel to provide documents, reports and/or expert testimony which include expenses for travel, lodging and meals at the rates stated in this agreement.

Assignments: If the lawyer and/or law firm he represents refers or assigns this case to another attorney at law, the consultant/expert will be provided written notice and all outstanding fees and reimbursements will be made at that time. Furthermore, if the lawyer and/or his law firm remain as direct participants in the case, then this agreement and contract will remain in force.

Out-of State Testimony: The lawyer/law firm will insure at the outset that there are no licensing conflicts that would prevent this expert from legally testifying in that state's court. The lawyer/law firm recognizes and is fully aware that my forensic expertise is not in the practice of medicine.

The signature of the lawyer below reflects agreement with all of the aforementioned terms. Please return one original signed copy of this agreement with appropriate fee on law firm check made payable to Matte Polygraph Service, Inc., 43 Brookside Drive, Williamsville, NY 14221-6915.

_____   _____
(Signature of Lawyer/Law Firm)   (Date)

_____   _____
(Signature of Consultant/Expert)   (Date)

Model PV Examination Report for the Quadri-Track Zone Comparison Technique

PRIVILEGED AND CONFIDENTIAL

John H. Doe, Attorney at Law   Date
111 Mason Blvd.., Suite 222
Buffalo, N. Y. l4202

Dear Mr. Doe:

At your request, _____ SSAN: was administered a psycho-physiological veracity (PV) examination using the polygrap on _____to determine whether or not_____

Before being administered a PV examination _____read and signed a statement assuring all concerned that the examination was being taken voluntarily.

A urine specimen was obtained from _____immediately (prior to) (after) the psychophysiological veracity examination. This specimen was transmitted to the __ _____ for forensic drug assay - urine, which revealed (no presence of any drug).

Upon completion of Test(s) A, B, and C above, _____ was transported to CPF MetPath Laboratories, Williamsville, New York, where a urine specimen was obtained from _____for forensic drug assay - urine, which revealed _____(no presence of any drug).

The Polygraph Quadri-Track Zone Comparison Technique employing non-current exclusive control questions and a numerical scoring system of chart analysis as recommended in the Validation Study on the Polygraph Quadri-Track Zone Comparison Technique[71] was utilized throughout the examination, using a Stoelting UltraScribe electronic polygraph instrument (a Lafayette LX-4000 Computerized Polygraph System) which indicated and recorded on a moving chart relative changes in blood pressure, rate and strength of pulse beat, exosomatic electrodermal activity, thoracic and abdominal breathing patterns (and covert body movement).

The following relevant questions were asked during the PV examination. Four polygraph charts were conducted on the target issue in this examination. A minimum of two polygraph charts are required by the protocol of the Quadri-Track Zone Comparison Technique in compliance with American Polygraph Association standards. A control-stimulation test was also administered prior to commencement of the tests regarding the target issue.

Three principal targets were covered in this examination which were administered as Test A, Test B, and Test C, in order of their combined information adequacy, target intensity, and distinctness of issue. A minimum of two polygraph charts were conducted in each test in accordance with the protocol of the Quadri-Track Zone Comparison Technique and American Polygraph Association standards. A control-stimulation test was also administered prior to commencement of the tests regarding the target issues.

TEST A. The following relevant questions were asked during Test A:
Preparatory/Sacrifice Relevant Question:
39.
Relevant Questions Quantified and Used for Determination:
33.
35.
answered in the affirmative to Preparatory Question 39 and in the (negative/affirmative) to Relevant Questions 33 and 35 in above test A.

TEST B. The following relevant questions were asked during Test B:
Preparatory/Sacrifice Relevant Question:
39.
Relevant Questions Quantified and Used for Determination:
33.
35.
answered in the affirmative to Preparatory Question 39 and in the (negative/affirmative) to Relevant Questions 33 and 35 in above Test B.

TEST C. The following relevant questions were asked during Test C:
Preparatory/Sacrifice Relevant Question:
39.
Relevant Questions Quantified and Used for Determination:
33.
35.
_____answered in the affirmative to Preparatory Question 39 and in the (negative/affirmative) to Relevant Questions 33 and 35 in above Test C.

(Model Opinion for the Truthful)

Conclusions:

In the opinion of the undersigned, _____'s polygrams in Test A above showed no strong or consistent unresolved responses to aforementioned relevant questions. Careful analysis and quantification of _____'s polygrams revealed a total score of plus 27 for 3 charts. A minimum score of plus 9 for 3 charts is required before a definite truthful conclusion can be rendered. It is therefore the opinion of the undersigned that _____ _____was Truthful when he gave the above indicated answers to aforementioned relevant questions 33 and 35 in Test A above.

According to the Predictive Table for Estimating Error Rates,[1] and based on the Statistical Table of Probability that a Deceptive subject will score this value (+27) or higher, the Potential for Error is 0.0 percent.

(Model Opinion for Deception)

In the opinion of the undersigned, _____ 's polygrams in Test A above showed strong and consistent unresolved responses to aforementioned relevant questions. Careful analysis and quantification of _____'s polygrams revealed a total score of minus l8 for 3 charts. A minimum score of minus l5 for 3 charts is required before a definite conclusion of Deception can be rendered. It is therefore the opinion of the undersigned that _____ was Deceptive when he gave the above indicated answers to aforementioned relevant questions 33 and 35 in Test A above.

According to the Predictive Table for Estimating Error Rates,[2] and based on the Statistical Table of Probability that a Truthful subject will score this value (-18) or lower, the Potential for Error is 0.0 percent.

(Model for Inconclusives)

In the opinion of the undersigned, _____'s polygrams in above test ( ) showed inconsistent unresolved responses to the above-listed relevant questions. Careful analysis and quantification of _____'s

polygrams revealed a total score of minus 3 for 4 charts. A minimum score of plus 12 for 4 charts is required before a definite truthful conclusion can be rendered. A minimum score of minus 20 for 4 charts is required before a definite conclusion of deception can be rendered. The results of_____'s psychophysiological veracity (polygraph) examination are therefore Inconclusive, which translated means that neither a finding of truthfulness or deception could be established from _____'s polygrams in above test ( ).

Please be advised that Indefinite conclusions are not uncommon in the polygraph community. A numerical scoring system in chart analysis as recommended in the Validation Study on the Quadri-Track Zone Comparison Technique[3] was employed which contains a conclusion table requiring a high truthful or deceptive score be attained before a definite conclusion can be rendered. This Inconclusive area is designed to prevent false positive or negative conclusions, so that conclusive results will enjoy exceptionally high validity and reliability.

Sincerely,

Enclosures: James Allan Matte, C.P.I.
1. Graph of Predictive Table   Forensic Psychophysiology Expert
2. Copy of Release Form signed   President
by _____

---

1. Validation Study on the Polygraph Quadri-Track Zone Comparison Technique, James Allan Matte, and Ronald M. Reuss, published in *Research Abstract* LD 01452, Vol. 1502, 1989, University Microfilm International (UMI), and *Polygraph*, Vol. 18, Nr. 4, 1989, Journal of the American Polygraph Association

2. A Field Study on the Validity of the Quadri-Track Zone Comparison Technique. Daniel J. Mangan, Thomas E. Armitage, Gregory C. Adams. *Physiology & Behavior*, 95 (2008) 17-23, Journal of the International Behavioral Neuroscience Society.

3. A Field Study on the Validity of the Quadri-Track Zone Comparison Technique. Tuvia Shurany, Einat Stein, Eytan Brand. *European Polygraph*, Vol. 1, Nr. 1(7), 2009, Journal of Krakow University College, Poland.

The American Society for Testing and Materials (ASTM) established the controlling standards for *Forensic Psychophysiology*, a title which it enacted for the discipline of psychophysiological veracity examinations using the polygraph.

APPENDIX H

MODEL POLYGRAPH LICENSING ACT

Section 6. Standards of Practice.

Page 666. Change paragraph F to read:

F. No polygraphist will administer more than five (5) polygraph examinations in any one day.

APPENDIX T

PRE-EMPLOYMENT POLYGRAPH EXAMINEE INSTRUCTION AUDIO TAPE EPPA
© 1988, 1997, 2002, 2011 by James Allan Matte

The following examinee instruction audio tape was designed primarily for use in pre-employment polygraph examinations that require certain notices be provided and read to the examinee in compliance with the Employee Polygraph Protection Act of 1988. Having these notices and a full explanation of the nature and characteristics of the polygraph test recorded on a audio tape for the examinee's listening, provides a record of proof that such notices were given and read to the examinee.

Instruction Audio Tape

Welcome to Matte Polygraph Service. Since this may be your first polygraph examination, we would like to assure you that your polygraph examination will be administered by a graduate of a polygraph school accredited by the American Polygraph Association, and a full member of that organization. James Allan Matte is a forensic psychophysiology expert with more than 39 years of experience in the conduct of psychophysiological veracity examinations, also known as polygraph tests, and is a former O.S.I. Agent with the Office of Special Investigations, US Air Force and a retired U.S. Army C.I.D. Agent. He is the author of three textbooks on polygraph. The first was published by Charles C. Thomas in 1980, entitled "The Art and Science of the Polygraph Technique" and the second book published by J.A.M. Publications in December 1996 entitled "Forensic Psychophysiology Using The Polygraph: Scientific Truth Verification - Lie Detection" is an 800-page volume considered a most comprehensive book written on the subject of truth-verification and lie-detection. A 2002 Supplement to the aforementioned textbook was published in March 2002. The third book published in December 2000, titled "Examination and Cross-Examination of Experts in Forensic Psychophysiology Using The Polygraph" provides attorneys with ideal formats to depose their experts when laying the foundation for the admissibility of psychophysiological veracity examination results. All three books should be available at your local library. James Allan Matte is the 1997 recipient of the prestigious "John E. Reid Memorial Award for Distinguished Achievements in Polygraph Research, Teaching and Writing" by the American Polygraph Association. In December 2003, he was presented with the Robert & Mary Ann Henson Memorial Award as the Outstanding Graduate of the Backster School of Lie Detection. Thus you may be assured of an objective, accurate and reliable examination.

The enclosed form that you have just completed will be thoroughly reviewed with you by the polygraphist in the examination room, therefore if you have a problem in filling out the enclosed form, the matter can be easily resolved during the review of the form with the polygraphist who is there to help you.

Not all of the test questions reflected on this form pertain to you, therefore do not answer them at this time. All of the pertinent test questions will be thoroughly reviewed with you before the test by the polygraphist in the privacy of the examination room.

During the review of the test questions, you have every opportunity to qualify any of your answers, of bringing out anything you feel might possibly bother you regarding any of the questions on the test. Once the test questions have been thoroughly reviewed with you to your satisfaction, then you will be seated in a very comfortable examination chair, at which time very sensitive electronic sensors will be placed at various areas of your person, over your clothing, to monitor and record such things as your heart beat, pulse rate and changes in your mean blood pressure, and your galvanic skin response which measures changes in sweat gland activity. Nothing hurts and nervousness does not affect the outcome of the test. Most people are expected to be nervous when they take a polygraph examination, that's perfectly normal. The polygraphist is an expert who is there to help you through the test. So you may have confidence that with your cooperation accurate and reliable results will be obtained.

The polygraphist is required to follow certain scientific procedures in order to obtain accurate and reliable results. Therefore, during the actual examination, you will be restricted to just a Yes or No answer to the same test questions that will have been previously reviewed with you. There are no surprise questions asked. You will only be asked those questions that will have been thoroughly reviewed with you prior to the test, and they will be word for word...not a word will be changed. So it is imperative that if you wish to explain something, or qualify one of your answers, that you do this during the review of the test questions prior to the actual test. The polygraphist is not witch hunting for small stuff, he simply does not want it to bother you on the test. As an example, if during the review of the test question..."Did you ever steal any money from any of your employers?" you stated that you had stolen one dollar from your last employer...no one would lose any sleep over it, however the polygraphist wouldn't want that to bother you on the test, therefore he would add a preamble or a few words in front of that test question which would sound like this on the test..."Besides what you have already told me, did you steal any other money from any of your employers?" Now you would be able to answer "No" truthfully on the test and no deception, no lie would be reflected on the polygraph chart...unless you had in fact stolen more than what you had told the polygraphist, in which case deception would be indicated on the chart. If deception is indicated on the polygraph chart, then we will have to assume as your prospective employer will also, that whatever it is that you withheld must be significant, otherwise you would have told the polygraphist about it during the review for him to eliminate from the test. The polygraphist doesn't expect to test angels, they-re all in heaven, on this earth we all suffer from human frailties...so the primary purpose of the test is to determine whether or not the polygraph program for the company you're applying for will be effective as a internal security measure, as a deterrent for you during your period of employment there. It's only going to be an effective deterrent if you have a healthy respect for it, and you show this by being truthful on the test. So to encourage you to be truthful on the test, the permission form that was given to you by our secretary or the polygraphist which requires your signature before we can test you, when you sign it, you will be authorizing us to give you the test, but you will also be restricting us in giving the results of this test only to the company whose name appears on that form that you sign.

Included in the aforementioned permission or release form is a Notice which the Employee Polygraph Protection Act of 1988 and the Department of Labor Regulation 29 CFR 801.22 require that it be read to you before you take a polygraph examination:

1. (a) The polygraph examination area does contain a camera through which you may be observed.

    (b) Another device, such as those used in conversation or recording, will be used during the examination.

    (c) Both you and the employer have the right, with the other's knowledge, to record electronically the entire examination.

2. (a) You have the right to terminate the test at any time.

    (b) You have the right, and will be given the opportunity, to review all questions to be asked during the test.

    (c) You may not be asked questions in a manner which degrades, or needlessly intrudes.

    (d) You may not be asked any questions concerning: Religious beliefs or opinions; beliefs regarding racial matters; political beliefs or affiliations; matters relating to sexual behavior; beliefs, affiliations, opinions, or lawful activities regarding unions or labor organizations.

    (e) The test may not be conducted if there is sufficient written evidence by a physician that you are suffering from a medical or psychological condition or undergoing treatment that might cause abnormal responses during the examination.

3. (a) The test is not and cannot be required as a condition of employment.

    (b) The employer may not discharge, dismiss, discipline, deny employment or promotion, or otherwise discriminate against you based on the analysis of a polygraph test, or based on your refusal to take such a test without additional evidence which would support such action.

    (c) (1) In connection with an ongoing investigation, the additional evidence required for an employer to take adverse action against you, including termination, may be (A) evidence that you have access to the property that is the subject of the investigation, together with (B) the evidence supporting the employer's reasonable suspicion that you were involved in the incident or activity under investigation.

    (2) Any statement made by you before or during the test may serve as additional supporting evidence for an adverse employment action, as described in 3(b) above, and any admission or criminal conduct by you may be transmitted to an appropriate government law enforcement agency.

4. (a) Information acquired from a polygraph test may be disclosed by the examiner or by the employer only:

(1) To you or any other person specifically designated in writing by you to receive such information;

(2) To the employer that requested the test;

(3) To a court, governmental agency, arbitrator, or mediator that obtains a court order;

(4) To a U. S. Department of Labor official when specifically designated in writing by you to receive such information.

(b) Information acquired from a polygraph test may be disclosed by the employer to an appropriate governmental agency without a court order where, and only insofar as, the information disclosed is an admission of criminal conduct.

5. If any of your rights or protections under the law are violated, you have the right to file a complaint with the Wage and Hour Division of the U. S. Department of Labor, or to take action in court against the employer. Employers who violate this law are liable to the affected examinee, who may recover such legal or equitable relief as may be appropriate, including employment, reinstatement, and promotion, payment of lost wages and benefits and reasonable costs, including attorney's fees. The Secretary of Labor may also bring action to restrain violations of the Act, or may assess civil money penalties against the employer.

6. Your rights under the Act may not be waived, either voluntarily or involuntarily, by contract or otherwise, except as part of a written settlement to a pending action or complaint under the Act, and agreed to and signed by the parties.

As I have mentioned earlier, this notice is included in the release form our secretary or the polygraphist gave you in two copies, one copy of which is for you.

While we are on the subject of rights, it must be remembered that the polygraphist also has rights some of which are worthy of enunciation at this time:

1. The polygraphist has the right to expect the examinee to be dressed in clothes that will not soil the examination chair with grease, oil or other contaminant that will adversely affect the next examinee.

2. The polygraphist has the right to expect the examinee to have clean hands in order for the sensors that will be placed on the examinee's hands to function properly.

3. The polygraphist has the right to expect the examinee to be courteous and polite throughout the examination.

4. The polygraphist has the right to expect the examinee to fully cooperate and follow test instructions necessary for the proper conduct of the polygraph examination.

5. No smoking, gum or tobacco chewing is permitted in the examination room.

6. The polygraphist has the right to terminate the interview and examination at any time he feels that any of the above mentioned conditions are not being met, and to report to the employer the reason for not conducting or terminating the test.

Now that we've got each other's rights squared away, let's discuss the polygraph instrument and what it records.

Initially, all polygraph instruments were mechanical. They operated on a series of levers and tambours producing chart tracings that reflected exactly what was obtained from the subject, a one-to-one ratio. Then came a new generation of polygraph instruments that are fully electronic - no moving parts except for the pens of course. Therefore with the use of amplifiers we are now able to increase or decrease the strength and amplitude of a tracing at will. We now also have computerized polygraph systems that record the same physiological parameters plus the added covert movement sensors.

There are four pens that write simultaneously on a chart or a roll of graph paper. Two of those pens record the upper and lower breathing patterns by the placement of a rubber pneumograph tube over your chest and one over your abdomen or stomach, over your clothing of course. The third pen records your pulse rate and changes in your mean blood pressure through the use of medical blood pressure cuff which is wrapped tightly around your left or right bicep over your shirt sleeve. Then the bladder inside the cuff is inflated with air and locked inside at a constant pressure for the duration of the test. The cuff is not inflated with as much air as a doctor would, but it is inflated with enough air to obtain a reading which is then amplified electronically to an ideal tracing on the polygraph chart. So during the test, don't be alarmed if your arm should fall asleep or you feel a little tingling sensation in the tip of your fingers, it's perfectly normal. The air in the cuff will be released at the end of each chart to give your arm a rest. Each chart only lasts about four minutes. As an alternative, the polygraphist may elect to use a cardio-activity monitor or a thumb blood pressure cuff instead of the biceps blood pressure cuff to record the same physiology. This cardio-activity monitor also known as a CAM is simply a small electronic transducer which is placed over one of your thumbs and held in place with a Velcro strap. The thumb blood pressure cuff is wrapped tightly around your thumb to obtain the same data as the bicep blood pressure cuff. Finally the fourth pen which is longer than the other pens and sits higher than the other pens is called the GSR pen. GSR stands for Galvanic Skin Resistance. Sudden increases in sweat gland activity may send the GSR pen into a wide chart excursion, therefore in order to avoid having the GSR pen collide with the other pens; it was made longer and higher so that it may ride over the other pens. The computerized polygraph system uses virtual pens to record on the monitor screen the same physiological data as the electronic polygraph instrument.

You're probably wondering why we record your breathing patterns. Well, if you attempt to control your breathing by slowing it down or speeding it up or manipulate it in any way, it will be recorded on the polygraph chart for later analysis but will become obvious to the polygraphist who knows what your normal breathing rate and pattern should be. Only the guilty person attempts to manipulate his or her breathing - the innocent want to cooperate to prove or confirm their innocence. Also, by monitoring your breathing patterns we know when you take a deep breath, sniff, cough, clear throat or even swallow, and this is all permanently recorded on the polygraph chart.

You're probably also wondering about nervousness and its effect on the outcome of the test. Let me assure you that nervousness won't affect the test. Most people who take a polygraph examination are nervous, even though they may be innocent. Think of it this way. If you have high blood pressure, it's constant throughout the test, right? if you are nervous, that's constant throughout the test also. Anything that is constant or consistent can be disregarded as a norm.

Some people ask - what if the machine malfunctions. Well first of all it's not a machine, it's an instrument. A machine connotes that it does all the work that the polygraphist merely operates a machine, that he simply pushes a button and the answer as to truth or deception comes out at the other end. That's where the term Operator came from, we were considered operators of a lie-detector machine. Nothing could be further from the truth. It's an instrument, a diagnostic tool. It merely records your physiology on a moving chart using a structured psychological test which is subsequently analyzed for a determination of truth or deception. We verify the truth as well as detect lies, in fact we do the former more often than the latter, hence we are properly called polygraphists or forensic psychophysiology experts and we actually conduct psychophysiological veracity examinations rather than the old term "polygraph examination" but the old term is better understood by the general public, thus continues to be used.

You may have observed that at this moment your hands may feel sweaty and your pulse rate may seem faster than normal just waiting to be polygraphed - will this cause the instrument to record erroneous results? The answer is a definite NO. I know it may be hard for you to understand so let me give you a brief description of the physiology involved, then perhaps you will better appreciate the scientificity and accuracy of the test.

About two millions years ago, man's actions were primarily governed by his limbic system, sometimes referred to as the 'old brain' which is primitive in nature. When primitive man perceived that there was a threat to his well-being, either by seeing a tiger running towards him, or hearing the roar of a lion in back of him, his sensory organs would immediately send a signal to the 'old brain' the limbic system which in turn would activate a self-preservation mechanism known today as the sympathetic system to prepare his body for fight or flight. Now, this sympathetic system is a subdivision of the autonomic nervous system over which we have no conscious control. It prepares our body for fight or flight by causing the adrenal glands to secrete hormones known as epinephrine and norepinephrine into our blood stream. The norepinephrine constricts the smooth muscles surrounding the arterioles in the extremities of our body, significantly reducing the volume of blood in our fingertips, the surface of the skin and other organs of the body where the blood is not needed to meet the emergency, such as the stomach for instance. This explains the butterflies an athlete or a fighter may experience shortly before the event. Pallor in the face of a victim facing a physical threat is another indicator of norepinephrine at work. By contrast, epinephrine dilates the blood vessels leading to those areas of the body where the blood is needed to meet the emergency, such as the large muscle groups. Of course today most of the threats we face are psychological rather than physical, but the 'old brain' doesn't know the difference. The moment the guilty examinee hears the crime question being asked on the test, the stimulus goes from the ear directly to the 'old brain' recognizing it as a threat to his well-being and does what it has done for millions of years...it activates its self-preservation mechanism, the sympathetic system.

In other words that sympathetic system kicks in when I'm in danger of harm, and it redistributes the blood in my body from my hands, feet, and surface of the skin to the large muscle groups such as my legs, back, shoulders and arms to fight off the thing that's threatening me, or else run from it. Since there's less blood at the surface of the skin and at the extremities, one would bleed less if a surface wound was sustained.

Other obvious effects take place when the sympathetic system is activated. The heart pumps blood harder and faster; increasing blood pressure, pulse rate, and strength, thus furnishing more oxygenated blood to those areas of the body where it's vitally needed to meet the emergency. The sympathetic system also affects overt symptoms such as the tensing of the involuntary muscles that in addition to causing a constriction of the cardiovascular system, causes a tightening of the involuntary muscles in the stomach thereby inhibiting the diaphragm-intercostal muscular complex, which causes a less than average enlargement of the chest cavity. So without realizing it, you would take in less air in your lungs because the muscles around your diaphragm would be inhibited by the sympathetic system.

The effects of the sympathetic system can last from a few seconds to as long as twenty seconds before the parasympathetic system overcomes it. It is usually so minute that you don't notice it, but on the polygraph chart the pens draw a dramatic picture of this activity, and if you attempt to control it, that too is drawn by the pens on the polygraph chart.

Earlier I mentioned that the GSR pen measures sweating, but that's an oversimplification. Let me explain. By placing two electrodes against the skin of your index and ring fingers and inducing a minute amount of electrical current - less than a small 9 volt pen flashlight battery - into the skin, we balance the general resistance of the skin against this electrical current. Now when the sympathetic system activates, it causes a sudden increase in sweat gland activity which momentarily raises the sweat bed in the skin at the fingertips. This increases the moisture of the skin which becomes less resistant to the electrical current, allowing more electricity thru the skin. This in turn causes the GSR pen to swing from mechanical center upward on the polygraph chart, indicating the degree of decrease in skin resistance. In other words, this sudden increase in sweat gland activity is detected, measured and recorded by the GSR pen which tells me that the sympathetic system has kicked in.

But that is just one of the parameters that tells me when the sympathetic system activates, and it also tells me the duration of the response as well. Therefore we have three parameters recorded by four pens to tell me when and for how long your sympathetic system activated. Now, whenever the sympathetic system activates, it's followed by the activation of the parasympathetic system which is antagonistic to the sympathetic system. The role of the parasympathetic system is to maintain the homeostasis of your body - the chemical balance if you will - you may think of the sympathetic as the accelerator of your car and the parasympathetic as the brakes. If you didn't have such a recovery system, your heart would beat itself right out of your chest - major arteries would rupture - you'd never survive your first emergency. So nature provided this parasympathetic to put the brakes on the sympathetic system and bring you back to normal. In doing so the parasympathetic system may overcompensate - for instance, when the sympathetic causes you to take less air in your system, you later must compensate by taking in more air than normal and n doing so you start to hyperventilate. Your pulse rate for instance may actually slow down below your normal rate. Oftentimes. before your heart has a chance to accelerate its heart rate, the parasympathetic system, in a quick reflex, slows down the heart rate during the reaction time - this is then followed by a dramatic increase in the pulse rate beyond the examinee's normal heart rate for as long as ten to fifteen seconds on the chart. So you see, we polygraphists are looking for physiological evidence of both sympathetic and parasympathetic activation on the polygraph chart telling us which question or questions are most threatening to you - obviously the ones you lie to are going to be the most threatening.

The American Polygraph Association standards and the Erie County Polygraph Licensing Act require that the polygraphist conduct a minimum of at least two polygraph charts on any test, that is, he must run the test questions by you twice on the test to establish consistency, hence, reliability, so please don't be alarmed when the test questions are asked a second time on the test...that's normal procedure.

In order to preclude having to conduct more than the required number of charts, you can assist the polygraphist by remaining perfectly still during the actual test. You should not move any part of your body during the actual test. There should be no gum chewing or any other mastication during the examination. Coughing or sniffing during the test should be avoided. In fact, if you suffer from a bad cold, it would be in your best interest to postpone the test until the cold symptoms are gone. In that case, consult with our secretary or the polygraphist who will gladly give you another appointment. Thank you. If you wish more information about the polygraph, we recommend you read "Forensic Psychophysiology Using The Polygraph; Scientific Truth Verification - Lie Detection" by James Allan Matte, which may be available at your local library.

Please ring the bell to notify the polygraphist that you have listened to this tape and are now ready for the second phase of the examination. If you wish to hear this tape a second time, please ask the polygraphist and he will rewind it for you to hear again. Thank you for your cooperation.

APPENDIX U

SPECIFIC-ISSUE POLYGRAPH EXAMINEE INSTRUCTION AUDIO TAPE EPPA
© 1989, 2002, 2011 by James Allan Matte

The following instruction audio tape was designed primarily for use in specific-issue polygraph examinations that require certain notices be provided and read to the examinee in compliance with the Employee Polygraph Protection Act of 1988. Having these notices and a full explanation of the nature and characteristics of the polygraph test recorded on an audio tape for the examinee's listening, provides a record of proof that such notices were given and read to the examinee.

Instruction Audio Tape
Welcome to Matte Polygraph Service. Since this may be your first polygraph examination, we would like to assure that every polygraphist employed by this firm is a Certified Graduate of a polygraph School accredited by the American Polygraph Association. The President of our firm, James Allan Matte, is the author of three textbooks on polygraph entitled "The Art and Science of the Polygraph Technique" published in 1980, "Forensic Psychophysiology Using The Polygraph" published in December 1996, and a 2002 Supplement to aforementioned textbook published in March 2002. The third book entitled "Examination and Cross-Examination of Experts in Forensic Psychophysiology Using The Polygraph" was published in December 2000. he is the 1997 recipient of the prestigious "John E. Reid Memorial Award for Distinguished Achievements in Polygraph Research, Teaching and Writing" by the American Polygraph Association. James Allan Matte is a former Special Agent of the Office of Special Investigations (OSI) United States Air Force and a retired U.S. Army C.I.D. Agent. He has more than 39 years of experience as a forensic psychophysiology expert. Therefore you may be assured that your polygraph examination will be the most accurate and reliable that science can provide.

You were given a permission—release form by the polygraphist for you to read and sign in two copies, one of these copies is for you to keep. Included in the aforementioned permission form is a Notice which the Employee Polygraph Protection Act of 1988 and the Department of Labor Regulation 29 CFR 801.22 require that it be read to you before you take a polygraph examination:

    1. (a) The polygraph examination area does contain a camera through which you may be observed.

(b) Another device, such as those used in conversation or recording, will be used during the examination.

(c) Both you and the employer have the right, with the other's knowledge, to record electronically the entire examination.

2. (a) You have the right to terminate the test at any time.

(b) You have the right, and will be given the opportunity, to review all questions to be asked during the test.

(c) You may not be asked questions in a manner which degrades, or needlessly intrudes.

(d) You may not be asked any questions concerning; Religious beliefs or opinions; beliefs regarding racial matters; political beliefs or affiliations; matters relating to sexual behavior; beliefs, affiliations, opinions, or lawful activities regarding unions or labor organizations.

(e) The test may not be conducted if there is sufficient written evidence by a physician that you are suffering from a medical or psychological condition or undergoing treatment that might cause abnormal responses during the examination.

3. (a) The test is not and cannot be required as a condition of employment.

(b) The employer may not discharge, dismiss, discipline, deny employment or promotion, or otherwise discriminate against you based on

the analysis of a polygraph test, or based on your refusal to take such a test without additional evidence which would support such action.

(c) (1) In connection with an ongoing investigation, the additional evidence required for an employer to take adverse action against you, including termination, may be (a) evidence that you have access to the property that is the subject of the investigation, together with (b) the evidence supporting the employer's reasonable suspicion that you were involved in the incident or activity under investigation.

(2) Any statement made by you before or during the test may serve as additional supporting evidence for an adverse employment action, as described in 3(b) above, and any admission of criminal conduct by you may be transmitted to an appropriate government law enforcement agency.

4. (a) Information acquired from a polygraph test may be disclosed by the examiner or by the employer only:

(1) To you or any other person specifically designated in writing by you to receive such information;

(2) To the employer that requested the test;

(3) To a court, governmental agency, arbitrator, or mediator that obtains a court order;

(4) To a U.S. Department of Labor official when specifically designated in writing by you to receive such information.

(b) Information acquired from a polygraph test may be disclosed by the employer to an appropriate governmental agency without a court order where, and only insofar as, the information disclosed is an admission of criminal conduct.

5. If any of your rights or protections under the law are violated, you have the right to file a complaint with the Wage and Hour Division of the U.S. Department of Labor, or to take action in court against the employer. Employers who violate this law are liable to the

affected examinee, who may recover such legal or equitable relief as may be appropriate, including employment, reinstatement, and promotion, payment of lost wages and benefits and reasonable costs, including attorney's fees. The Secretary of Labor may also bring action to restrain violations of the Act, or may assess civil money penalties against the employer.

6. Your rights under the Act may not be waived, either voluntarily or involuntarily, by contract or otherwise, except as part of a written settlement to a pending action or complaint under the Act, and agreed to and signed by the parties.

As I have mentioned earlier, this notice is included in the release form the polygraphist gave you in two copies, one copy of which is for you. While we are on the subject of rights, it must be remembered that the polygraphist also has rights. This is not an adversary proceeding. The polygraphist is not out to prove you guilty of anything. The polygraphist is a professional who assumes that each examinee is innocent of the offense or matter for which he or she is being polygraphed, and is dedicated to verify the truth as well as detect deception. His first responsibility, believe it or not, is to you the examinee, to administer the best and most accurate test possible. But in order for the polygraphist to do his job properly he expects the following to be observed by the examinee:

1. The polygraphist has the right to expect the examinee to be dressed in clothes that will not soil the examination chair with grease, oil other contaminant that will adversely affect the next examinee.

2. The polygraphist has the right to expect the examinee to have clean hands in order for the sensors that will be placed on the examinees hands to function properly.

3. The polygraphist has the right to expect the examinee to be courteous and polite throughout the examination.

4. The polygraphist has the right to expect the examinee to fully cooperate and follow test instructions necessary for the proper conduct of the polygraph examination.

5. No smoking, gum or tobacco chewing is permitted in the examination room.

6. The polygraphist has the right to terminate the interview and examination at any time he feels that any of the above mentioned conditions are not being met, and to report to the employer the reason for not conducting or terminating the test.

Now that the administrative matters have been explained and hopefully understood, let's discuss the polygraph instrument and what it records.

Initially, all polygraph instruments were mechanical. They operated on a series of levers and tambours producing chart tracings that reflected exactly what was obtained from the subject, a one—to—one ratio. Then came a new generation of polygraph instruments that are fully electronic - no moving parts except for the pens of course. Therefore with the use of amplifiers we are now able to increase or decrease the strength and amplitude of a tracing at will. We now also have computerized polygraph systems that record the same physiological parameters plus the added covert movement sensors.

There are four pens that write simultaneously on a chart or a roll of graph paper. Two of those pens record the upper and lower breathing patterns by the placement of a rubber pneumograph tube over your chest and one over your abdomen or stomach, over your clothing, of course. The third pen records your pulse rate and changes in your mean blood pressure thru the use of a medical blood pressure cuff which contains a rubber bladder. That blood pressure cuff is wrapped tightly around your left or right biceps over your shirt sleeve. Then the bladder inside the cuff is inflated with air and locked inside at a constant pressure for the duration of the test. The cuff is not inflated with as much air as a doctor would, but it is inflated with enough air to obtain a reading which is then amplified electronically to an ideal tracing on the polygraph chart. So during the test don't be alarmed if your arm should fall asleep or you feel a little tingling sensation in the tip of your fingers, it's perfectly normal. The air in the cuff will be released at the end of each chart to give your arm a rest. Each chart only lasts about four minutes. Finally the fourth pen which is longer than the other pens and sits higher than the other pens is called the GSR pen. GSR stands for Galvanic Skin Resistance. Sudden increases in sweat gland activity may send the GSR pen into a wide chart excursion, therefore in order to avoid having the GSR pen collide with the other pens, it was made longer and higher so that it may ride over the other pens.

You're probably wondering why we record your breathing patterns. Well, if you attempt to control your breathing by slowing it down or speeding it up or manipulate it in any way it will be recorded on the polygraph chart for later analysis but will become obvious to the polygraphist who knows what your normal breathing rate and pattern should be. Only the guilty person attempts to manipulate his breathing — the innocent want to cooperate to prove their innocence. Also, by monitoring your breathing patterns we know when you take a deep breath, sniff, cough, clear throat, or even swallow, and this is all permanently recorded on the polygraph chart.

You're probably also wondering about nervousness and its effect on the outcome of the test. Let me assure you that nervousness won't affect the test. Most people who take a polygraph examination are nervous, even though they may be innocent. Think of it this way. If you have high blood pressure, it's constant throughout the test, right? If you are nervous, that's constant throughout the test also. Anything that is constant or consistent can be disregarded as a norm.

Some people ask - what if the machine malfunctions. Well first of all it's not a machine, it's an instrument. A machine connotes that it does all the work, that the polygraphist merely operates a machine, that he simply pushes a button and the answer as to truth or deception comes out at the other end. That's where the term Operator came from, we were considered operators of a lie—detector machine. Nothing could be further from the truth. It's an instrument, a diagnostic tool. It merely records your physiology on a moving chart using a structured psychological test which is subsequently analyzed for a determination of truth or deception. We verify the truth as well as detect lies, in fact we do the former more often than the latter, hence we are properly called polygraphists or forensic psychophysiology experts.

You may have observed that at this moment your hands may feel sweaty and your pulse rate may seem faster than normal just waiting to be polygraphed — will this cause the instrument to record erroneous results? The answer is a definite NO. I know it may be hard for you to understand so let me give you a brief description of the physiology involved, then perhaps you will better appreciate the scientifically and accuracy of the test.

About two million years ago, man's actions were primarily governed by his limbic system, sometimes referred to as the 'old brain' which is primitive in nature. When primitive man perceived that there was a threat to his well—being, either by seeing a tiger running towards him, or hearing the roar of a lion in back of him, his sensory organs would immediately send a signal to the 'old brain' the limbic system which in turn would activate a self— preservation mechanism known today as the sympathetic system to prepare his body for fight or flight. Now, this sympathetic system is a subdivision of the autonomic nervous system over which we have no conscious control. It prepares our body for fight or flight by causing the adrenal glands to secrete hormones known as epinephrine and norepinephrine into our blood stream. The norepinephrine constricts the smooth muscles surrounding the arterioles in the extremities of our body, significantly reducing the volume of blood in our fingertips, the surface of the skin and other organs of the body where the blood is not needed to meet the emergency, such as the stomach for instance. This explains the butterflies an athlete or a fighter may experience shortly before the event. Pallor in the face of a victim facing a physical threat is another indicator of norepinephrine at work. By contrast, epinephrine dilates the blood vessels leading to those areas of the body where the blood is needed to meet the emergency, such as the large muscle groups. Of course today most of the threats we face are psychological rather than physical, but the 'old brain' doesn't know the difference. The moment the guilty examinee hears the crime question being asked on the test, the stimulus goes from the ear directly to the 'old brain' recognizing it as a threat to his well—being and does what it has done for millions of years ... it activates its self—preservation mechanism, the sympathetic system.

In other words that sympathetic system kicks in when I'm in danger of harm, and it redistributes the blood in my body from my hands, feet, and surface of the skin to the large muscle groups such as my legs, back, shoulders and arms to fight off the thing that's threatening me, or else run from it. Since there's less blood at the surface of the skin and at the extremities, one would bleed less if a surface wound was sustained.

Other obvious effects take place when the sympathetic system is activated. The heart pumps blood harder and faster; increasing blood pressure, pulse rate, and strength, thus furnishing more oxygenated blood to those areas of the body where it's vitally needed to meet the emergency. The sympathetic system also affects overt symptoms such as the tensing of the involuntary muscles that in addition to causing a constriction of the cardiovascular system, causes a tightening of the involuntary muscles in the stomach thereby inhibiting the diaphragm—intercostal muscular complex, which causes a less than average enlargement of the chest cavity. So without realizing it, you would take in less air in your lungs because the muscles around your diaphragm would be inhibited by the sympathetic system. The effects of the sympathetic system can last from a few seconds to as long as twenty seconds before the parasympathetic system overcomes it. It is usually so minute that you don't notice it, but on the polygraph chart the pens draw a dramatic picture of this activity, and if you attempt to control it, that too is drawn by the pens on the polygraph chart.

Earlier I mentioned that the GSR pen measures sweating, but that's an oversimplification. Let me explain. By placing two electrodes against the skin of your index and ring fingers and inducing a minute amount of electrical current less than a small 9 volt pen flashlight battery into the skin, we balance the general resistance of the skin against this electrical current. Now when the sympathetic system activates, it causes a sudden increase in sweat gland activity which momentarily raises the sweat bed in the skin at the fingertips. This increases the moisture of the skin which becomes less resistant to the electrical current, allowing more electricity thru the skin. This in turn causes the GSR pen to swing from mechanical center upward on the polygraph chart, indicating the degree of decrease in skin resistance. In other words, this sudden increase in sweat gland activity is detected, measured and recorded by the GSR pen which tells me that the sympathetic system has kicked in.

But that is just one of the parameters that tells me when the sympathetic system activates, and it also tells me the duration of the response as well. Therefore we have three parameters recorded by four pens to tell me when and for how long your sympathetic system activated. Now, whenever the sympathetic system activates, it's followed by the activation of the parasympathetic system which is antagonistic to the sympathetic system. The role of the parasympathetic system is to maintain the homeostasis of your body - the chemical balance if you will - you may think of the sympathetic as the accelerator of your car and the parasympathetic as the brakes. If you didn't have such a recovery system, your heart would beat itself right out of your chest - major arteries would rupture - you'd never survive your first emergency. So nature provided this parasympathetic to put the brakes on the sympathetic system and bring you back to normal. In doing so the parasympathetic system may overcompensate - for instance, when the sympathetic causes you to take less air in your system, you later must compensate by taking in more air than normal and in doing so you start to hyperventilate. Your pulse rate for instance may actually slow down below your normal rate. Oftentimes, before your heart has a chance to accelerate its heart rate, the parasympathetic system, in a quick reflex, slows down the heart rate during the reaction time — this is then followed by a dramatic increase in the pulse rate beyond the examinee ' s normal heart rate for as long as ten to fifteen seconds on the chart. So you see, we polygraphists are looking for physiological evidence of both sympathetic and parasympathetic activation on the polygraph chart telling us which question or questions are most threatening to you - obviously the ones you lie to are going to be the most threatening.

In this polygraph examination, I will be using a computerized polygraph system which uses virtual pens to record the same physiological parameters previously described to you.

I am now going to explain the polygraph procedure to you. The polygraphist will first review with you each and every test question before the examination is conducted . This will give you an opportunity of knowing what the test questions are, and of qualifying any of your answers to those questions, of explaining anything you wish. It also gives the polygraphist a chance to see whether you fully understand the meaning and formulation of the test questions before the test is actually administered. Now this is a psychological test that is designed to identify and/or eliminate any factors other than a deliberate attempt at deception that may activate the sympathetic and parasympathetic systems that we discussed earlier. In addition, the polygraphist will run a minimum of at least two polygraph charts on any test that is administered — this is to establish reliability through consistency. So don't be alarmed because the polygraphist is running several charts on the same issue or same test - it's perfectly normal - in fact - it is required by the standards of practice of the American Polygraph Association and the Erie County Polygraph Licensing Act. This means that all of the test questions are going to be asked at least twice on the actual test. You're going to be asked the test questions once - that's one chart, then the polygraphist will release the air pressure out of the cardio cuff which will be wrapped around your left biceps, so that your arm may get a rest. Then after your left arm is rested, the polygraphist will inflate the cardio cuff again and run a second polygraph chart in which you will be asked the exact same questions you were asked on the first chart. He may even run a third and a fourth chart with the same test questions. He will run at least two charts and as many more as required until he is satisfied that he has obtained charts that reflect your best physiological tracings. During the actual examination you will be restricted to just a Yes or No answer - that's all, therefore if you want to qualify any of your answers or explain something, you must do it during the review of those same questions before the test.

In order to preclude having to conduct more than required number of charts, you can assist the polygraphist by remaining perfectly still during the actual test. You should not move any part of your body during the actual test. There should be no gum chewing or any other mastication during the examination. Coughing or sniffing during the test should be avoided. In fact, if you suffer from a bad cold, it would be in your best interest to postpone the test until the cold symptoms are gone. In that case, consult with the polygraphist who will gladly give you another appointment.

Please notify the polygraphist that you have listened to this tape and are now ready for the second phase of the examination. If you wish to hear this tape a second time, please ask the polygraphist and he will rewind it for you to hear again. Thank you for your cooperation.

APPENDIX V-1

AUTORISATION POUR PASSER UN EXAMEN POLYGRAPHIQUE

Je, _____, consens volontairement à passer un examen polygraphique pour _____. Je le fais de mon propre gré, sans éprouver de contraintes et sans avoir reçu de promesses de récompense, d'immunité ou de tout autre genre. Je reconnais que je ne suis pas détenu(e), ni en état d'arrestation.

Le polygraphiste _____m'a expliqué de façon satisfaisante la procédure polygraphique et il a répondu à toutes mes questions concernant une entrevue utilisant la technique polygraphique.

Le polygraphiste m'a expliqué les points suivants et je comprends que :

1. La durée d'un examen polygraphique est d'environ 2 à 3 heures. Toutes les questions posées durant cet examen polygraphique seront formulées et révisées avec moi avant l'examen polygraphique.

2. Personne ne peut me forcer à me soumettre à un examen polygraphique; un examen polygraphique est sur une base volontaire. J'ai le droit de refuser de me soumettre à cet examen polygraphique.

3. Je peux exercer mon droit au silence et cesser de répondre aux questions du polygraphiste en tout temps. J'ai le droit de mettre fin à l'examen polygraphique, même si cet examen est dûment commencé, et de quitter la salle de polygraphie en tout temps.

4. Le résultat de cet examen polygraphique n'est pas infaillible.

5. Je serai questionné(e) par le polygraphiste avant, pendant et après l'examen polygraphique afin d'obtenir le résultat et de discuter de ce résultat. **Tout ce que je dirai** lors de cette entrevue peut servir de preuve devant une cour de justice.

6. J'ai le droit d'avoir recours sans délai à l'assistance d'un(e) avocat(e). Si je décide d'avoir recours à un(e) avocat(e), j'ai le droit de communiquer avec ce(tte) dernier(ère) avant, pendant ou après l'examen polygraphique afin d'obtenir des conseils légaux.

7. Si je décide d'avoir recours à un(e) avocat(e), j'aurai droit à une discussion en privé avec ce(tte) dernier(ère). Je peux contacter un(e) avocat(e) de l'aide juridique ou de garde sans égard aux moyens financiers en composant le : (numero the telephone)_____.

Au meilleur de ma connaissance, je ne suis présentement atteint(e) d'aucun problème de santé d'ordre physique ou mental qui m'empêcherait de passer cet examen polygraphique.

J'autorise le polygraphiste à enregistrer cette rencontre sur ruban magnétique vidéo et/ou audio. Je consens à ce que cet enregistrement puisse servir à des fins de formation.

J'autorise le polygraphiste à divulguer le résultat de cet examen polygraphique, ainsi que toutes mes réponses à ses questions, à : _____.

Je dégage et ne tiens aucunement responsable le polygraphiste _____ et sa compagnie, _____, de toutes poursuites civiles résultant de cet examen polygraphique.

IMPORTANT : Avez-vous bien compris <u>tout</u> ce qui est écrit sur cette page ? _____.

_____   _____
Nom du Sujet   Nom du Polygraphiste

                        _____
                              Date   Heure

(COURTESY OF GALIANOS POLYGRAPHE EXPERT, INC.)
www.galianospolygraph.com

APPENDIX V-2

AUTHORIZATION FOR A POLYGRAPH EXAMINATION

I, _____, voluntarily agree to submit to a polygraph examination
for _____   that   occurred   or
_____. I do so of my own free will, without coercion, duress, and promise of reward, immunity,
or of any other kind. **I understand that I am neither detained nor under arrest.**

The polygraphist has satisfactorily explained the polygraph procedure to me and he has answered all my questions
concerning an interview utilizing the polygraph technique.

The polygraphist has also explained the following points to me and I understand that:

1.   The duration of a polygraph examination is about 2 to 3 hours. All the questions that will be asked during the
      examination will be formulated and reviewed with me beforehand.

2.   No one can force me to submit to a polygraph examination because it is taken on a voluntary basis. I can exercise
      my right of refusal and not submit to a polygraph examination.

3.   I can exercise my right to silence and stop answering the polygraph examiner's questions at any time. I have the
      right to stop the polygraph examination, even if it is already in progress, and to leave the polygraph room at any
      time.

4.   The result of this polygraph examination is not infallible.

5.   I will be questioned by Mr. Galianos before, during and after the polygraph examination. I will be given the result
      of the examination and discuss this result. **Anything I will say** during this interview can be given in evidence
      before a court of law.

6.   I have the right to have recourse to a lawyer, without delay. If I should decide to have recourse to a lawyer, I
      have the right to communicate with him or her before, during or after the examination for the purpose of obtaining
      legal counsel.

7.   If I should decide to have recourse to a lawyer, I have the right to a private conversation with him or her. I can
      contact a legal-aid lawyer or duty counsel regardless of financial means.

To the best of my knowledge, I suffer from no physical or mental condition that would prevent me from submitting to a
polygraph examination.

I authorize Mr. Galianos to record this interview in its entirety on DVD. I agree that this video recording may be used as
part of a formal training program.

I authorize Mr. Galianos to release the result of this polygraph examination, as well as my answers to his questions, to:
_____.

I release and hold harmless Mr. John Galianos and the company, Galianos Polygraphe Expert Inc., of all civil lawsuits which
could result from this polygraph examination.

IMPORTANT: Do you fully understand **everything** that is written on this page? _____

_____   _____
        Name of Examinee   John Galianos
                                              Certified Polygraph Examiner

_____   _____
      Date   Time

(Courtesy of Galianos Polygraphe Expert, Inc.)
www.galianospolygraphe.com

APPENDIX W-1

DECLARACION PARA TOMAR LA EXAMINACION POLIGRAFO

Yo, _____, libremente y voluntariamente,
sin la compulsion o la coercion entiendo que esta entrevistada sera en conexion:

Acuerdo voluntariamente ser examindo por medio del poligrafo durante esta entrevista o cualquier parte de ella.

No se ha hecho nigunas amenazas o promesas en tomar esta examinacion.

Represento que estoy en buena saludud, mental y fisica.

Entiendo que las preguntas que se pediran seran repasadas con mi antes de la examinacion.

Entiendo que puedo parar esta entrevista y examinacion del poligrafo en cualquier momento.

Entiendo que este proceso sera grabada.

No sostendre a examinador obligado para ninguna ediciones fisica or psicologica que puedan resultar de esta examinacion.

Entiendo que los resultados de tal prueba y de las conclusiones dibujadas por _____, sus oficiales, agentes, y empleados pueden probar desfavorable a mí. También reconozco la posibilidad que el examinador no sera capaz de rendir una decisión basada en este examen. No obstante, sostengo _____ sus oficiales, agentes, y empleados libres e inofensivos de cualquier demanda que puede ser que tenga de otra manera contra ellos para cualesquiera daños a mi o cualquier responsabilidad resultando tomar de la prueba y acceso sus resultados y de las conclusiones dibujada por _____.

A nombre de me y mis herederos, lanzo, renuncio por este medio y descargo cada uno de las corporaciones susodichas, firmas, sus oficiales respectivos , agentes y empleados, de cualquiera y toda la acción o causa de la acción, demando por siempre, la demanda o la responsabilidad, que ahora tengo o puedo para tener resultar directamente o indirectamente de mi examinación dicha que toma y de las opiniones orales y escritas rendidas debido a el examen dicho. Estoy de acuerdo que no llevará a cabo en _____ o sus funcionarios responsables de cualquier violaciónes EPPA.

Doy mi consentimiento que los resultados de la entrevista y el examen del poligrafo se pueden entregar a:

Nombre: _____

Aceptación: Después de haber leído y comprendido la información anterior, doy _____ o su agente permiso para llevar a cabo una entrevista y / o el examen del poligrafo.

Persona Examinada:_____Fecha/Lugar:_____

Examinador:_____

Testigo:_____

APPENDIX W-2

POLYGRAPH EXAMINATION STATEMENT OF CONSENT

I, _____ consent freely and voluntarily, without duress or coercion to be interviewed in connection with the issue of:

I voluntarily agree to be examined by means of the polygraph during this interview or any part of it. No threats or promises of any kind have been made to me to obtain my consent to the use of the polygraph. I represent that I am in good mental and physical condition and I know of no mental or physical ailment which might be impaired by the examination.

I understand that the questions to be asked will be reviewed with me prior to the examination.

I understand that I can stop this interview and polygraph examination at any time.

I understand that this process will be video/audio recorded.

I will not hold the examiner liable for any physical or psychological issues that may result from this examination. I understand that the results of such a test and the conclusions drawn by _____, its officers, agents, and employees may prove unfavorable to me. I also acknowledge the possibility that the examiner may be unable to render a decision based on this exam. I do, none-the-less, hold _____ its officers, agents, and employees free and harmless from any claim I might otherwise have against them for any damages to me or any liabilities resulting from the taking of the test and disclosure of its results and the conclusions drawn by _____. On behalf of myself and my heirs, I hereby release, waive and forever discharge each of the above-named corporations, firms, their respective officers, agents and employees, from any and all action or cause of action, claim, demand or liability, which I have now or may have resulting directly or indirectly from my taking said examination and the oral and written opinions rendered because of said exam. All agreed upon fees verbal or written will be paid prior to testing. Any future court testimony (in person, telephonic or written) fees will be paid at the same rate of one hundred dollars per hour. I agree that I will not hold _____ or its officers liable for any EPPA violations.

I hereby give consent for the results of the Interview and/or Polygraph Examination to be given to:

Name: _____

Acceptance: Having read and understood the above information, I hereby give _____ or its agent permission to conduct an interview and/or polygraph examination.

Signed : _____ Date:_____

Examiner:_____

Witness:_____

(COURTESY OF CALIFORNIA FORENSICS)
www.californiaforensics.com

APPENDIX X
QUADRI-TRACK ZONE COMPARISON TECHNIQUE
Test Question Construction (ARABIC)

تقنية منطقة التعقب الرباعي

إنشاء سؤال اختبار

CHART NR USED ON 1 2 3 4 5   TARGET   ( )

               5 4 3 2 1   مستخدم في الرسم رقم   ( ) الهدف

IS YOUR FIRST NAME 13F 13 و اسمك الأول	IS YOUR LAST NAME 13L 13 ل كنيتك	WERE YOU BORN IN 14 J مكان ولادتك ي
(First Name) (اسمك الأول)	(Last Name)(كنيتك)	(Country of birth) (البلد الذي ولدت به)
DO YOU INTEND TO ANSWER TRUTHFULLY EACH QUESTION ABOUT THAT? هل تنوي الإجابة على كل سؤال بصدق بشأن ذلك؟		RE: WHETHER (OR NOT) YOU 39 الإشارة: ما إذا كنت (أو لم تكن) _____ _____ _____ _____

ARE YOU COMPLETELY CONVINCED THAT I WILL NOT ASK YOU AN UNREVIEWED QUESTION DURING THIS CHART?   25

هل أنت مقتنع تماما أني لن أسألك أي سؤال لم تتم مراجعته خلال هذا الرسم البياني؟

BETWEEN THE AGES OF ( ) AND ( ) – DO YOU REMEMBER: 46

هل تتذكر ما يلي عندما كان عمرك ما بين ( ) و ( ):

_____
_____   33
_____
_____

DURING THE FIRST ( ) YEARS OF YOUR LIFE – DO YOU REMEMBER: 47

هل تتذكر ما يلي خلال السنوات ( ) الأولى من حياتك:

_____
_____
_____

_____   35
_____
_____
_____

ARE YOU AFRAID AN ERROR WILL BE MADE ON THIS TEST REGARDING THE TARGET ISSUE?   23

هل تخشى أن يحدث خطأ في هذا الاختبار بشأن المسألة المستهدفة؟

ARE YOU HOPING AN ERROR WILL BE MADE ON THIS TEST REGARDING THE TARGET ISSUE?   24

هل تأمل أن يحدث خطأ خلال هذا الاختبار بشأن المسألة المستهدفة؟

IS THERE SOMETHING ELSE YOU ARE AFRAID I WILL ASK YOU A QUESTION ABOUT, EVEN THOUGH I TOLD YOU I WOULD NOT?   26

هل هناك شيء آخر تخشى أن أسألك سؤالا عنه، حتى لو كنت قد قلت لك أني لن أفعل ذلك؟

APPENDIX Y
QUADRI-TRACK ZONE COMPARISON TECHNIQUE
Test Question Construction (Chinese - Simplified)
四轨道区域对比法
测试问题说明

TARGET ( )
目标( )

USED ON CHART NR. 1 2 3 4 5
表格 NR. 1 2 3 4 5 所用

14J	WERE YOU BORN IN 您的出生地 ____ (Country of birth) (出生国)	13L IS YOUR LAST NAME 您的姓 ____ (Last Name) (姓)	13F IS YOUR FIRST NAME 您的名 ____ (First Name) (名)
39	RE: WHETHER (OR NOT) YOU 主题:您是否 ____		DO YOU INTEND TO ANSWER TRUTHFULLY EACH QUESTION ABOUT THAT? 您是否愿意 诚实地回答有关此事的每个问题?
25	ARE YOU COMPLETELY CONVINCED THAT I WILL NOT ASK YOU AN UNREVIEWED QUESTION DURING THIS CHART? 您是否完全相信，我不会问及从未谈论过的话题?		
46	BETWEEN THE AGES OF ( ) AND ( ) – DO YOU REMEMBER: 在( )岁至( )岁期间–您是否记得:____		
33	____		
47	DURING THE FIRST ( ) YEARS OF YOUR LIFE – DO YOU REMEMBER: 在您人生的头( )年–您是否记得:____		
35	____		
23	ARE YOU AFRAID AN ERROR WILL BE MADE ON THIS TEST REGARDING THE TARGET ISSUE? 您是否害怕在就此问题的测试中犯错?		
24	ARE YOU HOPING AN ERROR WILL BE MADE ON THIS TEST REGARDING THE TARGET ISSUE? 您是否希望在就此问题的测试中犯错?		
26	IS THERE SOMETHING ELSE YOU ARE AFRAID I WILL ASK YOU A QUESTION ABOUT, EVEN THOUGH I TOLD YOU I WOULD NOT? 您是否担心我会问其他问题，即便我已经告诉您我不会问及这些问题?		

APPENDIX Z
QUADRI-TRACK ZONE COMPARISON TECHNIQUE
Test Question Construction (Chinese - Traditional)
四軌道區域比對法
測試問題結構

TARGET 目標 (　　)   USED ON CHART NR. 用於表編號 1 2 3 4 5

14J	WERE YOU BORN IN 你出生於 (Country of birth)（出生國家）	IS YOUR LAST NAME 你的姓氏是 (Last Name)（名字）	13L	IS YOUR FIRST NAME 你的名字是 (First Name)（姓氏）	13F
39	RE: WHETHER OR NOT YOU 回覆：您是否		DO YOU INTEND TO ANSWER TRUTHFULLY EACH QUESTION ABOUT THAT? 您是否打算誠實地回答 每一項 關於它的問題？		
25	ARE YOU COMPLETELY CONVINCED THAT I WILL NOT ASK YOU AN UNREVIEWED QUESTION DURING THIS CHART? 你是否完全相信我不會在此表上向你訊問未經過審核的問題？				
46	BETWEEN THE AGES OF (　　) AND (　　) – DO YOU REMEMBER: 在 (　　) 與 (　　) 歲之間 — 你是否記得：				
33					
47	DURING THE FIRST (　　) YEARS OF YOUR LIFE – DO YOU REMEMBER: 在你生命中的前 (　　) 幾年 — 你是否記得：				
35					
23	ARE YOU AFRAID AN ERROR WILL BE MADE ON THIS TEST REGARDING THE TARGET ISSUE? 你是否害怕關於此目標問題的測試中可能發生錯誤？				
24	ARE YOU HOPING AN ERROR WILL BE MADE ON THIS TEST REGARDING THE TARGET ISSUE? 你是否希望關於此目標問題的測試中可能發生錯誤？				
26	IS THERE SOMETHING ELSE YOU ARE AFRAID I WILL ASK YOU A QUESTION ABOUT, EVEN THOUGH I TOLD YOU I WOULD NOT? 你是否還有其他擔心我會訊問你的問題，即使我已經告訴過你我不會訊問？				

APPENDIX AA
QUADRI-TRACK ZONE COMPARISON TECHNIQUE
Test Question Construction (English)

TARGET (   )   USED ON CHART NR. 1 2 3 4 5

14J	WERE YOU BORN IN _____ (Country of birth)	13L IS YOUR LAST NAME _____ (Last Name)	13F IS YOUR FIRST NAME _____ (First Name)
39	RE: WHETHER (OR NOT) YOU _____ _____ _____ _____ _____		DO YOU INTEND TO ANSWER TRUTHFULLY EACH QUESTION ABOUT THAT?
25	ARE YOU COMPLETELY CONVINCED THAT I WILL NOT ASK YOU AN UNREVIEWED QUESTION DURING THIS CHART?		
46	BETWEEN THE AGES OF ( ) AND ( ) – DO YOU REMEMBER:_____ _____ _____ _____		
33	_____ _____ _____ _____		
47	DURING THE FIRST ( ) YEARS OF YOUR LIFE – DO YOU REMEMBER: _____ _____ _____ _____		
35	_____ _____ _____ _____		
23	ARE YOU AFRAID AN ERROR WILL BE MADE ON THIS TEST REGARDING THE TARGET ISSUE?		
24	ARE YOU HOPING AN ERROR WILL BE MADE ON THIS TEST REGARDING THE TARGET ISSUE?		
26	IS THERE SOMETHING ELSE YOU ARE AFRAID I WILL ASK YOU A QUESTION ABOUT, EVEN THOUGH I TOLD YOU I WOULD NOT?		

XXXXXXXXXXXXXXXXXXXXXXXXXXXXXXXXXXXXXXXXXXXXXXXXXXXXXXXX

APPENDIX BB

QUADRI-TRACK ZONE COMPARISON TECHNIQUE
Formulation des Questions (French)

CIBLE ( )   UTILISE SUR TRACE NR. 1 2 3 4 5

14 J	ETES-VOUS NEE AU/AUX/ EN_____ (Pays de naissance)	13L VOTRE NOM DE FAMILLE EST-IL_____ (Nom de famille)	13F VOTRE PRENOM EST-IL_____ (Prenom)
39	OBJECT: SI OUI OU NON VOUS_____		AVEZ-VOUS L'INTENTION DE DIRE LA VERITE EN REPONDENT A CHAQUE QUESTION A CE SUJET?
25	ETES-VOUS COMPLETEMENT CONVAINCU QUE JE NE VOUS POSERAI PAS UNE QUESTION DONT NOUS N'AVONS PAS REVISEE LORS DE CE TRACE?		
46	ENTRE LES AGES DE ( ) ET ( ) – VOUS SOUVENEZ-VOUS:		
33			
47	AU COURS DES ( ) PREMIERES ANNEES DE VOTRE VIE – VOUS SOUVENEZ VOUS:		
35			
23	AVEZ-VOUS PEUR QU'UNE ERREUR SERA FAITE SUR CE TEST CONCERNANT L'ISSUE CIBLE?		
24	ESPEREZ-VOUS QU'UNE ERREUR SERA FAITE SUR CE TEST CONCERNANT L'ISSUE CIBLE?		
26	Y A-T-IL QUELQUE CHOSE D'AUTRE DON'T VOUS AVEZ PEUR QUE JE VOUS POSERAI UNE QUESTION, MEME SI JE VOUS AI DIT QUE JE NE LE FERAIS PAS?		

XXXXXXXXXXXXXXXXXXXXXXXXXXXXXXXXXXXXXXXXXXXXXXXXXXXXXXXXXXXXXXXX

APPENDIX CC
QUADRI-TRACK ZONE COMPARISON TECHNIQUE
Test Question Construction (German)
ZONENVERGLEICHSTECHNIK VON QUADRI-TRACK
Testfragenaufbau

TARGET ( )   **USED ON CHART NR. 1 2 3 4 5**
ZIEL ( )   **VERWENDET IN DIAGRAMM NR. 1 2 3 4 5**

14J	WERE YOU BORN IN SIND SIE GEBOREN IN (Geburtsland) (Country of birth)	13L IS YOUR LAST NAME LAUTET IHR NACHNAME (Nachname) (Last Name)	13F IS YOUR FIRST NAME LAUTET IHR VORNAME (Vorname) (First Name)
39	RE: WHETHER (OR NOT) YOU BETR.: OB SIE (ODER NICHT) _____ _____	DO YOU INTEND TO ANSWER TRUTHFULLY EACH QUESTION ABOUT THAT? BEABSICHTIGEN SIE, ALLE DIESBEZÜGLICHEN FRAGEN WAHRHEITSGEMÄSS ZU BEANTWORTEN?	
25	ARE YOU COMPLETELY CONVINCED THAT I WILL NOT ASK YOU AN UNREVIEWED QUESTION DURING THIS CHART? SIND SIE VOLLKOMMEN ÜBERZEUGT, DASS ICH IHNEN WÄHREND DIESER BEFRAGUNG KEINE UNGEPRÜFTEN FRAGEN STELLEN WERDE?		
46	BETWEEN THE AGES OF ( ) AND ( ) – DO YOU REMEMBER? ERINNERN SIE SICH AUS DER ZEIT ZWISCHEN IHREM (.) UND (.) LEBENSJAHR AN DAS FOLGENDE: _____		
33	_____ _____		
47	DURING THE FIRST ( ) YEARS OF YOUR LIFE – DO YOU REMEMBER: ERINNERN SIE SICH IN IHREN ERSTEN ( ) LEBENSJAHREN AN DAS FOLGENDE:		
35	_____ _____		
23	ARE YOU AFRAID AN ERROR WILL BE MADE ON THIS TEST REGARDING THE TARGET ISSUE? HABEN SIE ANGST, DASS BEI DIESEM TEST EIN FEHLER HINSICHTLICH DES PROBLEMS GEMACHT WIRD, AUF DAS DIESER TEST ABZIELT?		
24	ARE YOU HOPING AN ERROR WILL BE MADE ON THIS TEST REGARDING THE TARGET ISSUE? HOFFEN SIE, DASS BEI DIESEM TEST EIN FEHLER HINSICHTLICH DES PROBLEMS GEMACHT WIRD, AUF DAS DIESER TEST ABZIELT?		
26	IS THERE SOMETHING ELSE YOU ARE AFRAID I WILL ASK YOU A QUESTION ABOUT, EVEN THOUGH I TOLD YOU I WOULD NOT? GIBT ES SONST NOCH ETWAS, BEI DEM SIE FÜRCHTEN, ICH KÖNNTE IHNEN FRAGEN DAZU STELLEN, OBWOHL ICH IHNEN GESAGT HABE, ICH WÜRDE ES NICHT?		

XXXXXXXXXXXXXXXXXXXXXXXXXXXXXXXXXXXXXXXXXXXXXXXXXXXXXXXXXXXX

DD APPENDIX
QUADRI-TRACK ZONE COMPARISON TECHNIQUE
(werbeH) חיבור שאלות הבדיקה

לשימוש במדפסים מספר : 5 4 3 2 1   מטרה (   )

14J	האם נולדת ב.................	**13L** האם שם משפחתך הוא......	**13F** האם שמך הפרטי הוא.......
	(ארץ הלידה)	(שם משפחה)	(שם פרטי)

39	RE: האם אתה	האם בכוונתך לענות בכנות על כל שאלה בנושא זה

25		האם אתה משוכנע בוודאות שבמהלך בדיקה זו לא אשאל אותך שום שאלה שלא דיברנו עליה.

46		בין הגילאים ( ) ( ) ו ( ) האם אתה זוכר

33		

47		במהלך ( ) השנים הראשונות של חייך האם אתה זוכר

35		

23		האם אתה חושש מטעות כלשהי במהלך הבדיקה אודות הנושא הנבדק

24		אם אתה מקווה לטעות כלשהי שתתבצע במהלך הבדיקה אודות הנושא הנבדק?

26		האם יש נושא אחר שאתה חושש להישאל אודותיו למרות שאמרתי לך שלא אעשה כך?

APPENDIX EE

क्वाड्री ट्रैक ज़ोन तुलनात्मक तकनीक
परिक्षण प्रश्न बनावट (Hindi)

लक्ष्य (   )   चार्ट न. 1 2 3 4 5 पर उपयोग किया गया

14J	जहाँ आपका जन्म हुआ	13L	आपका अंतिम नाम है	13F	आपका प्रथम नाम है
	(जन्म का स्थान)		(अंतिम नाम)		(प्रथम नाम)

39	प्रत्युत्तर: चाहे (या नहीं) आप _____ _____ _____ _____ _____

क्या आप ईमानदारी से उस बारे में प्रत्येक प्रश्न का उत्तर देना चाहते हैं

25	क्या आप पूर्ण रूप से विश्वस्त हैं कि मैं आपसे इस चार्ट के दौरान कोई असमीक्षित प्रश्न नहीं पूछूँगा?
46	( ) और ( ) आयु के बीच – क्या आपको याद है:_____ _____ _____
33	_____ _____ _____
47	आपकी उम्र के पहले ( ) वर्षों के दौरान – क्या आपको याद है:_____ _____ _____
35	_____ _____ _____
23	क्या आपको भय है कि लक्ष्य समस्या से संबंधित इस परिक्षण में कोई त्रुटि उत्पन्न होगी?
24	क्या आपको लक्ष्य समस्या से संबंधित इस परिक्षण में किसी त्रुटि की अपेक्षा कर रहे हैं
26	क्या कुछ और है जिसके बारे में आपको भय है कि मैं आपसे पूछूँगा, जबकि मैंने कहा है कि मैं ऐसा नहीं करूँगा?

XXXXXXXXXXXXXXXXXXXXXXXXXXXXXXXXXXXXXXXXXXXXXXXXXXXXXXXXXXXXX

APPENDIX FF
QUADRI-TRACK ZONE COMPARISON TECHNIQUE
Test Question Construction (Italian)
TECNICA DI CONFRONTO DELLA ZONA QUADRI-TRACK
Costruzione della domanda del test

TARGET ( )   USED ON CHART NR. 1 2 3 4 5
OBIETTIVO ( )   USATO SUL DIAGRAMMA N.RO 1 2 3 4 5

14J	WERE YOU BORN IN LEI È NATO/A A _____ (Country of birth) (Paese di nascita)	13L IS YOUR LAST NAME È IL SUO COGNOME _____ (Last Name) (Cognome)	13F IS YOUR FIRST NAME È IL SUO NOME _____ (First Name) (Nome)
39	RE: WHETHER (OR NOT) YOU OGGETTO: SE (O MENO) LEI _____ _____ _____ _____ _____		DO YOU INTEND TO ANSWER TRUTHFULLY EACH QUESTION ABOUT THAT? INTENDE RISPONDERE SINCERAMENTE A TUTTE LE DOMANDE A RIGUARDO?
25	ARE YOU COMPLETELY CONVINCED THAT I WILL NOT ASK YOU AN UNREVIEWED QUESTION DURING THIS CHART? È ASSOLUTAMENTE CONVINTO/A CHE NON LE FARÒ UNA DOMANDA NON ESAMINATA IN QUESTO DIAGRAMMA?		
46	BETWEEN THE AGES OF ( ) AND ( ) – DO YOU REMEMBER: TRA LE ETÀ DI ( ) E ( ) - LEI RICORDA: _____ _____ _____		
33	_____ _____ _____ _____		
47	DURING THE FIRST ( ) YEARS OF YOUR LIFE – DO YOU REMEMBER: DURANTE I PRIMI ( ) ANNI DELLA SUA VITA - LEI RICORDA: _____ _____ _____		
35	_____ _____ _____		
23	ARE YOU AFRAID AN ERROR WILL BE MADE ON THIS TEST REGARDING THE TARGET ISSUE? TEME CHE SARÀ FATTO UN ERRORE IN QUESTO TEST RIGUARDO ALL'ARGOMENTO IN QUESTIONE?		
24	ARE YOU HOPING AN ERROR WILL BE MADE ON THIS TEST REGARDING THE TARGET ISSUE? SI AUGURA CHE SARÀ FATTO UN ERRORE IN QUESTO TEST RIGUARDO ALL'ARGOMENTO IN QUESTIONE		
26	IS THERE SOMETHING ELSE YOU ARE AFRAID I WILL ASK YOU A QUESTION ABOUT, EVEN THOUGH I TOLD YOU I WOULD NOT? LEI TEME CHE VI SIA QUALCOS'ALTRO SU CUI LE FARÒ UNA DOMANDA, ANCHE SE LE HO DETTO CHE NON LO FARÒ?		

XXXXXXXXXXXXXXXXXXXXXXXXXXXXXXXXXXXXXXXXXXXXXXXXXXXXXXXXXX

APPENDIX GG
QUADRI-TRACK ZONE COMPARISON TECHNIQUE
クアドリトラックゾーン比較手法
Test Question Construction (Japanese)
テスト質問の構築

TARGET (   )   USED ON CHART NR. 1 2 3 4 5
対象(   )   チャート番号1 2 3 4 5に使用

14J	WERE YOU BORN IN あなたは _____ (Country of birth) (出生国) で生まれましたか	13L IS YOUR LAST NAME あなたの姓は _____ (Last Name) (姓) ですか	13F IS YOUR FIRST NAME あなたの名は _____ (First Name) (名) ですか
39	RE: WHETHER (OR NOT) YOU あなたが次の事柄に該当するか（否か）について _____ _____ _____		DO YOU INTEND TO ANSWER TRUTHFULLY EACH QUESTION ABOUT THAT? あなたはそれに関する各質問に正直に回答する意向がありますか？
25	ARE YOU COMPLETELY CONVINCED THAT I WILL NOT ASK YOU AN UNREVIEWED QUESTION DURING THIS CHART? あなたは、このチャートでレビューされていない質問を私から問われることはないと完全に確信していますか？		
46	BETWEEN THE AGES OF ( ) AND ( ) – DO YOU REMEMBER: 年令( )才と( )才の間 – あなたは覚えていますか： _____ _____		
33	_____ _____ _____		
47	DURING THE FIRST ( ) YEARS OF YOUR LIFE – DO YOU REMEMBER: あなたの人生の最初の( )年間 – あなたは覚えていますか： _____ _____		
35	_____ _____ _____		
23	ARE YOU AFRAID AN ERROR WILL BE MADE ON THIS TEST REGARDING THE TARGET ISSUE? 対象事項に関してこのテストで誤りが犯されることをあなたは恐れていますか？		
24	ARE YOU HOPING AN ERROR WILL BE MADE ON THIS TEST REGARDING THE TARGET ISSUE? 対象事項に関してこのテストで誤りが犯されることをあなたは期待していますか？		
26	IS THERE SOMETHING ELSE YOU ARE AFRAID I WILL ASK YOU A QUESTION ABOUT, EVEN THOUGH I TOLD YOU I WOULD NOT? 私は質問しないとあなたに述べたにもかかわらず、あなたが私から質問されることを恐れている何か他のことはありますか？		

APPENDIX HH
쿼드리 트랙 (QUADRI-TRACK) 영역 대조 기술
테스트 문제 생성 (Korean)

타겟 (   )   챠트 번호 사용. **1 2 3 4 5**

14J 출생연도	13L 성(姓)	13F 이름
_____	_____	_____
(출생 국가)	(성(姓))	(이름)

39	RE: 본인 여부	관련 질문 항목에 대해 성실하게 답변해 주시겠습니까?
	_____	
	_____	
	_____	
	_____	

25	본 챠트 과정에서 사전에 검토되지 않은 질문은 없을 것이라고 확신하십니까?

46	연령 ( )세 - ( )세 – 기억하십니까: _____
	_____
	_____
	_____

33	_____
	_____
	_____
	_____

47	인생의 초기 ( )년간 – 기억하십니까: _____
	_____
	_____
	_____

35	_____
	_____
	_____
	_____

23	본 테스트의 타겟 관련 문제에서 발생할 수 있는 오류에 대해 우려하십니까?

24	본 테스트의 타겟 관련 문제에서 오류가 발생하기를 기대하십니까?

26	질문하지 않을 것이라고 미리 설명해 드린 내용이지만, 질문에 대해 우려되는 내용이 있습니까?

XXXXXXXXXXXXXXXXXXXXXXXXXXXXXXXXXXXXXXXXXXXXXXXXXXXXXXXXXXXXXX

APPENDIX II
QUADRI-TRACK ZONE COMPARISON TECHNIQUE
TECHNIKA PORÓWNAWCZA OBSZARU CZTERO-WYKRESOWEGO
Test Question Construction (Polish)
Konstrukcja pytań testu

RGET (   )   USED ON CHART NR. 1 2 3 4 5
                                                         WYKORZYSTANO NA KARCIE NR 1..2..3..4..5

J	WERE YOU BORN IN	13L IS YOUR LAST NAME	13L IS YOUR FIRST NAME
	CZY URODZIŁ (A) SIĘ PAN(I) W	CZY MA PAN(I) NA NAZWISKO	CZY MA PAN(I) NA IMIĘ
	(Country of birth)	(Last Name)	(First Name)
	(kraj urodzenia)	(nazwisko)	(imię)

RE: WHETHER (OR NOT) YOU   DO YOU INTEND TO ANSWER
ODNOŚNIE TEGO CZY PAN(I) _____   TRUTHFULLY EACH QUESTION ABOUT
_____   THAT?
_____   CZY ZAMIERZA PAN(I) ODPOWIEDZIEĆ NA
_____   KAŻDE PYTANIE NA TEN TEMAT ZGODNIE
_____(CZY TEŻ NIE)   Z PRAWDĄ?

ARE YOU COMPLETELY CONVINCED THAT I WILL NOT ASK YOU AN UNREVIEWED
QUESTION DURING THIS CHART?
CZY JEST PAN(I) CAŁKOWICIE PRZEKONANY(A), ŻE NIE ZADAM PANU(I) W TEJ KARCIE
NIEZWERYFIKOWANEGO PYTANIA?

BETWEEN THE AGES OF (   ) AND (   ) – DO YOU REMEMBER:
W WIEKU POMIĘDZY (   ) A (   ) ROKIEM ŻYCIA, CZY PAMIĘTA PAN(I): _____
_____
_____

_____
_____

DURING THE FIRST (   ) YEARS OF YOUR LIFE – DO YOU REMEMBER:
PODCZAS PIERWSZYCH (   ) LAT ŻYCIA, CZY PAMIĘTA PAN(I): _____
_____

_____
_____

ARE YOU AFRAID AN ERROR WILL BE MADE ON THIS TEST REGARDING THE TARGET
ISSUE?
CZY OBAWIA SIĘ PAN(I), ŻE W TYM TEŚCIE POPEŁNIONY ZOSTANIE BŁĄD DOTYCZĄCY
GŁÓWNEGO ZAGADNIENIA?
ARE YOU HOPING AN ERROR WILL BE MADE ON THIS TEST REGARDING THE
TARGET ISSUE?
CZY MA PAN(I) NADZIEJĘ, ŻE W TYM TEŚCIE POPEŁNIONY ZOSTANIE BŁĄD DOTYCZĄCY
GŁÓWNEGO ZAGADNIENIA?
IS THERE SOMETHING ELSE YOU ARE AFRAID I WILL ASK YOU A QUESTION ABOUT,
EVEN THOUGH I TOLD YOU I WOULD NOT?
CZY OBAWIA SIĘ PAN(I), ŻE ZADAM PANU(I) PYTANIE NA JAKIŚ INNY TEMAT, MIMO, ŻE
POWIEDZIAŁEM(AM), ŻE TEGO NIE ZROBIĘ?

APPENDIX JJ
QUADRI-TRACK ZONE COMPARISON TECHNIQUE
ТЕХНИКА СРАВНЕНИЯ С ОТСЛЕЖИВАНИЕМ ЧЕТЫРЕХ ЗОН
Test Question Construction (Russian)
Формирование вопроса для тестирования

TARGET ( ) ЦЕЛЬ ( )	USED ON CHART NR. 1 2 3 4 5 ИСПОЛЬЗУЕТСЯ В ТАБЛИЦЕ № 1 2 3 4 5

14J 14J	WERE YOU BORN IN ВЫ РОДИЛИСЬ В _____ (Country of birth) (Место рождения (страна))	13L IS YOUR LAST NAME 13L ВАША ФАМИЛИЯ (Last Name) (Фамилия)	13F IS YOUR FIRST NAME 13F ВАШЕ ИМЯ (First Name) (Имя)

39	RE: WHETHER (OR NOT) YOU ПО ВОПРОСУ: ДЕЙСТВИТЕЛЬНО ЛИ ВЫ _____ _____ _____ _____ DO YOU INTEND TO ANSWER TRUTHFULLY EACH QUESTION ABOUT THAT? БУДЕТЕ ЛИ ВЫ ЧЕСТНО ОТВЕЧАТЬ НА КАЖДЫЙ ВОПРОС НА ЭТУ ТЕМУ?
25	ARE YOU COMPLETELY CONVINCED THAT I WILL NOT ASK YOU AN UNREVIEWED QUESTION DURING THIS CHART? А ВЫ ПОЛНОСТЬЮ УВЕРЕНЫ В ТОМ, ЧТО Я НЕ БУДУ ЗАДАВАТЬ ВАМ НЕПРИЯТНЫЕ ВОПРОСЫ В ЭТОЙ ТАБЛИЦЕ?
46	BETWEEN THE AGES OF ( ) AND ( ) – DO YOU REMEMBER: КОГДА ВАШ ВОЗРАСТ БЫЛ ОТ ( ) ДО ( ), ПОМНИТЕ ЛИ ВЫ: _____
33	_____ _____ _____
47	DURING THE FIRST ( ) YEARS OF YOUR LIFE – DO YOU REMEMBER: КОГДА ВАМ БЫЛО ( ) ЛЕТ, ПОМНИТЕ ЛИ ВЫ: _____
35	_____ _____ _____
23	ARE YOU AFRAID AN ERROR WILL BE MADE ON THIS TEST REGARDING THE TARGET ISSUE? БОИТЕСЬ ЛИ ВЫ ТОГО, ЧТО В ЭТОМ ТЕСТЕ БУДЕТ СДЕЛАНА ОШИБКА В ОТНОШЕНИИ ВАШЕГО ЦЕЛЕВОГО ВОПРОСА?
24	ARE YOU HOPING AN ERROR WILL BE MADE ON THIS TEST REGARDING THE TARGET ISSUE? НАДЕЕТЕСЬ ЛИ ВЫ НА ТО, ЧТО В ЭТОМ ТЕСТЕ БУДЕТ СДЕЛАНА ОШИБКА В ОТНОШЕНИИ ВАШЕГО ЦЕЛЕВОГО ВОПРОСА?
26	IS THERE SOMETHING ELSE YOU ARE AFRAID I WILL ASK YOU A QUESTION ABOUT, EVEN THOUGH I TOLD YOU I WOULD NOT? А ЕСТЬ ЛИ КАКОЙ-ЛИБО ЕЩЕ ВОПРОС, КОТОРЫЙ ВЫ БОИТЕСЬ, ЧТО Я ЗАДАМ, НЕ СМОТРЯ НА ТО, ЧТО Я ВАМ СКАЗАЛ, ЧТО НЕ БУДУ ЗАДАВАТЬ?

APPENDIX KK
QUADRI-TRACK ZONE COMPARISON TECHNIQUE
Construccion de pregunta de prueba (Spanish)

OBJECTIVO (   )   USADO EN CARTA NR. 1 2 3 4 5

14J	ESTABA NACIDO EN	13L ES SU APELLIDO	13F ES SU NOMBRE
	(Pais de nacimiento)	(Apellido)	(Nombre)
39	RE: SI USTED		TIENE LA INTENCION DE CONTESTAR SINCERAMENTE CADA PREGUNTA SOBRE ESTO?
25	ESTA USTED COMPLETAMENTE CONVENCIDO QUE YO NO LE VAYA A PREGUNTAR UNA PREGUNTA QUE NO SEA RFEPASADA DURANTE ESTA CARTA?		
46	ENTRE LOS AÑOS DE ( ) Y ( ) – RECUERDA: _____		
33			
47	DURANTE LOS PRIMEROS ( ) AÑOS DE SU VIDA – RECUERDA:_____		
35			
23	TEME USTED QUE ALGUN ERROR SE PUEDA PASAR EN ESTE EXAMEN CON RESPETO AL ASUNTO CENTRAL?		
24	ESPERA USTED QUE ALGUN ERROR SE PUEDA PASAR EN ESTE EXAMEN CON RESPETO AL ASUNTO CENTRAL?		
26	HAY ALGO MAS QUE TEMA USTED QUE LE VAYA A PREGUNTAR, AUNQUE YO LE DIJE QUE NO SE LO PREGUNTARA?		

APPENDIX LL

MATTE POLYGRAPH SERVICE, INC.
SCIENTIFIC TRUTH VERIFICATION — LIE DETECTION

POLYGRAPH EXAMINATION WORKSHEET

CLIENT_____ DATE/TIME_____
PLACE TESTED_____
SUBJECT _____ OCCUPATION_____
PRESENT EMPLOYER_____
LENGTH OF EMPLOYMENT_____ POSITION_____
ADDRESS OF SUBJECT_____
SSAN _____ DPOB_____ AGE_____
TELEPHONE _____ DRIVER LICENSE NR._____
M F RACE_____ HT____ WT____ HAIR____EYES____ BUILD_____ S M D SEP W CHILDREN_____
SCHOOL GRADE FINISHED 1 2 3 4 5 6 7 8 9 10 11 12 GED COLLEGE 1 2 3 4 5 6 7 8 DEGREE_____
MILITARY SERVICE A N M CG AF FROM_____ TO_____ DISCH_____ RANK_____
COURT-MARTIALS/ARRESTS _____

PRESENT PHYSICAL CONDITION: GOOD O FAIR O POOR O LAST PHYSICAL EXAM_____
HOSPITALIZED PAST 2 YEARS_____
TROUBLE WITH NERVES REQUIRING MEDICATION _____
HEART DISEASE_____
TO SUBJECT'S KNOWLEDGE, BLOOD PRESSURE NORMAL O LOW O HIGH O _____
_____
_____

DIABETES (over 50 using 50 or more units of insulin by injection per day) _____
_____
EPILEPSY_____ PREGNANCY_____ PERMISSION FORM_____
EVER UNDER CARE OF PSYCHIATRIST_____ EVER PATIENT IN MENTAL HOSPITAL_____
ANY MEDICATION OR DRUGS IN LAST 12 HOURS _____
NR OF HOURS SLEEP LAST NIGHT_____ PERMISSION FORM SIGNED_____
PREVIOUS POLYGRAPHS_____
INTERRUPTIONS_____
REMARKS_____
_____

PREDICATION: Subject was administered a polygraph examination to determine _____
_____
_____
_____
_____

CASE INFORMATION/SUBJECT'S VERSION: SEE ATTACHED SHEET_____
PRE-TEST/POST-TEST ADMISSIONS: SEE ATTACHED SHEET/CONFESSION.
TEST CONDUCTED: 1. QUADRI-TRACK 2. SAT 3. STIM 4.SKG 5. KS POT 6. P POT 7. MITT

CONCLUSIONS: TARGET A ( ) TRUTHFUL/DECEPTIVE TO RELEVANT QUESTIONS NR _____
                 TARGET B ( ) TRUTHFUL/DECEPTIVE TO RELEVANT QUESTIONS NR _____
                 TARGET C ( ) TRUTHFUL/DECEPTIVE TO RELEVANT QUESTIONS NR _____
                 TARGET D ( ) TRUTHFUL/DECEPTIVE TO RELEVANT QUESTIONS NR _____
                 TARGET E ( ) TRUTHFUL/DECEPTIVE TO RELEVANT QUESTIONS NR _____

QUADRI-TRACK ZONE COMPARISON TECHNIQUE
Test Question Construction

TARGET (   )   USED ON CHART NR. 1 2 3 4 5

14J	WERE YOU BORN IN	13L IS YOUR LAST NAME	13F IS YOUR FIRST NAME
	_____	_____	_____
	(Country of birth)	(Last Name)	(First Name)
39	RE: WHETHER (OR NOT) YOU _____ _____ _____ _____ _____ _____		DO YOU INTEND TO ANSWER TRUTHFULLY EACH QUESTION ABOUT THAT?
25	ARE YOU COMPLETELY CONVINCED THAT I WILL NOT ASK YOU AN UNREVIEWED QUESTION DURING THIS CHART?		
46	BETWEEN THE AGES OF ( ) AND ( ) – DO YOU REMEMBER:_____ _____ _____ _____		
33	_____ _____ _____ _____		
47	DURING THE FIRST ( ) YEARS OF YOUR LIFE – DO YOU REMEMBER: _____ _____ _____ _____		
35	_____ _____ _____ _____		
23	ARE YOU AFRAID AN ERROR WILL BE MADE ON THIS TEST REGARDING THE TARGET ISSUE?		
24	ARE YOU HOPING AN ERROR WILL BE MADE ON THIS TEST REGARDING THE TARGET ISSUE?		
26	IS THERE SOMETHING ELSE YOU ARE AFRAID I WILL ASK YOU A QUESTION ABOUT, EVEN THOUGH I TOLD YOU I WOULD NOT?		

XXXXXXXXXXXXXXXXXXXXXXXXXXXXXXXXXXXXXXXXXXXXXXXXXXXXXXXXXXXXXX

The Quadri-Track ZCT Numerical Score Sheet and Conclusion Table

STIMULATION TEST DATA:	NUMBER SELECTED: CHART NUMBER:							

Quadri-Track Zone Comparison Quantification System Score Table

CHART 1	NDI +3 +2	INDEF +1 0 -1	DI -2 -3	=( )	(35)	NDI +3 +2	INDEF +1 0 -1	DI -2 -3	=( )	(24)	NDI +3 +2	INDEF +1 0 -1	DI -2 -3	=( )
PNE (33)	+3 +2	+1 0 -1	-2 -3	=( )	(35)	+3 +2	+1 0 -1	-2 -3	=( )	(24)	+3 +2	+1 0 -1	-2 -3	=( )
EDA (33)	+3 +2	+1 0 -1	-2 -3	=( )	(35)	+3 +2	+1 0 -1	-2 -3	=( )	(24)	+3 +2	+1 0 -1	-2 -3	=( )
CAR (33)	+3 +2	+1 0 -1	-2 -3	=( )	(35)	+3 +2	+1 0 -1	-2 -3	=( )	(24)	+3 +2	+1 0 -1	-2 -3	=( )
CHART 2 NDI	INDEF	DI			NDI	INDEF	DI			NDI	INDEF	DI	
PNE (33)	+3 +2	+1 0 -1	-2 -3	=( )	(35)	+3 +2	+1 0 -1	-2 -3	=( )	(24)	+3 +2	+1 0 -1	-2 -3	=( )
EDA (33)	+3 +2	+1 0 -1	-2 -3	=( )	(35)	+3 +2	+1 0 -1	-2 -3	=( )	(24)	+3 +2	+1 0 -1	-2 -3	=( )
CAR (33)	+3 +2	+1 0 -1	-2 -3	=( )	(35)	+3 +2	+1 0 -1	-2 -3	=( )	(24)	+3 +2	+1 0 -1	-2 -3	=( )
CHART 3 NDI	INDEF	DI			NDI	INDEF	DI			NDI	INDEF	DI	
PNE (33)	+3 +2	+1 0 -1	-2 -3	=( )	(35)	+3 +2	+1 0 -1	-2 -3	=( )	(24)	+3 +2	+1 0 -1	-2 -3	=( )
EDA (33)	+3 +2	+1 0 -1	-2 -3	=( )	(35)	+3 +2	+1 0 -1	-2 -3	=( )	(24)	+3 +2	+1 0 -1	-2 -3	=( )
CAR (33)	+3 +2	+1 0 -1	-2 -3	=( )	(35)	+3 +2	+1 0 -1	-2 -3	=( )	(24)	+3 +2	+1 0 -1	-2 -3	=( )
CHART 4 NDI	INDEF	DI			NDI	INDEF	DI			NDI	INDEF	DI	
PNE (33)	+3 +2	+1 0 -1	-2 -3	=( )	(35)	+3 +2	+1 0 -1	-2 -3	=( )	(24)	+3 +2	+1 0 -1	-2 -3	=( )
EDA (33)	+3 +2	+1 0 -1	-2 -3	=( )	(35)	+3 +2	+1 0 -1	-2 -3	=( )	(24)	+3 +2	+1 0 -1	-2 -3	=( )
CAR (33)	+3 +2	+1 0 -1	-2 -3	=( )	(35)	+3 +2	+1 0 -1	-2 -3	=( )	(24)	+3 +2	+1 0 -1	-2 -3	=( )

TARGET ( )   TOTAL: ( )   TOTAL: ( )   TOTAL: ( )
GRAND TOTAL: ( )
FOR ( ) CHARTS.

% Pop:_____
P.E.: _____

CONCLUSION TABLE

RESULTS FOR 1 CHART

CIRCLE APPROPRIATE NUMBER BELOW		
+27 to +3	+2 to -4	-5 to -27
TRUTH	INDEFINITE	DECEPTION

RESULTS FOR 2 CHARTS

CIRCLE APPROPRIATE NUMBER BELOW		
+54 to +6	+5 to -9	-10 to -54
TRUTH	INDEFINITE	DECEPTION

RESULTS FOR 3 CHARTS

CIRCLE APPROPRIATE NUMBER BELOW		
+81 to +9	+8 to -14	-15 to -81
TRUTH	INDEFINITE	DECEPTION

RESULTS FOR 4 CHARTS

CIRCLE APPROPRIATE NUMBER BELOW		
+108 to +12	+13 to -19	-20 to -108
TRUTH	INDEFINITE	DECEPTION

S-K-G TEST	13L		USED ON CHART NR._____
25	ARE YOU COMPLETELY CONVINCED THAT I WILL NOT ASK YOU AN UNREVIEWED QUESTION DURING THIS CHART?		
39	REGARDING THE:	DO YOU INTEND TO ANSWER TRUTHFULLY EACH QUESTION ABOUT THAT?	
42	SAME AS ABOVE	BEFORE THAT OCCURRED – DID YOU DEFINITELY KNOW IT WAS ABOUT TO HAPPEN?	
34	SAME AS ABOVE	AT THE VERY TIME THAT_____ OCCURRED – WERE YOU_____ (on the scene)	
48	DURING THE FIRST ( ) YEARS OF YOUR LIFE – DO YOU REMEMBER:		
33	SAME AS ABOVE	DID YOU (YOURSELF)	
32	SAME AS ABOVE	DO YOU KNOW FOR SURE (WHO)	
31	SAME AS ABOVE	DO YOU SUSPECT ANYONE IN PARTICULAR OF	
23	ARE YOU AFRAID AN ERROR WILL BE MADE ON THIS TEST?		
24	ARE YOU HOPEFUL AN ERROR WILL BE MADE ON THIS TEST?		
26	IS THERE SOMETHING ELSE YOU ARE AFRAID I WILL ASK YOU A QUESTION ABOUT, EVEN THOUGH I TOLD YOU I WOULD NOT?		

SEG-1
THE 42 Score ( ) 34 Score ( ) 33 Score ( ) 32 Score ( ) 24 Score ( )
GSR 42 Score ( ) 34 Score ( ) 33 Score ( ) 32 Score ( ) 24 Score ( )
CAR 42 Score ( ) 34 Score ( ) 33 Score ( ) 32 Score ( ) 24 Score ( )
SEG-2
THE 42 Score ( ) 34 Score ( ) 33 Score ( ) 32 Score ( ) 24 Score ( )
GSR 42 Score ( ) 34 Score ( ) 33 Score ( ) 32 Score ( ) 24 Score ( )
CAR 42 Score ( ) 34 Score ( ) 33 Score ( ) 32 Score ( ) 24 Score ( )
42 TOTAL ( ) 34 TOTAL ( ) 33 TOTAL ( ) 32 TOTAL ( ) 24 TOTAL ( )

S-K-G CONCLUSION TABLE
RESULTS FOR 1 CHART CIRCLE APPROPRIATE NUMBER BELOW
+ 2 or more   + 1 to - 2   - 3 or more
TRUTH   INDEF   DECEPTION
RESULTS FOR 2 CHARTS CIRCLE APPROPRIATE NUMBER BELOW
+ 4 or more   + 3 to - 5   - 6 or more
TRUTH   INDEF   DECEPTION

"KNOWN SOLUTION" PEAK-OF-TENSION TEST	USED ON CHART NR.	"PROBING" PEAK-OF-TENSION TEST	USED ON CHART NR.
PREPARATORY QUESTION		PREPARATORY QUESTION	
PREFIX QUESTION		PREFIX QUESTION	
BUFFER QUESTIONS (Must contain fictitious key only)		LEAST LIKELY CHOICES	
1		A	
2		B	
3		MOST LIKELY CHOICES	
BUFFER QUESTIONS (Plus True Key Only)		C	
4		D	
5		E	
6		F	
7		LEAST LIKELY CHOICES	
BUFFER QUESTIONS (Cannot contain either Key)		G	
8		H	
9		ALL INCLUSIVE CHOICE	
		I	

LATEST BOOKS AND COMPACT DISK
on
FORENSIC PSYCHOPHYSIOLOGY
by
James Allan Matte

Examination and Cross-Examination of Experts in Forensic Psychophysiology Using The Polygraph. ISBN: 0965579425. Published in December 2000. Hardbound 440-page book, provides attorneys with ideal formats to depose their experts when laying the foundation for the admissibility of psychophysiological veracity (PV) examination results. It also provides attorneys with examination and cross-examination scripts that will be of immense value in the identification of valid and faulty PV examinations. This book will provide experts in forensic psychophysiology with a cookbook of model scripts based on authoritative sources and research data that will prepare them for the most arduous trials involving PV examinations. A book Review in *The Champion*, The National Association of Criminal Defense Lawyers (NACDL), December 200-1, Vol XXV, No. 10, b Dick Wheelan, defense attorney on the advisory board of *The Champion* stated that "This text is intended to convince readers of the efficacy of the polygraph, but as its title implies, it is intended to assist the attorney to examine and cross-examine the polygraph expert. The book achieves its goal. In fact, the attorney who takes the time to study and understand this text might well know more about the use of the polygraph than the expert he is questioning." Book Reviews and Testimonials can be found at www.mattepolygraph.com or www.jampublications.com.

Forensic Psychophysiology Using The Polygraph: Scientific Truth Verification – Lie Detection. ISBN: 0965579409. Initially published in December 1996, Second Printing with corrective changes 1998. Hardbound 800-page volume, represents the most complete and comprehensive textbook ever written on forensic psychophysiology using the polygraph. Law professor Edward J. Imwinkelried in his book review in *The Champion*, NACDL, stated that "the text belongs on the shelf of any defense attorney who contemplates waging a polygraph war." This textbook was cited by the United States Supreme Court in *United States of America vs. Edward G. Scheffer* (1997). Book Reviews and Testimonials can be found on website at: www.mattepolygraph.com or www.jampublications.com.

CD-ROM version ISBN: 0965579417 (1998-00) of above title: *Forensic Psychophysiology Using The Polygraph,* works with all platforms (PC, MAC and UNIX) and with most operating systems (Windows 3x. 95, 98, 00, NT, XP, OX/2, Windows 7, System 7, System 8, and UNIXO. This CD-ROM includes a full text search and retrieval product and hyperlink images, plus many colored illustrations and a video introduction by the author.

SUPPLEMENT 2002-2012, ISBN: 9781469907932 to *Forensic Psychophysiology Using the Polygraph* (ISBN: 0965579409). This 184 page Supplement contains numerous significant changes to several chapters of aforesaid volume, including many illustrations and the translation of the Quadri-Track Zone Comparison Technique format into fourteen (14) foreign languages.

For more details, prices and shipping costs, please visit J.A.M. Publications at www.jampublications.com or call us at (716) 634-6645 – Fax (716) 634-7204 or E-Mail: editor@jampublications.com. All of aforementioned books and CD are also available at www.amazon.com.

Made in the USA
Charleston, SC
14 June 2012